THE EVERYTHING®

PARENT'S GUIDE TO

CHILDREN WITH ANXIETY

Dear Reader,

Although we are psychologists specializing in anxiety and children, we are also moms, and know firsthand what it feels like to have a child who is struggling with a health issue. We understand the confusion and overwhelming feelings that can come with all the information available out there. That is why we feel so grateful for the opportunity to share our insights with you in this book.

The doctor and founding humanistic psychologist Alfred Adler once said, "The whole is greater than the sum of its parts." Remember this wisdom when it seems like your child's anxiety is taking over his life, and yours. His fear of facing fear is just one part of the whole of his person; so much more is waiting to be discovered. Therefore, we hope this book is the first step of many to give you clarity and a road to travel, as you help your child become a confident and happy individual, ready to take flight and soar.

Ilyne Sandas   Christine Siegel

Welcome to

THE

EVERYTHING®

PARENT'S GUIDES

Everything® Parent's Guides are a part of the bestselling *Everything*® series and cover common parenting issues like childhood illnesses and tantrums, as well as medical conditions like asthma and juvenile diabetes. These family-friendly books are designed to be a one-stop guide for parents. If you want authoritative information on specific topics not fully covered in other books, *Everything*® Parent's Guides are your perfect solution.

 Alerts: Urgent warnings

 Essentials: Quick handy tips

 Facts: Important snippets of information

 Questions: Answers to common questions

PUBLISHER Karen Cooper

DIRECTOR OF ACQUISITIONS AND INNOVATION Paula Munier

MANAGING EDITOR, EVERYTHING SERIES Lisa Laing

COPY CHIEF Casey Ebert

ACQUISITIONS EDITOR Brielle Matson

SENIOR DEVELOPMENT EDITOR Brett Palana-Shanahan

EDITORIAL ASSISTANT Hillary Thompson

Visit the entire Everything® series at *www.everything.com*

THE EVERYTHING®

PARENT'S GUIDE TO

CHILDREN WITH ANXIETY

Professional advice to help your child
feel confident, happy, and secure

Ilyne Sandas, M.A., L.P., and Christine Siegel, M.A., L.P.
with Deborah D. White, Ph.D., L.P.

Avon, Massachusetts

*To every parent who suffers along with his or her
anxious child—this book is for you.*

• • •

An Everything® Series Book.
Everything® and everything.com® are registered
trademarks of F+W Publications, Inc.

Published by Adams Media, an F+W Publications Company
57 Littlefield Street, Avon, MA 02322 U.S.A.
www.adamsmedia.com

ISBN 10: 1-59869-686-6
ISBN 13: 978-1-59869-686-8

Printed in Canada.

J I H G F E D C B A

Library of Congress Cataloging-in-Publication Data
is available from the publisher.

*This book is available at quantity discounts for bulk purchases.
For information, please call 1-800-289-0963.*

*All the examples and dialogues used in this book are fictional, and have
been created by the author to illustrate disciplinary situations.*

►**anx-i-e-ty** (ăng-zī-ĭ-té) n. **1.** A treatable, yet overwhelming sense of apprehension, worry, and/or fear, marked by physical symptoms such as heart palpitation, nausea, tension, trembling, and sweating and psychological symptoms that include self-doubt about one's ability to cope.

Acknowledgments

Thanks to our agent, Mary Sue Seymour, and our editors at Adams Media, Kerry Smith, and Brielle Matson. A special thank you goes to Dr. Deb White, our technical reviewer, for her expertise, guidance, and friendship throughout the writing process. Moreover, a big shout-out of love to our families for their support: Jesse, Sara, Molly, Brian, Katie, Mike, Maddie, Jim, and Cheryl! We thank you for your understanding and willingness to give us the time and space to do this project.

• • •

Contents

Introduction

Congratulations! By picking up this book, you are already on the road to a life less encumbered by anxiety for your child, yourself, and your family. As with any serious health issue, learning to manage the symptoms of anxiety is a topsy-turvy journey, much like being swept up in a tornado where life can seem as if it is spiraling out of control. Like Dorothy and Toto in *The Wizard of Oz*, sometimes you will not know where you are going, and it may feel like you have landed in a surreal dream, ill-equipped to handle your new and unfamiliar surroundings. After you realize that your child is struggling with an anxiety disorder and the initial storm has passed, you may feel like the weight of it all has dropped on you like a house out of the sky.

Like the travelers in this familiar story, you and your child may encounter many trials and perhaps some distractions and deceptions on the road to recovery. At times, the journey may take twists and turns, and seem to double back on itself, while the wicked witch of anxiety and all of her minions lurk around the corner. Just as in Oz, the good witch cannot simply wave her wand and take all of the fear away; you, your child, and perhaps your family will need to travel the road together, gathering insight and experience to find your way back home. Although at times you might feel discouraged and exhausted, keep faith in the process with your sights on the horizon; its promise and glow will pull you forward during even the bleakest of times. Rest assured that, as the lessons in this book are presented in a spiraling fashion, sometimes repeated in new ways for your benefit, you will be weaving your way to the final destination. *The Everything® Parent's Guide to Children with Anxiety* will provide you with the resources, tools, and information you need to make the choices right for your child and family. You will gain courage, knowledge, and esteem as you both replace your current worry with a future filled with confidence and security. Though you may have to say goodbye to some familiar but unhelpful coping methods to make way for the new, you will come to realize that what you feared most was perhaps only an illusion, which vanishes as you acquire new information and tools to combat anxiety.

The lessons offered in the book are balanced between what is traditional and what is nontraditional, and what is informational, supportive, and therapeutic. They will guide you from diagnosis to the causes and forms of anxiety through how to find professional help, work with your insurance company, and create strategies and resources for the everyday management of anxiety. Sometimes, as life unfolds, everyone needs a little guidance and support along the way, much like the beloved characters in *The Wizard of Oz*. It is so easy to be consumed by the weight of your feelings that you do not realize the vast resources you have within. You forget to go in and grab them, even if that just means asking for help or reading something to get a better perspective. As you and your child work through the various issues related to anxiety, the contents of this book will lead you to the revelation that you both had the courage within, the heart of self-compassion, and the knowledge to come home to what was there all along.

CHAPTER 1

What, Me Worry?

It is true that kids today have to keep pace with a faster lifestyle than any other generation in the past. They are faced with greater academic expectations and responsibility, have additional pressures due to a changing family structure, and look forward to an uncertain worldview economically and politically. In short, growing up is probably very different from how you remember it and, for some, a lot more worrisome.

What's Happening to My Child?

It is hard for parents to think their child might be suffering in a physical or psychological way. If you are taking the time to read this, though, you must be concerned about how anxious your child is. Well, take heart; anxiety is one of the most common medical and psychological conditions in children and adolescents today. One in ten children may be affected by an anxiety disorder and it is the most frequent mental health diagnosis in America, surpassing depression. It is also the most treatable; 90 percent of children and adults successfully decrease their anxiety through lifestyle changes that foster empowerment, confidence, and independence. This has been achieved through a combination of psychotherapy, complementary and alternative medicine, and when necessary, medication.

How to Recognize Anxiety

Adults experiencing anxiety feel nervous, jittery, moody, and worried. You may not sleep well, and others might see you as agitated, irritable, or distractible. Children and teens can experience anxiety in much the same way. When young they often do not have the words to let you know what is going on for them, and teens get confused about how to balance what they know in their heads with the emotions they are feeling. So the anxiety creeps into their behavior, and shows itself in both overt and covert ways.

An example of covert anxiety is that while your child is studying for a test, he keeps biting his nails until they bleed. You see the damage, but do not know why. Or, your child complains he has a stomachache, which unbeknown to you disappears after a school test is over.

An example of overt anxiety is that before going to dance class your child has a meltdown when you ask her to put her dance gear in her bag. During the yelling, you hear things like; "I can't go to class, I will not have enough time to study tonight," or "Stop being on me about everything, I'm only one person, how much can I take?"

The first line of defense is to know the signs that set normal fears and worries apart from more serious and ongoing anxieties.

Alert!

Although some children are able to tell you how they are feeling, giving you clues how to help and diagnose, diagnosing an anxiety disorder in babies and toddlers is extremely difficult and underreported.

While every child occasionally feels stressed, worried, or fearful, an anxiety disorder is diagnosed when your child feels excessively, unreasonably, often uncontrollably, and persistently worried. This worry will take over your child's thoughts, sometimes lasting for an extended period, and the hardest part for your child is that he will not feel like he can make it stop. You can sit down and discuss your child's fears with him, showing him they are not warranted, but he still cannot seem to make the worry and apprehension stop. If the distress your child feels extends to all areas of life including home, school, and with friends, then it is no longer "normal or expected" anxiety. Specific areas of concern occur when anxiety has affected school attendance, academic motivation, learning, concentration, memory, friendships, activity level, or sleep patterns.

 Essential

If your child has unrecognized and/or untreated anxiety that continues over time, there is an increased risk for a pattern to develop. This pattern of internal reactions becomes part of the child's personality and carries into adulthood. This is because repeated avoidance of a fearful situation actually reinforces it, making the fear grow stronger.

The Two Components

Your child's anxiety typically will have two parts, physical sensations and emotional experiences. The most common physical sensations include stomachaches, headaches, back or neck aches, nausea, and sweating. The emotional component will consist of intense and constant nervousness, worry, and fear. Because there are physical symptoms, it is important to see your family doctor to rule out an illness first. Doctors have found that anxiety can be caused by thyroid disorders, encephalitis, hypoglycemia, irritable bowel syndrome, Group A Strep, or even pneumonia.

Is Fear the Same as Anxiety?

Although fear and anxiety are related, there is an important distinction between them. Fear is the appropriate reaction to a real danger or threat. One example is when a siren sounds to warn you of a tornado in your neighborhood and your child gets scared. In that scenario the brain is just responding to protect your child. Anxiety is the reaction to a *perceived* danger or threat, such as a thunderstorm in a neighboring county that your child has heard about on the news. Although there is no danger in your own neighborhood and you tell him that, his brain, which has been primed to overreact, jumps into action anyway and he gets anxious. Anxiety is more of a learned fear response that has been etched in your child's brain. This process will be discussed in detail in Chapter 2.

The Anxious Coping Style

Children can grow out of fears as they mature, and are generally resilient. How do you know when your child's reactions are the beginning of an anxiety disorder, especially when you consider that anxiety in children is expected and normal at specific times in development? From around eight months old through the preschool years, it is normal for your child to show intense feelings if separated from his parents, called separation anxiety. At two years old, your child may be scared of the dark, loud noises, animals, changes in the house, or strangers. At age five you can add "bad people" and fear of bodily harm to the above list. By age six it is common for children to still be afraid of the dark and have separation issues, as well as fear of thunder and lightning, supernatural beings, staying alone, or getting hurt. Kids ages seven through twelve often have fears that are more reality-based, like getting hurt because they are now more aware of the world around them, or of some kind of disaster happening.

Many children can be described as intensely oversensitive, or "high maintenance," which can be a normal expression of your child's developing personality too. The deciding factors then, as you look at your child, lie in the frequency and intensity of the fears, and how much the fear and worry interferes with life.

What Are You Looking For?

Here are some things to consider as you assess your child's level of anxiety in the home, school, or daycare setting, transitioning, or when socializing. It is important to note your child will need to have multiple symptoms over a length of time. This will be discussed in detail in Chapter 6. For now, ask yourself if your child shows:

- Inflexibility
- Shyness or nervousness when interacting with others
- Self-critical statements
- Inability to let go of worry
- Avoidance of new or challenging situations
- Difficulty transitioning
- Trouble falling or staying asleep
- Perfectionism

 **Question?**

Do you spend excessive time rearranging activities or reassuring your child? Do you fear the next outing or change in routine?
If so, make a chart of weekly activities and transitions and rate your child's level of distress over a month's time. This will help you see more clearly where the issues lie and what you need to address.

Doctors suggest the best time to watch for signs of an anxiety disorder is when your child is between the ages of six and eight. During this time you will notice changes that are important. He should grow less afraid of the dark and imaginary creatures, and instead become more anxious about school performance and social relationships. The ability he has during this time to grow through the unknowns of school responsibility and structure can be very telling.

Also, how he chooses to handle tests, friendships, and being on a team are clues as well. An excessive amount of anxiety in children this age may be a warning sign for the development of anxiety disorders later in life.

 Essential

Understanding the nature of anxiety and how your child experiences it will help you sympathize with your child's struggles. Check out the Web site *www.adaa.org*. An understanding parent is the first step to a healthier child.

Another litmus test of problematic anxiety in your child is when you reassure her, but she still cannot stop the worry in her head. What often results is that her distressed thoughts, feelings, and behaviors saturate her life and the functioning of the family as a whole. You can use the previous list to identify patterns of anxiety early so that her worry molehills do not turn into big anxiety mountains.

Worry Makes Anxiety Grow

Everyone worries. On the positive side, worry can motivate you to do well at a task, accomplish a goal, or take care of a problem. Chronic worry though turns into trouble when it becomes the focus of your child's life; when he seems unable to let go of the worry and enjoy his day. Additionally, as your child grows and learns through experience, he usually realizes there are no monsters hiding in the closet; if you make a mistake, you will live; and sometimes you have to keep trying to get what you want. However, for some children, anxiety is so overwhelming that it becomes paralyzing and prevents any forward movement. Children who are anxious can't see options clearly and either find it difficult to ask for help and withdraw or freeze, or constantly ask for help, seeing themselves as incapable. Your child might have a tendency to lose his sense of subjective control over the world, and become consumed with the worry. He may also drop an acquired developmental skill, such as toilet training, or taking turns at school if the worry starts to traumatize him. Take note, though: temporarily losing a developmental skill often occurs just prior to acquiring a new skill as well. It can be confusing, so be sure to look for other evidence of anxiety and, if the skill does not return within a week, consider a problem with anxiety.

What Does Worry Look Like?

Worry involves both thoughts and feelings and is defined as a lasting preoccupation with past or future events. This type of thinking causes your child to feel as if she were reliving an event repeatedly, or constantly readying herself for the worst outcome in a future event. When you see your child "becoming her anxiety," you might think to yourself, "I do not get it, where did this come from?" The worried thoughts will often seem out of proportion to you and sometimes seem as if they came out of nowhere. You will see your child get stuck in a vicious cycle that in turn increases her dread, and nothing you say or do seems to help. Instead, when your child is trapped in worry you will often hear the phrases "If only . . ." and "What if . . . ," over and over.

The "What Ifs"

"What If" refers to thoughts about the future. In the case of worry, these thoughts are about any number of possible emotionally charged things that could happen. "What if I am not liked by the other kids, do not do well on the test, cannot hit the ball in gym, or do not get chosen for the team?" When the worry starts and your child cannot stop it, it grows in intensity like a runaway train, and your child ends up with, "What if no matter what I do, it is not enough?" It is an endless pursuit that can never be satisfied and often results in negative self-talk, low self-esteem, and ultimately, being unsure of who they are. It also shows itself behaviorally; when the What Ifs take hold over your child's life, he may seem paralyzed, unable to participate in activities for fear of the What Ifs, or unable to perform up to his capability. You then will hear phrases like, "What if I don't catch the ball when it comes my way, I can't be on the team," or "I can't try out for the play, what if I forget my lines? Everyone will make fun of me—I'll just die."

The "If Onlys"

"If only . . ." refers to thoughts about an unhappy event that your child wishes had not happened. Maybe your child said something to a friend she now wishes she had not, or did something she looks back on with regret. The event has ultimately left her with an unresolved emotional feeling, and worry is how her mind tries to resolve it, by trying to figure out what went wrong and how to fix it. "If only" will sound like this, "If only I had kept my mouth shut when Sara asked me what I thought of her new haircut, now she will never talk to me again," or "If only I listened in class, I would have gotten a better grade on this test."

 **Question?**

Are you constantly trying to soothe and reassure your child?
If you find yourself managing your child's feelings, often repeating calming and positive statements to no avail, this is one of the signs she is overly anxious and you probably need to schedule an appointment with your child's doctor.

Unfortunately, in many cases, because the event has already happened and your child cannot control the past, nothing can be done, and worry cycles on like a gerbil on a wheel. Your child can become consumed with guilt, hypersensitive to criticism, and hesitant to take action for fear of "yet another failure." The "if only" becomes a "what if . . . I fail . . . " and the cycle begins again.

Your Child's Identity

Identity is who you are, and who you are not. Healthy identity is another key part of your child's development. Identity is self-awareness and other-awareness; how much your child knows about her likes and dislikes, her beliefs about who she is and what she thinks her capabilities are. As your child's sense of self develops, so does her ability to blossom in school and in social relationships. Just as self-esteem is how she *feels* about herself, identity is how she *thinks* about herself. A child with a strong sense of identity might state, "I am a short person, I like pizza, and I am funny."

Anxiety, because it is so overpowering, interferes with your child's ability to make that distinction, and to see herself clearly. Filled with a sense of "I can't . . . " or "I do not . . . " your child with anxiety cannot even begin to see her way clear to a strong sense of self. This lack of foundation will magnify negative self-statements and prevent her from developing into a competent and confident adult.

Autonomy

An important skill for your child to learn in order to develop a healthy identity and be less affected by stress and anxiety is to grow in autonomy. Autonomy is defined as self-awareness, a sense of identity, the ability to act independently, and the ability to exert control over the external environment. If you have ever heard a three-year-old say, "I can do it myself!" you have experienced a child experimenting with autonomy. Your child's sense of knowing he can make it on his own, and knowing what type of person he is and is not become building blocks for future success and happiness.

Internal Strength

For children in a difficult environment, such as a family with alcoholism, overprotective parents, fighting, divorce, or mental illness, a strong identity means the ability to distance oneself from the family chaos and still see the future as positive. These children will be able to identify how to differentiate "what is about me," from "what is about them," and to make independent judgments about life events. This internal strength creates a buffer against stress by allowing a child not to internalize, or take on, others' problems. A strong identity, as you can see, is the key to combat stress and anxiety, and cope well through adversity.

Your Child's Self-Esteem

Self-esteem is the collection of beliefs and feelings that your child has about himself, combined with a general sense of whether or not he sees himself as basically good, worthy, and competent. It is a collection of ideas about who he believes he is, what he is capable of, and what makes him special and unique from others. Self-esteem encompasses how your child will define himself, his attitudes and behaviors, and how he sees his ability to affect the world around him. The two key ingredients for your child's strong self-esteem are that he feels he is both lovable and capable. Do you remember when a respected adult praised you for an accomplishment, or for just being you? That event was a building block in your ability to experience self-esteem, and your children build their self-esteem, bit by bit, in the same way.

The Happy Child

The patterns of self-esteem begin developing soon after birth and are a life-long process. For example, when a baby or toddler reaches a developmental milestone, he experiences a sense of accomplishment that bolsters self-esteem. In a healthy family, this sense of pride and accomplishment is reflected back to the child by parents and other family members. It is this learning process of attempts and mastery that teaches your child a "can-do" sense of self.

A healthy self-concept is no doubt your child's shield against the challenges of the world. Kids who feel good about themselves will most likely have an easier time moving through conflicts and fighting back negative influences. They tend to be hopeful, energetic, and have positive thoughts about the future. They are more likely to be able to solve problems on their own, and to ask for help or support when they need it.

The Self-Critical Child

In contrast, if your child has low self-esteem, challenges can become a source of major anxiety and frustration, fueling the already burning fire inherent in an anxiety disorder. When your child is plagued by worry and anxiety, he will develop self-critical thoughts such as, "I'm no good," "I can't do anything right," and "What's the point?" Ultimately, he might become passive, withdrawn, and depressed. Children with a deflated sense of self see small setbacks as permanent, intolerable conditions. The immediate response to challenges becomes, "I can't." Making matters worse, to fight off the "I can't" feeling, your child might strive for perfection and control.

 *Fact*

The National Institute of Mental Health (NIMH) has conducted research and developed treatment protocols for anxiety disorders. They suggest a combination of medication and specific types of psychotherapy, which are called cognitive behavioral and behavioral therapy.

Perfection

Perfection in a child's world might look like an inability to appreciate what she does well or to tolerate her limitations. Your child will see her mistakes as huge, creating a negative outlook full of personal criticisms. The negativity will translate to seeing herself as incompetent, inadequate, imperfect, and can also lead to a black and white, rigid view of people and life. The types of statements you might hear are "How could I have missed that, I'm so stupid," or "I didn't get invited . . . nobody likes me." Often, if what your child did accomplish is not 100 percent, she considers herself a failure. This thinking becomes a crippling and painful way to live and restricts your child's opportunities to be human and grow from mistakes. Worry, stress, and anxiety take their toll. Anxiety leads to perfectionism, which is unattainable and thus inevitably leads back to anxiety via self-blame and possibly self-hatred. In the end, mistakes become criticism, shortcomings become failure, and relationships with both the self and others can become impaired.

The Stress and Anxiety Connection

Stress can come from any situation or thought that causes your child to feel frustrated, angry, nervous, or tense. What is stressful to one child will not necessarily be stressful to another. Stress is subjective, and often parents do not experience stress the same way their children do. Parents also do not feel stress about the same things as their children do. Understanding what is stressful for your child and responding, even if the issue seems trivial, will help your child build his overall sense of security. For example, if your child tells you he is "afraid of the dark and wants to sleep with a light on," it will not be helpful to say, "Oh, that's silly, there is nothing out there, I already checked." The child who feels stress or anxiety will know that you do not know what you are talking about, he might feel confused about how to trust you or himself, and his symptoms will grow. Stress is one of the biggest risk factors in children who feel anxiety, and it can lead to depression, eating disorders, or a host of other difficulties. The impact is usually cumulative, adding up over time before it becomes an anxiety disorder. This gives you many opportunities to interrupt the cycle and redirect your child's sense of security, self, and competence. Becoming aware of what seems stressful in your child's life gives you the power to intervene and stop the cycle of anxiety before it begins.

The following are the typical emotional or behavioral signs of a stressed child: Worry, inability to relax, new or recurring fears (fear of the dark, being alone, of strangers), clinging or unwilling to let go of mom or dad, unexplained anger, unwarranted crying, aggressive or refusal behavior, regression to a behavior that is typical of an earlier developmental stage (like bedwetting or thumb sucking), unwillingness to participate in family or school activities, and shyness that limits activities.

 Fact

According to Mental Health America, an advocacy group that recently conducted a nationwide survey on how people manage stress, most Americans manage stress by watching TV, skipping out on exercise, and choosing junk food over a healthy meal.

It is common for your child to be stressed if he sees you are stressed. This is something you might need to talk to yourself about. Are you overbooked or overwhelmed, constantly worried, or not sleeping? Or, are you not eating well, unable to set boundaries to take time for yourself, or do you allow your child to hear information that is upsetting to you? Research has suggested parents who are not emotionally available for their children, or who lack positive coping mechanisms themselves, often have children who are stressed out. You are the most powerful model for your children and need to provide examples of healthy stress management and self-care.

Possible Reasons for Stress

It is normal for your child to feel stress when she is starting school or a new school year, or changing from one school phase to the next, such as between elementary and middle or junior high school. Moving, changes in peer groups, or families with high expectations in academics or other activities have also been found to be highly stressful. If your child has been abused, neglected, deprived, or has had a major loss that threatened her security, she is also at risk for stress or anxiety. Additionally, when there has been a demand for a child to carry responsibility that would normally belong to a parent, like dealing with a family member's chemical abuse or chronic illness, children often feel stressed and anxious. This is because they have to overfunction by taking on chores and emotional responsibility greater than their years, and this may lead to patterns of perfectionism and rigidity as a result. This method of coping is how your child maintains a sense of control when life feels out of control.

Fight or Flight

Just like anxiety, when your child is under stress, her body will react. It produces certain hormones to deal with a real or perceived threat. Some of the hormones that are released are called adrenaline, noradrenalin, and corticosteroids. The chemical processes set off the flight or fight response, compelling either escape or self-defense. Your child's heart rate will increase so it can pump more blood to his muscles and brain, and his lungs will take in air faster to supply his body with the added oxygen it thinks it needs. The process is automatic, happens in seconds, and is almost impossible to stop. Later, in Chapters 13 and 16, there are tools to help mitigate this process.

The typical physical signs of a child experiencing stress are headaches, upset stomach, sleep disturbances, new or recurrent bedwetting, stuttering, or changes in eating habits.

 Essential

One of the immediate ways to reduce stress and alleviate anxiety is to ask your child to take three long, slow, deep breaths and repeat as necessary. If you join your child in the process, it will enhance your child's sense of calm as well as your own! More than three deep breaths can create a sense of lightheadedness, which could increase the child's anxiety, so be sure not to overdo it.

Take a Breather

Breathing is essential as a way to help reduce stress when your child's body has kicked into high gear. Here is how it works: When your child takes a deep breath and exhales slowly, although he will not be aware of it, his heart rate just slowed down. When he inhales, it beats faster, and when he exhales, it will beat slower. You can explain to him that it is a rhythm that will help his heart stay healthy and is an excellent way to be in better control of his feelings. Other benefits of deep breathing include increased oxygen flow to the brain and other organs, decreased muscle tension, increased energy and focus, and a general sense of well-being.

 Essential

Play is necessary for children to learn. Studies show it helps them learn how to control themselves, how to interact with others, improves intellectual skills, and fosters decision-making, memory, thinking, and speed of mental processing.

Sleep and balanced nutrition are also excellent ways to combat the effects of stress. Replenishing your child's body goes hand in hand with a happy and healthy child. Sleep varies according to age. Doctors give, for the most part, the following recommendations: children birth to age six need ten to thirteen hours of sleep a night, six- to nine-year-olds need ten hours, ten- to twelve-year-olds need nine hours, and adolescents need approximately eight to nine hours of sleep a night; depending on their schedules it can be more.

Remember, this list is only a recommendation, not an absolute. It is also understood that daily life can affect bedtimes and mealtimes and that you do your best on any given day. Your doctor's suggestions are important information to keep in mind as you work toward maximizing your child's potential.

The Well-Meaning Parent

Many professionals feel that children today are too busy, too scheduled, and do not have time to play creatively or have fun. Between school, dance, soccer, hockey, football, track, and music lessons, putting aside how stressful it is for parents to manage that with their own schedules, where is the opportunity to learn how to socialize in an unstructured and relaxing way?

It is best, not only for the child, but for the parent as well, to live a balanced life. Be open if your child complains about the number of activities she is involved in or refuses to go. She may be trying to let you know through a temper tantrum that she is overwhelmed or feeling stress. For that matter, if your child's schedule is stressing you out, you also get to say "This is not working." As a parent you want to provide your child with the best opportunities, but you do not want to sacrifice something more important in the process—your sanity.

CHAPTER 2

Causes of Anxiety

Anxiety occurs for a variety of emotional, biological, and environmental reasons. It is built on risk factors that are interrelated. Literature reveals the jury is getting closer to confirming that there is also an inherited or genetic component. Although this chapter breaks down the causes of anxiety into categories, they can, and often do, overlap.

How Common Is Anxiety?

Anxiety was first acknowledged by the American Psychiatric Association in 1980 as a mental disorder. It is not that anxiety didn't exist before that, but doctors used the terms "suffering with nerves," or neurosis, instead. Since then, anxiety has become the most widely recognized mental health problem in the general population. Estimates show 10 to 15 percent of American children are affected by, meet the criteria of, or are diagnosed with, some form of an anxiety disorder. In adults that figure rises, ranging from 16 to 18 percent.

For children ages six to eleven, research shows one in ten as having some form of anxiety disorder. Social anxiety has the highest percentage, with between 8 to 11 percent being affected, followed by generalized anxiety disorder at 3 to 4 percent, then separation anxiety disorder, post-traumatic stress syndrome, and obsessive-compulsive disorder.

Coexisting Conditions

A coexisting condition occurs when your child has more than one disorder at the same time. An example would be a child who feels anxious and is depressed about it. Research shows that a large percentage of children and adolescents who have anxiety, 50 to 89 percent, are diagnosed with another disorder as well. *The American Journal of Psychiatry* found that children who had a social anxiety disorder had an additional diagnosis:

- 20 percent had other specific phobias
- 16 percent had generalized anxiety disorder
- 8 percent had depression
- 16 percent had attention deficit hyperactivity disorder
- 16 percent had learning disabilities

Another study evaluated a group of children who had a panic attack by the age of fourteen. Researchers were able to project that by the time the children in the study were twenty-four years old:

- 33 percent still had an anxiety disorder
- 24 percent had a mood disorder
- 29 percent had a substance abuse disorder

 Essential

A National Institute of Mental Health survey conducted in 2007 found that half of all adults with an anxiety disorder had a psychiatric diagnosis in youth. Other literature suggests it is as high as 90 percent. If you suspect your child has an anxiety disorder, it is best to have a doctor check her symptoms.

Common Personality Traits and Characteristics

Certain traits appear to have an influence on the development of anxiety disorders in children. Common characteristics shared by those who suffer with anxiety include:

- Strong sense of responsibility
- Need to please others
- Oversensitivity to criticism
- Perfectionism
- Overachievement or low achievement
- Tendency to worry

Although anxiety can lead to distress and difficulty in your child's capacity to cope, there is another side to this; those same traits can produce some excellent kids. The characteristics listed above can also create children who are well-behaved, sensitive toward others, easily connected to their feelings, motivated to do well, work toward high achievement, and are bright, mindful, and concerned about pleasing others, not just themselves. Just as with most things in life, there are always two sides to a story.

Comparing Boys and Girls

Researchers have found that girls are twice as likely as boys to suffer from generalized anxiety disorder, social phobias, specific phobias, and panic attacks at some point in their lives. Obsessive-compulsive disorder is equally common in boys and girls, and more girls than boys suffer from post-traumatic stress disorder. Although far from finding a clear-cut reason for these gender differences, medical professionals suggest that maybe girls have an imbalance in hormones, an increase in emotional, mental, physical, or sexual abuse, and a higher sensitivity to others' struggles. A connection between abuse suffered in childhood and long-term changes in the brain's structure and chemistry has been found. Researchers looking at the brains of sexually abused girls found that they had abnormal blood flow in the hippocampus, which triggers memories and emotions. These girls were found to be more moody and depressed, and suffered more anxiety attacks.

Scientists also believe sex hormones may play a role in why more girls than boys feel anxiety. Estrogen, a female hormone, is known to interact with serotonin, one of the brain chemicals implicated in both depression and anxiety disorders. Additionally, girls are more likely than boys to seek help. This may reflect the fact that it is more socially acceptable for girls to both express and address their emotional states.

 **Question?**

My child complains before school that she does not feel well. How do I know if she is really sick?
For morning tummyaches, see if there are any other symptoms. If there is only one symptom, the bellyache, then do not worry. Two or more symptoms, bellyache and fever, or bellyache and vomiting, should be taken more seriously.

Psychological Aspects

It is helpful to keep in mind that your child learns primarily by imitation. Studies have found most of children's learning, actually 95 percent of it, occurs unconsciously, while children are simply living life. This makes it hard as a parent because it means you are being watched, and your outcomes are being used to make judgments about what life looks and feels like to your child. If you do not have open communication with your kids, or are not aware of their perceptions as they go through their learning process, the decisions they make about life are happening largely without your knowledge.

Feelings in the Family

Growing up in a family where fear, worry, and anxiety are consistently modeled by parents or family members can teach a child to be anxious. In addition, if a child grows up in a home where a parent or sibling is terminally ill, in an abusive or alcoholic home where she is walking on eggshells around a parent, or constantly in an over-alert state, she may learn to expect the worst, or actually *look* for the worst. The child ends up living in a state of constant worry.

The psychological state of fear and trauma can also be present when a child is bullied at school, in the neighborhood, or on the school bus. The continuous state of anxiety that results creates children who, to protect themselves, might freeze up or withdraw. They have a tendency to lose their sense of belonging and separate themselves out from friends. A typical example is the child who is standing off on his own during lunch or recess. It is also common for a child feeling anxiety to fall into a world of his own where he might feel he has to create plans for how to safeguard himself, "just in case." When this happens, the body and mind are sidetracked, and your child's growth may become interrupted.

 *Fact*

According to the National Child Traumatic Stress Network, more than one-fourth of all American youths have experienced some sort of a traumatic event by age sixteen. It has also been found that 1.7 million adolescents between the ages of twelve and nineteen were victims of a violent crime.

Internal Versus External Stressors

The term *internal* refers to the vulnerability that comes from genetics and temperament. It also means how your child feels inside about what happens outside of her. Internal triggers are more likely to affect a child who has strong emotions or who has a tendency to be a sensitive child. Examples of internal cues that can lead to anxiety are guilt, anger, shame, perfection, negative thinking, and frequent thoughts that are centered on should, must, and never.

External influences are events that happen outside of the child and have a point of origin. Examples of some external triggers are divorce, violence at home, school, games or TV, injury, illness or death of a family member, abuse, or a disaster. These examples will be addressed in detail later in this chapter.

Understanding the differences between the external and internal environment can be confusing. This is an area where communicating with your child, in an effort to help him understand where his fear accurately lies, would be helpful. It can be a first step in making a plan to be proactive for future issues, as discussed in Chapter 15.

 Essential

A hard, but significant, job as a parent is to understand that your child is constantly adding to her fears by how she thinks. Distorted thinking and an inability to stop the thinking are common. Once this process of worry, fear, or anxiety over an issue has begun, your child will continue to frighten herself with her own thoughts.

The amount of anxiety your child will feel from these triggers will be based on how she processes it. Therefore, it will be important for you to take the time to help your child separate out what is a real danger outside of her as compared to what she is creating internally, through her thoughts.

Biological Aspects

Fear and panic are normal reactions to danger. When fear or panic is felt, this reflects a chain of events in your child's autonomic nervous system. Let's take a look at how your child's body works, biologically speaking, as an aid to understanding how normal fear and panic become an anxiety disorder.

Neurotransmitters

A person's brain is a network of billions of nerve cells called neurons that communicate with each other to create thoughts, emotions, and behaviors. This process is called cell-to-cell communication, in which a transfer of information from one part of the brain to another is made possible by chemicals called neurotransmitters. The two primary neurotransmitters that affect your child's feelings are serotonin and dopamine. Also important in the cause and treatment of anxiety are the brain chemicals norepinephrine, acetylcholine, and gamma-aminobutyric acid (GABA), corticotrophin-releasing hormone (CRH), and cholecystokinin, all of which play a role in the regulation of arousal and anxiety.

This information is complex, but remember that it is helpful to be familiar with this process and the chemicals that play a part in panic and anxiety. That way, if you do end up at the doctor's office, you can feel informed and confident to make decisions. When a doctor recommends medication, he will suggest an anti-anxiety medication that affects one or more of the neurotransmitters discussed earlier to correct the imbalance in your child's brain. Medications are discussed fully in Chapter 11.

The Locus Ceruleus

The locus ceruleus, located in the lower part of the brain, is the structure that controls emotional response and triggers a defensive reaction for the purpose of protection. When your child is feeling anxious, the locus ceruleus sets the sympathetic nervous system (SNS) in motion, and chemical messengers like adrenaline, norepinephrine, and serotonin are released. The cause of the panic attack is simply the arousal of the SNS because of anxious feelings, even if there is no external threat present. Eventually, the parasympathetic nervous system (PNS) will kick in, and the symptoms will diminish.

Scientists have discovered they can provoke an anxiety attack if they stimulate the locus ceruleus electronically, and they can stop it with medication.

The Autonomic Nervous System

This system controls your child's breathing, digestion, and temperature regulation. It is composed of two parts; the sympathetic nervous system and the parasympathetic nervous system. As stated earlier, the job of the SNS is to rev your child up, and the job of the PNS is to calm your child down, each balancing the other out. When your child gets frightened the SNS releases adrenaline, his heart pumps faster, sometimes racing, his blood pressure goes up, he might get tingling in his hands and feet because blood flows away from them to his brain, and his lungs will work harder to get more air. This release allows him to focus more intently on the real or perceived danger and sets off the fight-or-flight reaction discussed in Chapter 1.

The Amygdala and Hippocampus

When the fight or flight response is triggered it occurs in the parts of the brain called the amygdala and hippocampus. The amygdala is the part of the brain where feelings and emotions lie. So if your child is feeling fearful and anxious, the amygdala will send this information throughout your child's body in an alert. The hippocampus holds memory, time, and place, especially for situations that are highly emotional. Once the amygdala jumps into action, your child can become overly sensitive to certain stimuli, responding to fear and anxiety in an instant, even in a safe situation.

An example might look something like this: You moved last month and your child was very upset about it. He now cannot find his teddy bear that he sleeps with every night. He becomes frantic even though you told him you know where it is and will go get it. His heart starts to beat faster and he is becoming sweaty and tingly all over anyway. Although you persist in reassuring him, your child has a panic attack.

Genetic Causes

Investigations into the causes of anxiety are clear that anxiety, panic, and depression can be hereditary, and that usually, anxiety disorders are a concern for several members of the same family. If a parent or sibling has certain anxiety disorders or panic attacks, a child's risk increases four- to six-fold for developing an anxiety disorder himself. This is because the structure of the brain and its processes are inherited. However, many people who have no family history of the disorder can develop anxiety as well.

 Fact

Incredibly, 19 million people are suffering from an anxiety disorder. Of those, about 20 to 25 percent have close relatives who have also struggled with a panic disorder sometime in their lives.

Studies have found that certain genetic variations lead to chemical imbalances in the brain that lie dormant until awakened by stress or trauma. The scenario used earlier illustrates this. Before you moved your son was good-natured, calm, and flexible. As a result of the move, he has difficulty with even the slightest bit of change without having intense anxiety. This finding has caused many researchers to investigate the interaction between genes and environment in causing anxiety, not just one or the other.

The Role of Temperament

Temperament is your child's nature present at birth. Many parents can tell almost immediately whether their child will be peaceful, irritable, sociable, or more introverted. At the forefront of temperament research is Dr. Jerome Kagan of Harvard University. The research has connected the dots between four personality traits: timid, upbeat, melancholic, and bold to patterns in brain activity. What he discovered in timid children is that the amygdala is more easily aroused in those prone to fearfulness, creating children who are more anxious and uneasy. Compared to children in the other groups, their hearts beat faster when confronted with stressful situations, they were more finicky about eating, were introverted around strangers, and were reluctant to try anything new. Kagan found that from birth, these children had a hyperexcitable right temporal lobe in their brains, and if fear was triggered in the child, those pathways became stronger. More research is needed, but other studies have shown that the hippocampus is smaller in people who have had a significant trauma.

The brain is constantly changing. It will reshape based on information it receives, changing itself in order to learn and respond. It is a work in progress and becomes stronger through repetition and time. Parents who are more successful in reducing their child's fearfulness and anxiety will allow the child to face fears so the pathways can become stronger. It is best to challenge your child in small increments, no matter how uncomfortable, while being encouraging and loving. Reshaping as soon as you notice your child is having difficulty, even in infancy when children tend to be more flexible in their thinking and have less to unlearn, works best.

 Fact

Dr. Kagan and his team found only 10 to 15 percent of children who were shy, fearful, irritable, and introverted as babies had social anxiety throughout their adolescence. That means the majority of the kids they studied did not. Having an introverted child is not a sure bet for later issues.

Changing your child's temperament is much less difficult when the brain is still developing. The greatest influence will occur between birth and five years old when neural pathways can still be easily sculpted.

As discussed, the research for heredity and genetics is strong and a great help toward understanding the foundation of your child's anxiety. The environment is a potent source as well.

Environmental Factors

Many of the environmental factors that contribute to anxiety are discussed in detail later in the book, but here is a general understanding. The environment is all events, people, circumstances, desires, needs, and situations that have a point of origin outside of your child. Any situation that disrupts your child's sense of structure and order in their world creates a change internally.

Life Events

It is common when children start school or transition to a new grade or daycare for them to become emotional, scared, or clingy for a brief period. Usually, parents will find a few weeks are normal for the transition, and are able to hang in there. It is when the reaction becomes protracted and your child cannot move past her feelings about the incident that intervention will be necessary. Some common examples of stressful life events (which are external stressors) are:

- A trauma
- Seeing violence at home, school, or on TV
- School issues
- Divorce
- Moving
- Loss
- Anxious, overprotective, or critical parenting style
- Difficulty with friendships
- Death of a family member, friend, or family pet

Uncertainty of outcome, along with transitions and ambiguous situations, often create the most stress. In addition, if a child grows up in an environment that is actually scary or dangerous, such as when there is violence in the family or the community, as discussed earlier, the child may learn to be fearful or expect the worst.

Uncertainty

When a situation lacks a clear outcome, your child might feel a lack of control and significant stress. Uncertain as to what type of coping response will be needed to deal with a particular situation, your child might be convinced he does not have what it takes to get through it, especially when he remembers difficulties he had in the past. A study of adolescents anxious about the future, a stressor marked by uncertainty, found they expressed their anxiety by trying to alter their mood. Often they resorted to drug-taking and impulsive or dangerous behavior to help them cope.

Children can learn how to manage environmental stressors through watching parents, siblings, friends, teachers, and peers at school. If they observe people who respond to stressful situations with uncertainty, worry, nervousness, extreme caution, and overemphasis on danger, this can influence how they themselves will react, and create a pessimistic worldview. This pattern is discussed further in Chapter 15.

Parental Influence

First, it is important to note that most parents do not *cause* their children to be anxious, rather they unwittingly help to perpetuate it. We say *most* parents because this statement does not hold true if there is intentional violence or abuse in the home. Sometimes in your efforts to do the best you can with what you have been taught or know, you are unaware that your efforts might be hindering your children. For example, if your seven-year-old child is afraid to make new friends, you might "help" him by making the phone call to set up a play date, instead of assuring him he can get through it on his own. Parents can also affect how a child chooses to cope though their anxiety by watching the choices they make. For example, if you come home from work stressed, does your child see you reach for a glass of wine or a beer to relax, or do you yell at others and then say, "Sorry, I had a stressful day"?

Alert!

According to a National Television study on violence, a child will have viewed 8,000 murders and 100,000 other acts of television violence by the time he is eleven years old. It is important to use parental controls and limit what is available for viewing to minimize the impact of trauma on your child and decrease sources of anxiety.

Research shows that inconsistency, harsh and rigid attitudes, ambiguity, and family conflict appear to be among the primary predictors of the development of anxiety. Also identified as associated with a child's anxiety is a lack of clear family rules, strong parental concern for a family's reputation, a poor relationship with the father, and an inability for the child to bond in infancy.

Trauma

Early traumatic experience can block the normal growth and development of coping skills, and affect your child's emotional and social growth. At the time of the event, intense feelings of fear and helplessness can overcome your child, causing him to feel he cannot think clearly or function well. If your child has experienced a life event that is out of the realm of normal human experience and continues over time, even with your care, concern, and discussions with him, he may be on his way to an anxiety disorder or post-traumatic stress disorder (PTSD and trauma are discussed fully in Chapter 6).

Your child's reaction to a trauma is affected by her age, what life has felt like so far, temperament and personality, and when the trauma happened. This can result in feelings of loss of control and stability, worry about personal safety, and grief reactions. When the trauma has been long-lasting or a sense of hopelessness develops, as in the case of abuse or bullying, you might see school refusal, or even suicidal thinking. Bullies are discussed further in Chapter 17.

Food

When foods are full of sugar or caffeine, contain food additives, or if your child is lacking vitamins and minerals, anxiety, feelings of panic, an inability to sleep, night frights, and/or depression can develop. These foods can influence your child's thought process by altering her ability to concentrate or learn new material; they can also lower her level of awareness, weaken the growth process of her brain, increase how sick she becomes when ill, and unbelievably, even increase the duration and intensity of a cold. More on the importance of nutrition is to come in Chapter 18.

 Essential

A number of conditions can occur when your child's body is low in potassium, including diarrhea, vomiting, and sweating, which are also symptoms of anxiety. To keep potassium levels balanced, be sure to give your child bananas, meats, fruits, fish, beans, and vegetables.

Because anxiety affects blood sugar levels, it can cause sensitivities and stomach problems such as pain, a bloated or distended stomach, discomfort, indigestion, and symptoms of hyperglycemia and hypoglycemia. When your child overeats, especially sweets and desserts, it can affect her nervous system. This can trigger moodiness, anxiousness, sleepiness, or depression. It is important to note that some people can control their anxiety disorder almost completely though a reduction of sugary or caffeinated foods and drinks.

Sleep

Sleep is a basic human need important at any age, as fundamental to feeling healthy as good nutrition and exercising regularly are. A good night's sleep, as you probably know, can make a world of difference in your child's ability to handle himself. It can refuel his body's energy, give his active brain the rest it needs, and all around put him mentally in a better mood. On the flip side, lack of sleep is known to disrupt the body's ability to replenish hormones that affect both physical and mental health. For children with anxiety, lack of sleep is linked to learning problems, slower emotional and physical growth, bedwetting, and high blood pressure. Details on sleep routine and insomnia will be presented in Chapter 18.

Behavioral Aspects

As mentioned before, the fight-or-flight response prepares the body for action, either to attack or to run. Studies on the amygdala and stress hormones point to the "freeze reaction," too. This occurs when stress continuously bathes the body and brain with cortisol and adrenaline, and will cause your child to become aggressive, unresponsive, or retreat; whatever he feels he needs to do to avoid feeling bad. In the end, he might make choices based on fear and anxiety about what he thinks will happen, rather than on reality.

The Good and the Bad

Although anxiety has some positive benefits such as increasing awareness and motivation, on the negative side, in addition to avoidance, a child might choose to isolate, skip school, become an excitement seeker, and reject rules, or use alcohol and other drugs. In extreme cases, a pattern of school refusal can result. Your modeling, support, and intervention as a parent can make a world of difference in the life of a child with anxiety.

Other Behavioral Issues

You may also recognize your child looking hesitant, acting passive, or avoiding or refusing to go places or do things. Telephone calls to friends can become difficult and initiating conversations with teachers, or even you, can feel stressful for them. Notice also if your child avoids eye contact as well, or becomes aggressive with you when requested to do something if neither of these behaviors were seen previously.

CHAPTER 3

Signs and Symptoms
of Anxiety

Children with anxiety show telltale signs of the turmoil hidden below the surface. These indicators fall into several categories, but the underlying theme is that your child feels that he simply cannot meet the demands of life because they are too difficult or frightening. This chapter describes typical signs that might indicate that your child is having anxiety issues. Pay attention to the frequency, intensity, and duration of the behaviors in your child. In addition, the more signs your child displays, the more likely the underlying cause is anxiety. It is also helpful to keep in mind the ways that your child may seem different from his peers.

Behavioral Issues

Because children are less likely to be able to identify and verbalize feelings of worry and anxiety, they are more likely to show anxiety through their behaviors. Keep in mind that the older your child, the more likely he will be able to talk about his internal states. Children act out feelings as a normal expression of their development, which can sometimes be frustrating. As a result, parents often mistake a child's behavioral troubles for stubbornness, laziness, or willfulness. In fact, the overall message a child with anxiety communicates through behavior is a state of hopelessness.

Meltdowns

A meltdown can be best described as a "total emotional break-down." Your child may sob, wail, refuse to move or respond, or talk nonstop about an event he found upsetting. He may seem inconsolable, or unable to "rally" for the next demand, like homework, an outing, or dinnertime. Adolescents may "freak out," lamenting about issues that may seem trivial or even insensible from the adult point of view.

 Essential

> It is typical for parents bringing a child with anxiety to therapy to identify behavioral troubles as their main reason for seeking therapy. A good therapist will look beyond these clues for an underlying emotional issue that causes disruptions in behavior, and then help you and your child develop a plan to manage both the problem behaviors and the emotions driving them.

Tearfulness

Tears in response to disappointments, loss, or injury to the physical or emotional self are normal and expected in children (and adults, too!) If your child is tearful for no apparent reason, cannot seem to stop crying in response to an upset, or seems to "cry at the drop of a hat," anxiety could be the cause.

Trouble Transitioning

Many children with anxiety have difficulty switching gears between activities. This may occur at school between subjects, at particular times during the day, such as between playtime and dinner, or when a new set of skills or attention is required. A child may dawdle or show one of the behaviors discussed earlier when he is having trouble with a transition.

Opposition

Opposition is the refusal to meet requests, obligations, or deadlines. Your child may refuse to do her chores, get ready for bed, or participate in family activities. Children who are afraid they cannot do something well may express their fear by becoming oppositional.

Avoidance

Avoidance is one of the hallmarks of anxiety in both adults and children. Because your child wants to shy away from what is uncomfortable, she may resist doing things that take her out of her comfort zone. Anxious children may avoid social situations or occasions in which they fear they will be called upon to use skills they are certain they do not possess, such as a class presentation. To avoid feeling inadequate, your child may procrastinate or even shut down entirely. Parents may respond by either pushing or coddling or by avoiding the issue themselves. Research shows that parents of children with anxiety tend to do tasks for children or respond in a way that does not increase and encourage autonomy. This increases avoidance of independence in the future because the child is blocked from experiencing an internal sense of competence or mastery.

 Fact

Procrastination is a specific form of avoidance, with an "I'll do it later" attitude. Unfortunately, procrastination actually increases anxiety by delaying the inevitable need to confront the proverbial dragon. When procrastination becomes a pattern, it may indicate underlying issues with anxiety.

Feeling Isolated

One of the most debilitating aspects of anxiety is its power to cause people to feel different, isolated, and cut off from the world. This feeling of alienation can come in many forms and tends to feed on itself. Often, feelings of being different and separate from others can lead to increased anxiety and withdrawal. Left unaddressed, these are overpowering feelings that can lead to depression in a child with anxiety. Overlap between anxiety and depression will be discussed more fully in Chapter 5.

Alone in the Family

Children who are anxious may shy away from contact with family as well. Although it is common for teens or children who are more solitary or introverted to spend time alone in their rooms, the anxious child will avoid family contact more often than not. Your child may try to opt out of family outings, especially when extended family is included. He may appear to be indifferent, may "hang back," or may be slow to warm when extended family or company is present. Anxious children may opt for solitary activity, even when the opportunity for more interesting group interaction is available. It is important to note that some children are naturally more introverted than others. If your child has anxiety, he will have issues in several of the areas highlighted in this chapter.

Question?

How can you learn more about what is typical for your child at a given age or stage?
A trip to your local library or bookstore can uncover excellent resources for determining whether your child differs from developmental norms. Books in the child development and parenting sections can be enlightening and reassuring. Early Childhood Family Education programs, available in many communities, are also great resources for parents.

Alone at School

Because they are often highly sensitive and may overreact to challenges or disappointments, anxious children can feel isolated at school. They have difficulty making and keeping friends, and may come home from school teary and overwhelmed by social demands they feel they cannot meet. Your child may make statements such as "no one likes me" or "everybody's mean to me." Because she may be afraid to try new things, like the monkey bars or the newest dance step, she may actually end up ostracized by her peer group, magnifying her sense of aloneness. Because peer relationships are so important, they will be addressed more fully in the section entitled "Trouble with Friends."

I'm Different

A child with anxiety issues often feels that he is not like other children. The cycle of negative thinking that so often occurs in a child with anxiety may cause him to magnify his fears and shortcomings. Because his experiences are perceived as more intense or overwhelming than those of his peers, he is left with a sense of "otherness" that may prevent him from identifying with and learning from his peers. Behavioral issues such as tearfulness or frequent meltdowns can alienate the child with anxiety further from his peers. It is not uncommon for children to avoid or reject kids who seem immature or have low self-esteem.

They Can Do It, Why Can't I?

The child with anxiety has a tendency to see the world through the lens of "not good enough." As a result, your child may give the achievements of others more importance than is due, and may downplay his own accomplishments. Because he may be afraid of failure, he may not attempt to master new skills and may see himself as unable to measure up to the expectations of his peer group. He may give up entirely on learning a new skill, like the child who becomes afraid of trying to ride a bike and who will not ride at all because his friends have already mastered the skill. A child with anxiety may believe that others accomplish things easily and then give up on a task, believing he is a failure because the task wasn't easy. If you believe this is true for your child, try modeling persistence in the face of trouble or ask other children to share their struggles about how difficult something was.

 Essential

Encourage your child to master small skill sets that will enable her to meet larger demands. For example, if she is resistant to a sleepover, start "smaller" by arranging daytime get-togethers. Confidence builds on itself, and the goal in addressing anxiety is to encourage your child to stretch, without increasing anxiety. The successes your child experiences will build on themselves, creating a mindset of capability.

School Refusal

One of the most troubling patterns that can develop in children with anxiety is refusing to attend or stay at school. Separation anxiety, generalized anxiety, social fears, and peer issues all contribute to school avoidance, and will be discussed in detail in Chapters 6 and 17. A pattern of school refusal, once established, can be extremely difficult to change, and may require intensive therapeutic intervention and close cooperation with the school. The best defense for this potential pitfall is a good offense, which you will find in Chapter 17.

What Are the Signs?

Most children who attempt to avoid school will do so by complaining of physical symptoms. Headaches, stomachaches, and vague complaints of not feeling good are extremely common in children with anxiety and will be detailed in the final section of this chapter. Complaining, pleading, dawdling, "disappearing," and repeated attempts to avoid or be absent from school (for example, by regularly missing the bus) are common. Increases in these behaviors when tests or projects are due may indicate test anxiety.

What Are the Consequences?

The most obvious consequence of missing school is that your child may get behind in her schoolwork. For the child who is already anxious, missing homework can become overwhelming, spiraling into more physical complaints and additional attempts to avoid school. Another consequence, particularly for a child who is socially anxious, involves missed opportunities to build competence in peer interactions. The longer a child is away from school, the more daunting it becomes to go back into the fray of social demands. In this case, the proverbial "getting back on the horse after a fall" applies directly. The longer your child is away from school, the less confident and motivated she will be to return.

 **Fact**

Classical conditioning is one of the strongest factors in the development of avoidant behavior. When your child experiences the repeated association of unpleasant emotions and school, this will increase the odds of school avoidance. Similarly, when your child connects feelings of relief with not being in school, odds are that he will repeat the pattern of avoidance.

What Can You Do?

If you feel your child attempts to stay home from school more than she should, you can use several approaches, depending on your child's particular pattern. Sometimes, friends or siblings attending the same school can be excellent supports for your child. You may wish to spend some extra time at your child's school, for example, by volunteering, if this encourages her to stay in school. However, be prepared to wean your involvement at some point so that your child can learn to tolerate being at school on her own. School nurses, psychologists, or social workers may also be called upon to help encourage a child with anxiety to stay through the day.

When All Else Fails

If you have followed the tips above and your child continues to avoid or refuse to attend school, try involving the school social worker, who likely has experience encouraging children with anxiety. You can also offer your child a small reward for regular school attendance. This could be as simple as having a chat and snack with your child after he returns from school, focusing on the positive events of the day. For an approach with a bit more bang, see the strategies for positive reinforcement in Chapter 19.

 **Alert!**

If your child continues to struggle with school avoidance after using the tactics discussed earlier, focus your attention on Chapter 17, which deals specifically with school issues. You might also want to consider seeking help from a qualified professional therapist at this juncture.

Homework Refusal

Children avoid and refuse homework for a number of reasons. An anxious child may fear failure or be caught in a frustrating cycle of perfectionism. He may simply be too emotionally overwrought to call upon the attention and focus needed to complete the work. He may need supervision and reassurance from a parent who is busy preparing a meal, or is tired from the day's demands. It is important to rule out learning challenges or attention deficit disorder (ADD) before concluding that homework troubles are anxiety related. Overlap with other mental health issues are detailed in Chapter 5.

What Does It Look Like?

Typical patterns of homework refusal may include procrastination or dawdling, forgetting assignments or materials needed to complete the work, defiance, excessive need for reassurance, and inability to work independently. Some children become great at the disappearing act by running off to a friend's house or holing up in their rooms. As surprising as it seems, some children may even offer to do chores or help with food preparation in an effort to avoid doing their homework.

What Can You Do to Help?

First, be aware of your child's assignments and obligations for school. Make checking your child's backpack or folder a daily part of your routine, such as when she first comes home from school or when you come home from work. Communicate your belief that your child can do the work on her own, but that you will be happy to assist her if she gets stuck.

If your child routinely does homework in an area with multiple distractions, consider the following tips:

- Turn the TV or radio off.
- Choose an area that is well lighted and clear of clutter.
- Have your child do homework routinely in that area, at about the same time each day.
- Try to make sure your child is not hungry or overly tired when tackling homework.
- Consider reading a book or magazine nearby so that you are available for support. You are also modeling good study habits!
- Encourage younger siblings to draw or do projects in the same area, but only if they do not overly distract your child.
- Be positive and reinforce your child's efforts.

When and How to Talk to the Teacher

If your child is experiencing anxiety-related concerns at school, be prepared to increase your level of contact with his teacher. Keep in mind that some teachers are more receptive than others are to emotional concerns, and it may be necessary to enlist the school social worker or other helpers to advocate for your child. Generally, it is a good idea to let your child know that you plan to talk with his teacher. But some children will be embarrassed by this as it can increase their anxiety if they feel the teacher is watching them closely. As such, you may wish to involve your child directly in problem solving, or enlist the help of a therapist who can "run interference."

 **Question?**

My daughter needs help at school but got very angry at me for suggesting I would call the teacher. What do I do now?
The importance of respecting your child and not increasing anxiety makes this a tough call. It is best to explain that, out of love, you will make the call, and that if you did not care, you wouldn't bother. Offer to make the call in her presence, and discuss what you will say. Reassure your child that even though she is upset at this moment, you know that once everyone is on the same page, she will get relief and actually feel better.

If homework becomes a daily struggle, or if you find yourself needing to talk with the teacher more than once or twice a month, it may be time to seek professional help to identify underlying anxiety.

Trouble with Friends

Social difficulties can plague children with anxiety for a number of reasons. Anxious children may shy away from social interaction because of their fear of failure. They may feel alienated from or rejected by their peers, and these feelings may or may not be an accurate assessment of the reality of the situation. Your empathy and understanding of your child's frustrations, along with your persistent and gentle encouragement, can go a long way to improving your child's social experiences. It is important for parents of children with anxiety not to minimize the enormous power social frustration and discomfort play in a child's developing sense of independence and self-esteem. Middle school (grades six through eight) can be a particularly difficult time for children as they navigate through puberty and the resulting new social and emotional demands.

No One Wants to Play with Me

Because children with anxiety are often shy and quiet compared to their more outgoing peers, they may have difficulty initiating social interaction or including themselves in a situation where other children are already involved in an activity. Your child may end up feeling that she is unwanted. Conversely, as you have already learned, peers can reject children with anxiety when their behavior is seen as immature, disruptive, or odd. Start by talking with your child about her fears, and encourage her by modeling ways to interact more effectively. You might say, "Why don't you try telling Susie that you would like to run through the sprinkler with her? Maybe you could bring popsicles over to share with her, you make the call and I will walk you over."

I Can't

Anxious children create mental mountains, which prevent them from the opportunity to have new and enjoyable experiences with their peers. Older children may compare themselves negatively to others, and may feel they have little or nothing of value to offer as a friend. Younger children may simply feel restless or uneasy around peers for reasons they are not yet able to identify.

Your child may fear doing things other more gregarious children do, such as sports, videogames, or sleepovers. To help your child overcome this roadblock, encourage and reward baby steps. You can also play a game or sport with your child to help increase confidence and ability and lessen fears.

 Essential

> Take the time to help your child introduce himself to other children in the neighborhood, or ask him to invite a classmate over to share in something he is interested in or does well. Don't forget to ask the teacher for a class list to help your child get started making new friends at school.

They Make Fun of Me

Younger children may lack social tact, and refer to your anxious child as a "crybaby" or "fraidy-cat." Unfortunately, the aftermath of repeated teasing can be serious, even leading to symptoms of post-traumatic stress disorder if the teasing is especially brutal, sadistic, or widespread. Be as supportive as possible if your child complains of teasing, and try to "check out the facts" whenever possible. With younger children, you may be able to intervene by increasing supervision, talking with the other parents involved, or limiting contact with specific friends. With older children, it may be necessary to speak to school personnel or neighborhood parents about your concerns, or assist your child in working out an assertive solution. Keep in mind that if this intervention is not handled delicately, it may backfire and lead to increased ostracism. In extreme cases, when a pattern of teasing or alienation cannot be broken, it may be necessary to move your child to another school.

Body Bugaboos

Children with anxiety can experience physical pain and discomfort as a part of their condition. In fact, bodily, or somatic, concerns are one of the most common characteristics in children with anxiety. As you read the next section, keep in mind that your child's complaints should be unrelated to sports or other injuries. The following complaints are among the most commonly experienced as an expression of underlying anxiety.

Aches and Pains

Aches and pains cover a relatively diffuse variety of physical sensations. They most typically include:

- Muscle aches
- Joint pain
- Tightness or tingling, most commonly in chest or extremities
- Back and/or neck pain

If your child experiences more than one or two of the above more than once or twice a week, start with your family physician to rule out any underlying physical conditions that could be causing the discomfort. If a trusted physician rules out physical causes, it may be time to seek psychological help.

 *Alert!*

Studies show somatic complaints are strongly associated with physical disorders in girls and with disruptive behavior disorders in boys. Researchers found that stomachaches, headaches, and musculoskeletal pains were common with anxiety disorders in girls. For boys, stomachaches were associated with oppositional defiant disorder and attention deficit hyperactivity disorder (ADHD).

Tummy Troubles

For many parents, the first indication of a child's anxiety involves one or more trips to the doctor to investigate digestive upsets.

Referred to as gastrointestinal complaints, these symptoms are of several different types:

- Nausea
- Stomachaches
- Indigestion or heartburn
- Vomiting
- Diarrhea
- Constipation

 Fact

Tandem breathing can be an effective distraction from body buga-boos. To start, sit side by side or hold your small child in your lap. Next, close your eyes. Pace your breathing together, matching your inhalations and exhalations. You can deliberately slow your own breathing and encourage your child to do the same. After a few minutes, stretch and return to your activity, noticing how much calmer you both feel.

Nervous Habits

Have you ever watched someone chew her fingernails, bounce her leg incessantly, twirl her hair, or snap chewing gum? These are all examples of nervous habits, which, interestingly enough, can cause onlookers to feel anxious or frustrated. Other nervous habits include knuckle-cracking, tapping fingers or objects, biting the lips, picking at the skin, or straightening clothing or other objects. Although most people have one or two nervous habits, in children these habits can go from distracting to debilitating if they are incessant and become a focus of teasing. Some children with anxiety can develop twitches or tics, which should be professionally evaluated to rule out concerns that are more serious.

CHAPTER 4

Is There a Test for This?

Unfortunately, anxiety, like most mental health conditions, is not something that can be detected by a single test. Depending on the seriousness of your child's anxiety, finding a compassionate therapist who can assess and treat your child might be enough, and formal testing won't be necessary. It is wise to rule out any underlying medical conditions as a first step because certain ailments can cause symptoms that mimic anxiety. Once you are sure your child is physically healthy, a trusted physician, friends, parenting groups, and your insurance providers are all good resources for taking the next steps.

Self-Evaluation and Charting

You are the best expert on your child's behavioral and emotional patterns, and your observations are invaluable tools. Tracking your child's behavior will allow you to determine whether it is getting better or worse over time. In addition, research has shown that the process of observing and charting a behavior may in itself reduce how often it occurs.

How Tracking Helps

Tracking your child's behavior can help you to feel more in control of his struggles by helping you understand the signs of the underlying turmoil and by pinpointing the areas in which he most needs help. Record-keeping provides baseline information for teachers and therapists so that they can design and implement strategies to reduce problem behavior and monitor whether the behavior is changing. Charting can also help you and your child build confidence as you achieve goals and track positive changes in behavior.

How to Start

An easy way to start is to look at the descriptions in Chapter 3, and make a list of any behaviors your child has shown. You may wish to add other areas of concern specific to your child or family. When observing a behavior, take into account the frequency, intensity, and duration of the behaviors you wish to track. You can use this "master list" as a sort of road map to navigate through the changes your child makes as you work with her to decrease her anxiety.

 Essential

When observing your child's behavior, it is important to focus on the two or three symptoms that you and your child find the most troublesome. For example, you might want to track the number and length of meltdowns, number and type of bodily complaints, or the number of nights your child does not fall asleep easily. Once you have tracked the top two or three, you can move on to others.

Charting 101

The easiest way for many parents to record a child's behavior is to copy a calendar page, and track directly on the page. You can use a key if this is helpful, for example using H for home, S for school, or other relevant abbreviations. You can engage your child in the process by using bright colors or different stickers to note events or progress. If you wish to use your chart to reward your child's progress, you will find tips on behavioral reinforcement in Chapter 19.

Clinical Interview and Diagnosis

Often, the first time a parent hears that their child has a diagnosis of anxiety is in a therapist's office. Usually after one to two sessions, a skilled therapist will be able to make a clinical diagnosis and begin to establish a treatment plan so that you and your child can begin to have some relief from the anxiety merry go round. Formal or structured testing is not always necessary, and in fact, can actually raise anxiety for some children. Chapter 8 will assist you in finding a counselor that you and your child are comfortable with.

What Is a Diagnosis?

A diagnosis is a kind of shorthand that medical and mental health practitioners use to describe particular groups of symptoms that occur together over a specific length of time. Symptoms can be emotional, behavioral, or physical, but usually come in combination. In order to be considered diagnosable, a symptom must reflect a change from normal functioning and be observable by others. Because much of your child's anxiety is hidden below the surface, the trick is to look for changes in behavior, like a decrease in your child's energy level, unwillingness to spend time with friends, or to try new things. Generally, a symptom must either cause distress or discomfort, or interfere with certain areas of functioning, such as friends, family, or school. As you read on, keep in mind that the medical model, despite being the most common approach when insurance is involved, is just one way to approach anxiety and other mental health issues. Chapter 13 will detail alternative approaches to anxiety management.

How a Diagnosis Is Used

A diagnosis helps those helping you and your child to efficiently capture a snapshot of your child's experience. It allows professionals to communicate easily with each other and with medical or insurance providers to understand your child and plan for her care. A specific diagnosis will also determine which interventions are most likely to be of help to you and your child to reduce her anxiety. For example, a child who experiences panic attacks will benefit most by relaxation therapy, and a child who has social fears may benefit more from role-play and group therapy.

Getting to a Diagnosis

A diagnosis is made by gathering information from parents and the child about the frequency, intensity, and duration of symptoms and the degree to which those symptoms affect the child's ability to function on a day-to-day level. Professionals will also gather background information, such as family, medical, and school history. The most common tool used in making mental health diagnoses is the *DSM-IV*, or *Diagnostic and Statistical Manual, Fourth Edition*. This manual details specific criteria that need to be met for each diagnosis. If a diagnosis is unclear or complicated, a therapist may request further evaluation using the assessment strategies outlined below.

 Fact

The *DSM-IV* is used by qualified therapists and psychiatrists to diagnose mental health conditions. Developed by the American Psychological Association, it provides detailed descriptions of criteria that must be met in order for a diagnosis to be given. Full diagnosis is based on five "axes," which include behavior, emotions, personality, medical concerns, sociological stressors, and overall level of functioning.

Where to Start

If you suspect your child has an anxiety disorder, the first place to start may be with your child's pediatrician or primary care doctor. Depending on your insurance plan, your doctor may request you bring your child in for a visit to determine if a referral to a specialist is in order.

Clinical Inventories

Professional therapists use clinical inventories as a way to assess the particular fears and dynamics underlying your child's anxiety issues. A review of the literature reveals almost as many inventories as there are therapists to administer them, and therapists vary in their skill and comfort in using these tools. As managed care has become more widespread, many insurance providers require that therapists use some sort of standardized measure of anxiety to establish a baseline of symptoms, direct treatment, and measure improvement as therapy progresses.

Anxiety and Depression

Pen-and-paper measures of depression and anxiety are among the most commonly used screening tools of therapists. Although they are not diagnostic in and of themselves, they can confirm a diagnosis of anxiety when taken together with the other information you provide. Unfortunately, simple tools for anxiety are not generally available for young children. For older children and adults, the most widely used are the Beck Depression and Anxiety Inventories. The Burns inventories of Anxiety and Depression are also commonly used. Therapists may use other tools such as a symptom checklist, given their preferences and the requirements particular to their setting. The Y-BOCS, or Yale-Brown Obsessive Compulsive Scale can be used to measure the severity of obsessions and compulsions.

Behavioral Inventories

Behavioral inventories are used for developmental screening and to identify different types of problem behavior a child might exhibit. Some inventories measure adaptive behavior, that is, the skills your child has that allow him to be independent in the world, such as self-care, problem solving, and following directions. Behavioral inventories are usually completed by parents, teachers, or trained observers. They can be used to determine which behaviors should be addressed first and can measure whether behaviors are changing over time. The Child Behavior Checklist (CBCL) is among the most common, and, again, your particular provider may have standard tools he uses to assess behavioral issues. Other useful parent-teacher rating scales include the Connors' Rating Scales and the Achenbach Inventories.

Self-Esteem

As you remember from Chapters 1 and 2, self-esteem is one of the building blocks of mental health. Self-esteem can be impaired in a number of ways, and inventories that allow your child to examine her feelings about herself, her sense of identity, and her sense of worth can build a base for change to occur in therapy. Self-esteem inventories are available to assess children at various ages. The Coopersmith Self-Esteem Inventory is one such instrument. Others include the Culture-Free Self-Esteem Inventory and the Martinek-Zaichkowsky Self-Concept Scale for Children (MZSCs).

 Fact

Self-esteem inventories are commonplace in the self-help industry and widely used in therapy and treatment settings. In general, they measure a person's perceptions of their competence, comfort, and worth both internally and in the settings of home and family, school or work, and social life.

Sentence Completion

The sentence completion technique is a useful way for a therapist to identify specific patterns of fears, worries, and areas of interest or vulnerability that may need to be addressed in therapy. The therapist will ask your child to "fill in the blank" to questions that will help in assessing behaviors, mannerisms, and areas of concern. Versions vary, but all include open-ended questions such as "When I was younger . . . ." Sentence completion is often used to create "talking points" for therapy, and can be presented in a playful format, which puts a child at ease.

Drawing

Therapists and evaluators use drawing exercises and inventories to analyze what a child communicates about hidden motives and struggles through his drawings, as well as to evaluate self-esteem and look for signs of trauma. Shape, size, and placement of body parts and other elements in the drawing provide clues a skilled therapist can use during therapy. It is an excellent way to establish rapport with a child and have fun as the therapist is doing his job. There are several standardized systems used to analyze and understand children's drawings. Among the most popular are the books *Children in Distress*, by Peterson and Hardin, and *Children Draw and Tell*, by Klepsch and Logie.

 **Alert!**

Because drawing is a projective technique and highly subject to the therapist's interpretation, it is important that a practitioner has training, experience, and supervision in interpreting your child's drawings.

Formal Testing

Formal testing and evaluation is usually only warranted if your child's anxiety has affected his functioning to the point that he cannot meet the demands of school, social, and family life. Formal testing is also indicated when simple anxiety becomes more complex and overlaps with conditions such as depression, ADHD, seizure disorders, or migraine headaches. Testing may be available in a clinic setting where your child is receiving therapy. Because formal testing can be costly and may not be covered by your insurance, it is best to check with your provider and insurance company before proceeding.

 Essential

Both diagnosis and formal testing are based on the process of standardization, or the statistical comparison of your child's symptoms or responses to those of others. Your child is measured against comparison groups to determine if he differs in a significant way, and the resulting findings help distinguish problems in specific areas. Sports offer a real-life example of standardization, when an athlete has to meet specific criteria to compete in a particular class or level.

Intelligence Testing

Intelligence testing was originally developed to assist in identifying mental retardation and learning issues. As such, it is designed to assess both general knowledge, and the ability to learn in our educational system. More recent advances in testing are designed to assess "multiple intelligences," such as creativity and imagination, and are less culture-bound than original intelligence tests. Despite limitations, intelligence testing can point to possible anxiety problems when specific patterns are found in the testing. In particular, measures of memory and attention, as well as foresight and problem solving, can be impacted by anxiety. The most commonly used intelligence test for younger children is the Stanford-Binet, which is more concrete and play-oriented, requiring no reading. For older children, the Wechsler Intelligence Scale for Children, Revised (WISC-R) is used most often.

IQ, or the Intelligence Quotient, is measured by standardized tests, which use subtests to assess particular aspects of intelligence such as recall, general knowledge, and pattern recognition. Taken together, the results of the subtests produce a number, which is then compared with samples of scores from the general population. The average IQ is said to be 100, with most people scoring between ninety and 110.

Personality Testing

The field of personality testing developed as psychologists became more interested in emotional well-being, interpersonal relationships, and self-understanding. The term "personality test" is in some way a misnomer for many tools that fall into this category. These tests are often used to identify traits, such as introversion versus extraversion, or logical versus emotional. Many of you have seen examples of this type of test in magazines or online. Generally, personality testing is used for adolescents and adults, once the personality has become more solidly defined. However, self-esteem and social inventories used in therapy with children can be considered personality tests. There are many forms of personality testing, but one of the most widely used is the Minnesota Multiphasic Personality Inventory, Second Edition (MMPI-II). The MMPI is often used to diagnose anxiety, depression, and other mental health conditions in adolescents and adults. The adolescent version, MMPI-A, is used for ages fourteen to eighteen. In some cases, this measure can also be used for young adults if they are still living at home or are delayed in school.

Projective Testing

Projective tests are abstract or symbolic in nature, and evoke responses said to be "projections" of thoughts, fears, emotions, and wishes that might be below your child's level of awareness. The famous inkblot test, called the Rorschach Inkblot Test, is a projective test. An evaluator carefully analyzes responses, and can then make observations about your child's internal world. Other projective tests include the Children's Apperception Test, and various standardized drawing exercises. Projective tests are more subjective than intelligence or personality tests; that is, they leave a bit more room for the evaluator to use her own clinical judgment in making conclusions. As such, it is important to ensure that the person evaluating your child is experienced and/or receiving good supervision and consultation.

Neuropsychological Evaluation

A neuropsychological evaluation is performed by a Ph.D. specialist called a neuropsychologist, and is a specific and extended battery of tests that look at brain function, intelligence, learning, memory and attention, sensorimotor responses, and information processing. This type of evaluation can rule out underlying issues with brain functioning that might account for symptoms such as moodiness or personality change. One to two sessions of an hour or more are required to complete a neuropsychological evaluation, and a subsequent session to review results generally follows. Neuropsychological evaluations can be especially useful when a child is having seizures, migraine headaches, or tics, or shows an abrupt change in mood or personality that is not related to changes in his environment. A common reason a parent would seek a neuropsychological evaluation is if a child has had a recent injury such as a diving mishap or car accident.

SENSORY EVALUATIONS

Sensory evaluations are most commonly used for children with autism or pervasive developmental disorders, mental challenges, and brain injury. Because anxiety often involves sensory overload or oversensitivity to various stimuli, your child will likely only need this type of testing if he is especially sensitive to taste, touch, sound, smell, or movement. You will want to be sure to check with your insurance provider to find out if this service is covered or if you need a referral. Specially trained occupational or physical therapists do sensory evaluations. The therapist may then recommend a sensory integration diet to help you, your child, and the school to develop techniques your child can use to minimize sensory overload or to learn how to self-soothe.

CREATIVITY TESTING

Creativity is highly complex, encompassing not only knowledge and skill, but also memory, common sense, intuition, and the ability to generate and express new concepts and ideas. Creativity testing was developed as researchers began to move past the constraints of academic learning, verbal ability, gender, race, and other factors that limited the usefulness of basic intelligence testing. Creativity testing is a close cousin to the tests of multiple intelligences, which measure qualities like interpersonal and musical intelligence. Tests of creativity and multiple intelligences can be used to identify gifted students and to augment the results of intelligence testing. They can be especially helpful if anxiety is suspected in a highly intelligent or creative child. Among the most commonly used are The Torrance Tests of Creative Thinking and The Barron-Welsh Art Scale, or BWAS.

GIFTEDNESS

Tests for giftedness in children may be as many as the schools they attend. Giftedness, like creativity, is complex and troublesome to measure. Often gifted children are assessed using several of the methods described above. The results are then taken together to form an overall picture of the gifted child's particular strengths and weaknesses. One tool that can be used to measure creativity is the Gifted and Talented Evaluation Scales, or GATES. If your child complains of being bored or fidgety in school, or gets in trouble because she "marches to her own beat," you may want to look into the possibility that she is gifted.

CULTURE-FAIR TESTING

Concerns about the limitations and bias of intelligence testing have lead to the development of culture-fair testing. This type of testing is considered culture fair because it is generally not dependent on language, yet measures abilities such as nonverbal reasoning and problem solving, regardless of native language, education, or cultural background. The Naglieri Nonverbal Ability Test (NNAT) is used for children in grades K–12, and can be administered in a group setting.

School-Based Evaluation

When a child has emotional or behavioral difficulties at school, there are a number of resources available to pinpoint the nature of the problem and determine possible solutions. Sometimes private schools have limited resources, but may be able to enlist outside help or refer you to specialty centers the school can coordinate with.

Teacher Observation

Your most valuable asset for your child at school is, of course, his teacher. Teachers can observe your child's level of attention and focus, his interaction with his peers, motivation and issues in learning, general mood, and self-esteem. School psychologists may assist teachers by providing inventories or questionnaires for teachers to fill out, and by helping the teacher to work effectively with your child once issues have been identified.

Alert!

If you find your child has begun to cling more to you or refuse to go to school, ask yourself if you have just gone through a period of time in which you became closer to her. Examples include after a family vacation, summer break, or a brief illness. It is also common for a child to act this way following a stressful occurrence such as a death or a move.

Behavioral Specialists

Behavior specialists are trained to observe and evaluate children in the school setting, and to plan interventions when behavior problems are an issue. They may have various degrees, and usually serve your child's educational team by noting and categorizing the positive and negative behavior your child shows while in school. They will help you identify particular triggers to your child's emotional or behavioral difficulties in school, and recommend the best ways to reduce their impact on your child's social and learning experience.

Social Observation

Social observation is a specific intervention in which a behavioral specialist, social worker, or therapist watches your child as she interacts with others in the classroom. Specific inventories and measures are available to help the specialist identify patterns of interaction that help or hinder a child with anxiety navigate the social waters. The specialist will then provide recommendations for change, such as including your child in a friendship group or creating a buddy system to support her.

Learning Evaluations

School psychologists and social workers complete learning evaluations, with the assistance of other team members as necessary. They involve intelligence testing and academic testing, and may include health and speech evaluations and analysis of your child's learning style. Often, medical and mental health records are used to make a complete evaluation of your child's strengths, weaknesses, challenges, and needs in the school setting. The results are then presented to you and a plan is developed to address the findings.

Projective Techniques

Projective techniques are named for the fact that they are used to interpret and increase understanding of the emotional dynamics driving your child's thoughts, emotions, and behavior that he "projects" to the world. For example, a child with anxiety might perceive danger or failure when shown a relatively neutral picture of a family. Projective techniques have a twofold purpose: to investigate, and to provide direction for therapy. Projective techniques help you and your child's therapist understand your child's experiences and identify themes that are used to direct therapy so that it will be most helpful for him. More information on play techniques in therapy is to come in Chapters 8 and 9.

 Fact

> Keep in mind that the younger your child, the more likely it will be for the therapist to use projective techniques in evaluation and treatment. These techniques are powerful and effective for children because they are more symbolic and less verbally loaded, and meet younger children at the appropriate developmental level.

Play

Play is used to assess and treat children and even some adolescents. Play is helpful in both evaluating and treating children because it allows adults to "speak the same language" of the child with whom they are interacting. Therapeutic play is different than "regular" play in that therapists are trained to use the symbols, metaphors, and themes your child introduces into her play to empathize with and assist her in removing anxiety roadblocks. Because play is highly subjective and open to interpretation, you will want to make sure that your provider has had adequate training in the use of play for assessment and therapy.

Art

Art materials used by play-oriented therapists include clay, paper, paint, glue, chalk, beads, collage work, bookmaking, and any other medium your child is interested in. Your child's artistic expressions can be a great way for him to communicate his fears, needs, and motivations in therapy. Kids also gain a sense of mastery as they complete projects and receive positive feedback on them.

Stories

Storytelling, like the sentence completion technique described previously, provides a blank canvas upon which your child can project his wishes, fears, and areas of vulnerability. Tandem storytelling, in which your child and the therapist create a story together, can provide a sense of camaraderie and mastery, as the story helps your therapist more fully understand your child's inner life. The Children's Apperception Test is an evaluation technique in which a child creates stories based on standard picture cards the therapist presents.

 **Question?**

Does your child love to draw, write, or create projects?
If so, this can be a special window into your child's true desires and motivations. Ask your child about her drawings and, without judgment, be positive and supportive about what she's presenting. If she is in therapy, she may wish to share her creations with her therapist as well.

Games

Many therapists use games to provide a nonthreatening approach for your child to identify, discuss, and resolve problem areas. Games are useful in that they require structured interaction with the therapist and can point to anxious patterns of interaction such as a need for control or intolerance for feedback. Therapeutic games also help therapists and children identify themes such as family and school, which are areas of special concern. There is a plethora of therapeutic games, and therapists that are more creative will often develop games with a child to clarify and address particular concerns. Games that allow children to identify and express feelings or to answer self-searching questions improve their ability to assert their opinions and take pride in them.

CHAPTER 5

If It's Not Anxiety, Then What?

Because anxiety can be subtle and pervasive, it can either mimic or overlap with other mental health conditions. Research shows that overlapping conditions are both more difficult to identify and to treat. In this chapter, you will find the most common conditions that anxiety is a symptom of, or can be confused with. As such, you will want to have your child professionally evaluated if you suspect she has multiple issues.

Overlap with ADHD

Attention deficit disorder (ADD) is a neurobiological condition that interferes with a child's ability to focus attention, stay organized, resist impulses, and follow through on tasks. Attention deficit hyperactivity disorder (ADHD) has the additional component of hyperactivity, which involves restlessness, impulsivity in speech and action, and an internal sense of being "revved up." Many parents may suspect that their child has ADHD at some time. In fact, a survey of the literature reveals that ADHD is the most commonly diagnosed childhood disorder, affecting some 3 to 5 percent of all school-aged children.

A child with ADHD may feel an internal sense the world is moving too fast, and he may have trouble paying attention because his mind is wrapped up in his multiple thoughts and worries. Children with anxiety can also suffer from thoughts and worries that seem unstoppable, and they may appear inattentive as a result. Similarly, children with ADHD may experience depression or anxiety because it is so difficult for them to meet the demands of their topsy-turvy world. To help you clarify things, as you read the descriptions below, focus on whether your child seems to have more difficulty than other children his age.

Alert!

Because ADHD can seriously affect your child's ability to learn, socialize, and develop the confidence, organization, and self-management skills he will need in adulthood, it is especially important to address this factor. However, it is just as important not to leap to conclusions without supporting facts.

Academic Problems

Most children with ADHD show signs of their distractibility and or impulsivity in the school setting. They may be unable to stay at their desks, focus on the teacher, or work for more than a few minutes without needing redirection. This applies to doing homework as well. It is typical for students with ADHD to have trouble managing assignments, and completing and turning in homework. You or someone close to your child may see this as laziness or underachievement, but it is not. Children with ADHD have physiological differences that prevent them from focusing. The overall effect is often reflected in poor grades or failure to progress in subjects. Children with anxiety often show restlessness and inattention as well and may have trouble with homework if they feel overwhelmed.

Your child's teacher can usually tell you whether she suspects that ADHD, rather than anxiety, is at the root of your child's trouble with schoolwork, or is an issue in the classroom. Keep in mind that ADD, because it lacks the behavioral component of hyperactivity, can be difficult to detect and may be more likely to mimic anxiety.

Behavior Problems

Children with ADHD or anxiety may have behavioral problems at home or school because of high levels of frustration. Typically, children with both disorders have more trouble transitioning between activities. For a child with ADHD it might be because it is so difficult for him to organize and sequence his thoughts and actions. For a child with anxiety it is due to fear, anticipation of failure, or feelings of being out of control. What you will see behaviorally is tantrums or meltdowns.

 Essential

> If your child's anxiety has obsessive qualities, he might spend hours writing one paper and not be able to complete any other work. This can look like laziness, procrastination, or ADD-style disorganization to you. However, it is important to realize that, in this instance, your child's anxiety is driven by a need for perfection and the fear that whatever he does is never good enough and must be redone.

Social Problems

Children with ADHD often have trouble making and keeping friends because of their impulsivity, which others see as odd or immature. Children with anxiety can also have unusual habits or ways of relating to others that can seem puzzling or unacceptable to their peers, as shared previously. For children who struggle with either, the rejection they feel can cause low self-esteem or depression, which leads to a sense of isolation and hopelessness about the future.

Temperament

Developments in the study of temperament have identified characteristics of children who do not quite seem to "fit the mold." One of the most significant patterns child specialists have identified is the active-alert child.

 Fact

Research suggests that as many as four times more boys than girls have ADHD, showing both attention difficulties and hyperactivity. Girls are more likely than boys to have ADD, without hyperactivity. This can be a dilemma for girls, who are often diagnosed at later ages because they are less likely to show behavior problems.

Linda Budd, Ph.D., in *Living with the Active Alert Child* identifies active-alert children as having these traits as well as others: They are active, alert, bright, controlling, fearful, intense, can need attention, and have difficulty getting along with others. Notice the overlap with the symptoms of the child with anxiety. Active-alert children are often considered gifted as well, so if you feel your child has these qualities, be sure to pay attention to the section on giftedness below.

Overlap with Depression

Depression is a mood disorder that can cause your child to feel tired, sad, lonely, bored, hopeless, or unmotivated for an extended period of time. In order for a clinical diagnosis in children, a depressive episode must last longer than two weeks and must interfere with daily functioning and/or be a change that is observable by others. Some researchers view anxiety and depression as two sides of the same coin. This is in part because both conditions involve disruption to the same neurotransmitters in the brain. In addition, symptoms of depression and anxiety overlap and may imitate each other. For example, many people with anxiety experience periods of depressed mood or other depressive symptoms such as guilt and feelings of worthlessness. Conversely, those with depression can experience states of agitation and worry that are very similar to the symptoms of anxiety.

The Irritability Factor

Because children and adolescents aren't always capable of identifying and communicating their feelings and internal experiences to others, they are more likely than adults to show irritability when they are depressed. Irritable children and teens can be very difficult to be around as they never seem content and may be negative or argumentative. Irritability is often contagious, and may snowball into conflict if it is persistent or extreme.

 Essential

Persistent feelings of worthlessness or excessive and unwarranted guilt can be very intense in both children and adults who are depressed. Guilt is also a strong component of anxiety, particularly if a child is old enough to feel she does not measure up to the expectations of peers, parents, and teachers.

Physical Considerations

When depression and anxiety are more serious, they can affect your child's ability to sleep and eat regularly. Children suffering from depression can experience loss of appetite, marked weight loss, or failure to make expected weight gains, while children with anxiety may have trouble with their appetite and weight loss. Insomnia involving both the ability to fall and stay asleep can occur in both anxiety and depression, as can a diminished ability to think clearly, concentrate, and make decisions. Children with anxiety are more likely to show agitation, while depressed children are more likely to experience fatigue and lethargy.

Substance Abuse

People with depression and anxiety are at risk for developing alcohol or drug abuse. The use of chemicals to alleviate emotional distress is referred to as "self-medication." Teens with anxiety may be especially vulnerable, particularly if they use alcohol or drugs as a "social lubricant." Talk frankly with your children about your values and expectations regarding chemical use, and be alert for sudden changes in sleep, eating, energy level, and choice of friends, as these can all be indicators of chemical abuse.

 Fact

Dysthymia is a sub-type of depression, which is experienced much like a "low-grade fever." That is, it can linger on and cause a person to feel just a bit ill at ease or raw around the edges. Some theorists say that dysthymia may even occur because a person's senses and emotions are overly sensitive and prone to overload.

Adjustment Disorders

As previously mentioned, it is common for children to experience changes in behavior and emotional upheaval when the world around them changes suddenly, as in a divorce or change of schools. In a child with anxiety, these challenges can be especially difficult because both her inner and outer world feel out of control at the same time. Both children and adults can experience adjustment disorders, and in fact, they are among the most commonly diagnosed mental health issues. In an adjustment disorder, there is a specifically identifiable stressor, which must have occurred no more than three months before the onset of emotional or behavioral symptoms. Adjustment disorders are generally short-lived, resolving in about six months after the original stress occurred. An adjustment disorder can involve depression, anxiety, or both. Behavioral disturbances can be common, especially in children, who are more likely to "show" their feelings through their behaviors. Common events that might cause a child to experience an adjustment disorder are outlined next. If you are concerned that your child is having more trouble adjusting to change than she should, use the tips provided to help her cope, so that her anxiety does not become problematic.

Moves

Moving to a new home is stressful for all families, and can be especially troubling if a child has to leave good friends or change schools. These transitions can be especially difficult in the middle-school years, when kids are working so hard to define who they will be and choosing a solid base of peers. For children with underlying anxiety, a move can be highly traumatic. If your child has anxiety, do your best to give him all the information you can and familiarize him with the new neighborhood. If the move is not long distance, maybe you can take a walk through the new neighborhood, especially when a school bus is picking up or dropping off other children, or drive around and visit a nearby park and restaurants. After the move, be sure to take the time to go back and visit old friends. Above all, let your child know that moving is not easy and listen to his fears. Validate the losses he will experience, and find ways he can be included in the team to make it a success.

Illness or Death in the Family

Both sudden and chronic illnesses are highly stressful for families, and of course, the loss of a loved one is among the most stressful events a person can experience. When family life becomes upset or unbalanced, this can be very destabilizing for a child with anxiety. Children who spend excessive amounts of time away from their parents, because of lengthy hospitalizations for either themselves or a family member, can develop symptoms of anxiety and have more difficulty with developmental transitions.

Illness and death are mysterious and scary, especially for younger children. Experts say that it is best to give your child whatever information is available, but in a form that fits his level of development. There are many great books and other resources that can help younger children grasp serious life events at a level they can understand. Medical providers, places of worship, friends, and family are also great resources and support, and can buffer both you and your child from the anxiety inherent in managing illness and death.

Birth of a Sibling

Though the birth of a sibling is a new beginning for all families, it can be an especially difficult time for older children, particularly if they are already anxious. They now have to share mom and dad's attention, and they can sometimes feel alone and isolated when the rest of the world pays too much attention to the new baby. Children with anxiety may show increased trouble with separation, or regress (lose skills) in managing their emotions and behavior. Helpful tips include making sure you continue to spend one-on-one time with your child, and include him as much as you can in the new daily routines you are establishing. Avoid making older children responsible for the care of their younger siblings on a regular basis, as this can cause resentment and tension between the siblings.

 Fact

Research has also shown that because higher expectations are placed on the oldest child in a family, first-borns experience more guilt, anxiety, and difficulty in coping with stressful situations.

Blended Families

Divorce, separation, and remarriage are childhood events that naturally create a wealth of feelings, including anxiety. Sometimes even positive changes, such as a parent marrying a person the child really likes, can cause stress. General fears of the unknown, or uncertainty of where a child "fits" in the new family are often undercurrents in children with anxiety. There are multiple resources on the Internet, at bookstores, through places of worship, or through community education to assist blended families.

Other Points to Consider

The following are additional issues that relate to children with anxiety that deserve mention, either because they have anxiety as a central component or because they can produce anxiety in children. Understand as you read this that information is an excellent defense against an illness that at times can feel so all-encompassing. That means the more you know the better—it will help you realize the path you need to take with your particular child.

PANDAS

PANDAS is an abbreviation for pediatric autoimmune neuropsychiatric disorders associated with streptococcal infections. Though rare, this term is used to describe children who develop obsessive-compulsive disorder (OCD) and/or tic disorders such as Tourette's syndrome. These symptoms worsen following strep infections such as strep throat and scarlet fever, and often have a dramatic or "overnight" presentation. Moodiness and separation anxiety are also common in PANDAS.

Oppositional Defiant Disorder

ODD stands for oppositional defiant disorder. A child with ODD resists or refuses the demands of authority figures, and is generally negative, hostile, and defiant. Children with ODD can be argumentative, prone to losing their tempers, blaming, resentful, and spiteful or vindictive. In addition, children with ODD sometimes deliberately annoy others and can be touchy and easily annoyed themselves.

Though it is clear that the general presentation of ODD is an angry one, anxiety sometimes lurks below the surface. Children with ODD can also suffer from depression or other mood issues, which should be thoroughly evaluated as a possible cause of acting-out behavior. For example, children with anxiety may refuse to go to school, which can look like defiant behavior when in fact it is fearful behavior.

Differently Abled

Children with physical disabilities or disabling medical conditions (severe allergies or asthma, diabetes, and so on) are prone to anxiety because the demands of the physical body both tax and are overtaxed by the emotional system. Additionally, some of the medicines used to treat chronic conditions can produce the side effects of anxiety or depression.

Social rejection can be common, and socializing can be difficult given your child's specific needs. Group therapy can often be a way for kids who feel different because of these circumstances to experience a sense of belonging and support, which helps them reduce anxiety or depression related to their condition. Check with your child's physician to see if he knows of groups or organizations that might be helpful to you and your child.

Is My Child Gifted?

As seen in Chapter 4, giftedness, like creativity, is complex and troublesome to measure because it is multidimensional, affecting many areas in your child's life. Generally, if your child is gifted, he may show many of the signs of active-alert children. He may complain of being bored or get in trouble for being restless at school. He may refuse to do "busywork" that requires little creative effort. He may sleep little, and read, draw, or want an opportunity to be more creative while doing projects or homework. Gifted children can sometimes be anxious or perfectionist as well, and may show a low frustration tolerance when their abilities do not always match what their minds create. There are many resources for gifted children at school and in the community. At home, try to provide opportunities for both focused work and unstructured time, and remember to help your child put on the brakes if she seems to be overfocused, over-stimulated, or overly perfectionist.

Developmental Transitions

Your child is consistently learning, growing, and changing. This is hard work, and sometimes children can become snagged at particular stages in their development. The following sections detail some especially difficult times for children. Look back to the section on adjustment disorders for reference if you feel your child has more trouble in a particular area than most children her age. If your child does not seem to adjust well after two to four weeks, you may need to look into a possible problem with anxiety.

Daycare

Going to a new daycare, especially if it also involves a new home or school, can cause anxiety in even the most well-adjusted children. Certainly, dropping a child off at daycare for the first time can be one of a parent's most difficult days. To ease transition, try to check in with your child each day after you pick her up, and send some small comfort items, depending on your child's age. Examples might be a picture of you and your child together, pocket-sized toy, stuffed animal, or blanket. Be sure to keep in regular contact with your daycare provider to track your child's adjustment and discuss any concerns either of you may have. Generally, if your child appears happy when you pick her up at the end of the day and is excited to return the next, you can be assured that she is doing well in the new setting.

Preschool

Preschool can be a troublesome time for children and parents alike. If your child has not been in daycare, it may be among the first times you and your child are apart for more than a few hours. It can be unsettling to leave your child with strangers, even when you have chosen your child's preschool with confidence. To minimize your child's anxiety, try to have a routine both before and after preschool, and ask your daycare provider to accommodate. It helps if you drop off and pick up your child on time so that he does not have to feel rushed or nervous during these transitions.

 Essential

Transitional objects are meaningful personal items that represent a parent or caregiver for a child when the caregiver is absent. A classic example is the teddy bear, toy, or blanket a child takes to bed with her each night. For a child with anxiety, it can be important to use transitional objects when she is away from home, such as at grandma's and grandpa's or summer camp.

Kindergarten

The transition to kindergarten, if difficult, may be the first sign your child could have issues with anxiety. That is not to say that starting kindergarten is not a tough task for any child. As they start their "official" school experience, children are exposed to more time away from home, larger groups of kids, busing, and more adults to tell them where to be and what to do. Children with separation anxiety can be especially vulnerable at this time. Try to keep your routine the same at home, and talk to your child regularly to support and encourage her. It may be helpful to check in with your child's teacher or offer to help in the classroom if your child is struggling with separation.

Middle School Transition

Many children transition to larger schools with unfamiliar children during middle school, and the demands for responsibility and self-motivation increase academically. The results are often frustrating, painful, emotional, and at times, even comical. It is utterly important, however, not to minimize your child's interests in and struggles with friends, choice of leisure pursuits, dress, or music. Many anxious children at this age benefit from a mentor, older sibling, or therapist with whom they can entrust their trials and tribulations.

Alert!

Middle-school age (grades five or six through grade eight) can be one of the most tumultuous periods for children, even for those children who do not have anxiety. Puberty brings on physical changes involving surging hormones and developing brain and emotional systems, and life brings new demands for personal and social awareness and responsibility.

Shyness and Introversion

Introversion and shyness are considered issues of temperament, much like the traits of gifted or active-alert children described above. Sometimes, it is difficult to determine whether a child is shy, introverted, or truly has anxiety. Consistent avoidance of activities or chances to meet new people may signal that you need to look into this issue more carefully to rule out debilitating shyness or underlying anxiety.

What Is Shyness?

Shyness is a term often used to describe those who avoid (shy away from) contact with others. A shy person may want to be social, but may experience physical symptoms of anxiety, which makes interaction with others uncomfortable. Shyness is actually a personality trait, and it can have many positive qualities. People who are shy often make good listeners who are sensitive, empathic, and are easy to be around. To sort out this issue, watch your child or teen in social settings and see if she is able to make eye contact and listen politely. If she seems happy with herself, and others feel comfortable around her, she may simply be introverted. If interacting with others seems painful or if your child routinely avoids opportunities to socialize, pay special attention to the section on social phobia in Chapter 6.

What Is Introversion?

Introversion is closely related to shyness, but introverts do not generally feel physically uncomfortable in social situations. Instead, introverts simply prefer to spend time in solitary pursuits, and "recharge" by spending time alone. Like those who are shy, introverts are often highly observant and introspective. It is typical for adolescents to appear quite introverted at times, as they may spend hours in their rooms gaming, grooming, or connecting with friends. Many gifted children can be introverted because their drive for learning and creativity pulls them inward. If you suspect your child's introversion is related to anxiety about social or other demands, this trait may need further exploration.

What Is Extraversion?

An extravert is a person who delights in being in large groups of people and recharges by connecting with others rather than being alone. Extraverts can sometimes appear to be the life of the party, but they can also simply need a higher level of social contact than their more introverted peers. Even extraverted children who appear confident and savvy on the outside can suffer from anxiety. If your child has frequent meltdowns after social gatherings, or if you suspect she is a "great actor," look further into whether she may have an underlying issue with anxiety.

The Overextended Child

As mentioned in Chapter 1, professionals and parents today are concerned that their children are overextended. Though researchers agree that some structured activity is good for kids, the goal is to balance structured time with free time. If your child has anxiety, you'll want to be especially sensitive to how he seems to handle the demands of his schedule to help him from becoming overwhelmed. Conversely, some children with anxiety have trouble with unstructured time because they have trouble making choices and initiating activity. As such, you may need to coach your child a bit on how to create structure for himself. The tips below will help you determine if you or your child are overprogrammed.

Signs Your Child Is Overextended

Signs that your child might be overprogrammed include frequent fatigue, resistance, or refusal to attend activities, complaints about or lack of enjoyment of activities, aches and pains, frequent irritability, persistent feeling that there is not enough time, and worry.

If your child regularly experiences more than one or two of the above, it may be time to have a sincere talk with her about how to cut back on activities.

 Fact

If, as you watch your child interact with others such as teachers, friends, and family, he seems to be overwhelmed, unfocused, or "not himself," this may indicate that it is time to start assessing your child's schedule and ability to cope. The same can be said for your own responses to the demands of your schedule.

Signs You May Be Overextended

If you as a parent are overextended, you may experience any of the above. Some additional questions to ask yourself include: Do I feel like I spend my life in the car, going from one activity to the next? Do I skip meals or eat them while driving? Do we have time to be together as a family? Do I create time for hobbies and leisure? Am I getting enough sleep?

Depending on your answers to these questions, it might be time to consider reducing the amount of activity you and your child are involved in. Sometimes eliminating even one obligation can reduce stress dramatically and help everyone to breathe a bit easier. To maximize a child with anxiety's sense of control, allow her to make a choice about what she would like to let go of.

CHAPTER 6

Common Types of
Anxiety in Children

According to the American Psychiatric Association and the American Academy of Child and Adolescent Psychiatry there are seven groups of anxiety. This text will concentrate on panic disorder, phobias, general anxiety disorder (GAD), obsessive-compulsive disorder (OCD), and post-traumatic stress disorder (PTSD) and will not review anxiety disorder due to a general medical condition or substance-induced anxiety disorder. Additionally you will find information on separation anxiety and night terrors because they are so common in children. If you find your child meets the criteria for one of the disorders present it is not a diagnosis, it is a guideline to let you know if it is time to see a doctor or qualified therapist.

Separation Anxiety Disorder

A young child who is scared of new people and places is normal. However, if a child has continued intense fear that something is going to happen to someone he loves and he stops normal activities, this could be a sign of a larger issue. Separation anxiety disorder affects about 4 percent of children ages six through twelve, and research shows treatment is often successful.

Factors to Consider

Environmental and temperamental factors that seem to characterize children who suffer from separation anxiety disorder are an extremely close-knit family, a fearful or extremely shy temperament as an infant, shyness or passivity in girls aged three to five years old, or an insecure parent who found it difficult to attach in infancy.

The Developmental Process

When your baby was born, you might have noticed she easily adapted to new surroundings and people, which is typical of babies six months old or younger. Actually, with infants, it is usually the parents who have more anxiety than the child when being left with a babysitter or in a new environment! Normal separation anxiety typically occurs between eight months and one year although some children experience it later, between eighteen months and two and a half years old, and some may never experience it at all. During this time, you may find you cannot leave the room for even a moment without your child becoming agitated and upset.

 Essential

Some degree of separation anxiety in a preschooler is normal, and it is a sign of healthy attachments to loved ones. If the distress continues past three to four minutes, though, this could be a sign of a developing anxiety disorder, and it is time for you to look more closely at other behaviors that may point to anxiety.

Stranger anxiety can also develop during this time. You know it is stranger anxiety when your child clings onto you for dear life; her huge panicky eyes looking like you are going to feed her to a dinosaur if you even try to give her to another person. As time goes by and your child learns to feel safe and secure that you really are going to return, and she really will be given back to you, the anxiety usually fades. It is when she continues to experience excessive fear that seems out of proportion at the start of her elementary school years, that you want to be concerned.

Symptoms

Separation anxiety disorder has a variety of physical and behavioral signs. Your doctor or therapist will look for at least three or more of the following symptoms that must begin before the age of eighteen, be present for at least four weeks, need to cause significant distress in the child, and/or must interfere with social and/or academic functioning. The symptoms also cannot be due to another anxiety or psychiatric disorder:

- Excessive distress when separated from you
- Worry about losing you, or harm coming to you
- Ongoing worry that some awful event such as kidnapping will separate her from you
- Recurrent reluctance to go anywhere, even out to play with friends, or to watch TV in a room if you are not present
- Ongoing distress about being alone at home or outside the home
- Reluctance to go to sleep without you nearby
- Difficulty falling asleep without you, or waking from nightmares about separation from you
- Repeated physical complaints, such as stomachaches, nausea, and headaches when separated from you or expecting to be separated from you

Risk Factors

Separation anxiety can look like or develop into depression because your child might be withdrawn, seem irritable, have difficulty sleeping, or experience difficulty concentrating. Symptoms of separation anxiety may be prompted by a scary experience or something your child heard about, such as child abduction or a fire in the community. For your child to be able to resolve the feelings of separation anxiety it is important he develop a sense of safety in his world, trust people other than parents, and be able to understand that even though his parents have left, they are coming back. When a fracture in the ability to bond or attach in infancy through adoption, illness, or return to work has occurred, it can predispose a child to develop this disorder. Some studies suggest children and teenagers who live in dangerous neighborhoods might be inappropriately diagnosed with separation anxiety disorder, even though it is reasonable for them to have fears about leaving their homes.

Panic Disorder

If your child has abrupt, intense fear that comes intermittently, unpredictably, and is recurrent, she might have a panic disorder. A panic attack happens very fast, is intense, and will reach its peak within ten minutes. Panic disorder is not common in young children and affects most people beginning in late adolescence, up to midlife.

Physical Symptoms
In order to be diagnosed with panic disorder your child must experience recurrent attacks with at least one episode that is followed by one month of persistent worry about future attacks. The attacks must be experienced as having an apparent onset and reach a peak in ten minutes. There needs to be a sense of imminent danger as well as four or more of the following symptoms:

- Pounding heart rate or chest pain
- Trembling or shaking and/or dizziness
- Shortness of breath
- Nausea or stomachaches
- Choking feeling
- Fear of losing control or dying
- Numbness or tingling
- Chills, sweating, or hot flashes
- Feeling of unreality

Learning disorders may co-exist with panic disorders and should not be overlooked. If your child is having a hard time with school, it might not be just about his panic. If after you see a doctor and the panic disorder is treated, your child is still upset about going to school, this may be an indicator of an undiagnosed learning disability.

Risk Factors

While 10 percent of children will have at least one panic attack, only 1 to 2 percent will develop panic disorder. However, the experience of panic is so scary that your child or adolescent may live in dread of another attack. He may also go to great lengths to avoid situations that may bring on another attack. This can cause him to want to stay home from school and have anxiety when separated from his parents. Another risk factor is school avoidance. As seen in Chapter 3, school avoidance can be complicated and difficult to treat, so it is best to intervene at the first sign of trouble.

 Fact

As with other anxiety disorders, there is a genetic component to panic attacks. Researchers have concluded that when a parent has a panic disorder, her children will be four to seven times more likely to develop one as well.

Of those adolescents who continue to have panic disorder as they go into adulthood, many will develop other psychiatric difficulties. Statistics show about half will develop agoraphobia and/or depression, and 20 percent will make suicide attempts, and/or develop alcohol or substance abuse issues. This disorder can also cause your child to believe he is unhealthy, go to the doctor often, and show significant social impairment.

The random nature of panic attacks is powerful and confusing. Since there is no reason outside her body for the worry, your child could start thinking there is something wrong inside her body. Left untreated, this could cause your child to stop most activity, especially outside the home, out of fear the panic will reoccur.

 **Question?**

Does your tween or teen feel anxious when she is supposed to visit at someone else's house?
Agoraphobia is the pattern of avoiding certain places or situations to control anxiety. It occurs when your child has an inability to go beyond known and safe surroundings because of intense fear and anxiety that she will not be able to get help or escape. This condition quickly builds upon itself, so try to seek help quickly.

AGORAPHOBIA OVERLAPS WITH PANIC DISORDER

Panic disorder can develop into agoraphobia. Your child's irrational fear of being in places he might feel trapped in or unable to escape from may cause him to feel like he has to stay at home so he can keep the panic away. Left untreated, this avoidance can build on itself and become quite debilitating.

Social Phobia

Social phobia is also known as social anxiety disorder or SAD (not to be confused with seasonal affective disorder which can also be known by the acronym SAD). This disorder is diagnosed when your child has a persistent fear of social situations, performing, and talking in front of others, especially if she will be around unfamiliar people. Your child may be terrified of being criticized, judged harshly, or embarrassed. Social phobia affects one in every twenty-five children, and it seems girls are diagnosed about twice as often as boys. Conversely, clinical samples are either equal on gender or show more males with the diagnosis. Children, especially adolescents, can be preoccupied with how they compare to their friends, so being a little self-conscious is normal. SAD is diagnosed when the symptoms are extreme. Parents can also exacerbate social anxiety disorder if they are fearful, withdrawn, or shy, or if they unintentionally reward their child's fearful behavior.

Symptoms

To be diagnosed with social phobia, a child's symptoms must last at least six months, which distinguishes it from the short-term social discomfort that many children briefly experience in new situations. There is no one sign that indicates that a child has social anxiety. However if your child experiences several of the following, SAD may be part of the picture:

- Fearing scrutiny by other people in social situations
- Avoiding situations that trigger the fear
- Crying, throwing tantrums, clinging, and freezing in specific social situations
- Complaining of sickness to avoid going to school
- Feeling unwilling or unable to participate in school activities such as sharing with the class, group projects, reading in front of the class, or raising hand
- Isolating at the playground, feeling outside of the group and not joining in, having no friends or one or two friends

 Fact

Approximately four out of every ten, or 43 percent, of children with social anxiety refuse to attend school because of their anxiety. If your child is refusing to go to school or goes and then spends most days in the nurse's office, it is time to seek help from a psychologist and possibly a psychiatrist.

When your child is faced with something she fears, she may have physical symptoms like blushing and sweating, dizziness, heart palpitations, tense muscles, dry mouth, trembling, and nausea. These symptoms magnify anxiety, and may even produce it over time.

Risk Factors

If your child has social phobia, he may have trouble speaking up in class, making or keeping friends, taking tests or keeping up with schoolwork, possibly fail exams, not feel able to turn in homework, and feel isolated. You also might notice he is afraid that others will see his anxiety and think he is weak or immature. Your child might fear that he will faint, lose control of bowel or bladder functioning, or not be able to concentrate. Looking ahead, according to the World Psychiatric Association, social anxiety sufferers are more likely to be single, attain lower education, contemplate or commit suicide, be on social security payments or on a disability pension, have other psychiatric disorders, abuse drugs or alcohol, and have an erratic work history.

As you can see, treating social anxiety in children is imperative. Researchers Beidel and Turner developed an approach for "shy" kids called Social Effectiveness Training. Instead of exploring underlying childhood issues for their shyness or putting the children on medication to see if their symptoms went away, they helped children develop the skills necessary to handle social situations competently. After twelve weeks, the study found two-thirds of the kids were no longer shy or frightened socially. At six months, the effectiveness of skill training increased to 75 percent.

Generalized Anxiety Disorder

In children, generalized anxiety disorder (GAD) is also called overanxious disorder. Children and teens with GAD will have excessive concern and worry about the past or future, look for the worst in situations, and often have fears that are out of proportion to what you might have expected. GAD affects approximately 3 to 5 percent of children age six to eleven years old. From early adolescence on, girls outnumber boys with this condition approximately two to one, and 50 percent of adults diagnosed with GAD had it during their childhood or adolescence.

Causes

GAD can be linked to an overactive thyroid gland, and a malfunction of this gland can cause the symptoms associated with anxiety. Children with chronic conditions, such as diabetes or high blood pressure, can be prone to anxiety as well. Frequently this disorder starts out slowly and then sneaks up on your child, so exact causes have been difficult for researchers to confirm.

Symptoms

Your child may be filled with self-doubt that he feels he is unable to control and be highly critical of himself. He may be preoccupied with being on time and adamant about doing things "perfectly." Children with generalized anxiety disorder do not have occasional worries or fears; for them this disorder weaves throughout their entire day and all they do—schoolwork, appearance, money, friends, their health, the future, the past, what they said and did, and to whom. Unfortunately, as you can imagine, these symptoms can make living life, having friends, or enjoying a hobby or activity pretty difficult. To be diagnosed with GAD, your child must have difficulty controlling the worry, and the anxiety and worry must be associated with one of the following, for at least six months:

- Restlessness and inability to relax
- Lack of energy
- Trouble falling asleep or staying asleep
- Muscular tension, aches, or soreness
- Trouble concentrating
- Irritability

Also, be on the lookout for "What Ifs," excessive perfectionism, frequent need for approval, trouble shutting off anxious thoughts, stomach problems, grinding of teeth, and dizziness.

Risk Factors

Generalized anxiety disorder, like other types of anxiety, can co-exist with depression, phobias, and panic attacks. Substance abuse in teenagers can be a problem if they are trying to self-medicate as a way to alleviate their symptoms. In addition, many people who meet a child, especially a teen, with GAD will see how concerned they are with time, schedules, finances, and health and think they are older than their years. Be careful; you do not want to encourage or reinforce these signs of over responsibility. Certainly, for the moment it is nice to hear your child described in a positive, mature way, but keep in mind that you know that his "impressive" behavior is based on fear and worry, which is actually hurtful for him.

Certain factors may increase your child's risk of having generalized anxiety disorder. A buildup of stress, a physical illness, and a tendency toward being anxious are among the most common culprits. In addition, as previously mentioned, generalized anxiety disorder occurs more frequently in children who have medical issues like diabetes and high blood pressure. Multiple moves, losses, or transitions can also set the stage for GAD.

 **Question?**

My child can't sit still. How do I know if this is generalized anxiety disorder or attention deficit hyperactivity disorder?
If your child has anxiety, she might have difficulty paying attention and be hyperactive or fidgety. A key difference to look for is in the "worry." Children with ADHD do not worry more than children without ADHD, whereas children with GAD are compelled to worry about many things throughout the day.

Obsessive-Compulsive Disorder

For some parents, having a child who is neat, organized, cautious, and careful would be a dream come true. Obsessive-compulsive disorder (OCD) is diagnosed when your child takes the positive qualities of neatness, organizational skills, being careful, or cleanliness to the extreme. With this mindset, she is trapped in a pattern of time-consuming, repetitive thoughts and behaviors and she cannot necessarily accomplish what you might think she should. For instance, she will take an hour-long shower that she is hoping will give her a cleaner body; unfortunately, instead she will get red, raw skin, and might walk out of that shower still thinking she needed to clean herself more. Young children find it difficult to recognize their behavior as useless, but older children are more aware but still find the pattern impossible to stop. These maladaptive obsessions (thoughts) and compulsions (behaviors) can easily imprison your child, and sometimes, your entire family.

 Fact

Obsessive-compulsive disorder usually starts between the ages of six and fifteen for boys, while for girls it often begins later, between the ages of twenty and thirty. It affects between 1 to 2 percent of children.

There is no evidence that OCD is learned or caused by childrearing choices. Interestingly, OCD is more common among people of higher education, IQ, and socioeconomic status. When in adolescence or older, men and women are affected equally.

The Obsession

An obsession is an unwanted thought or impulse that repeatedly occurs in the mind of the child. Repeatedly, the child experiences a disturbing thought, such as, "My teeth are yellow, I have to brush them"; "I think I left my homework on my desk at home, I am going to fail this class"; or "I am going to mess up this relationship with my friend, I know it." These beliefs are felt to the point of being intrusive, consuming, and unpleasant. The obsessions seem uncontrollable to your child and if she does not manage the thoughts through behaviors, she feels she might lose control of herself. Obsession with germs or body fluids and reoccurring doubts are among the most common.

The Compulsion

Compulsions are repetitive behaviors that are clearly excessive, but temporarily lessen the tension and anxiety caused by the obsession. Compulsions can include hand washing or checking behaviors, such as repeatedly making sure their belongings are where they should be, hoarding objects, counting, repeating words, or praying. Because compulsions become rituals, they take long periods of time, even hours, to complete (particularly if interrupted), which can feel very frustrating to the parent or others who don't understand the child's behavior.

 Essential

Children who engage in repeated hand washing intended to lessen anxiety about contamination commonly end up with raw skin and dermatitis. Lip-licking and sucking on hands or fingers can have similar results. Be sure to treat these signs early on.

Symptoms

Being able to recognize if your child has obsessive-compulsive disorder can be challenging. Sometimes your child's behaviors will appear obstinate or even lazy. When children obsess, it makes it hard for them to get anything done, especially if there are many items on a list, like chores. All you see as a parent are the hours they spend in the bathroom, or their bedroom, without much being accomplished. At home, children with OCD may have a combination of the following symptoms along with those presented earlier for generalized anxiety:

- Intrusive thoughts and repetitive behaviors
- Extreme distress if their rituals are interrupted
- Difficulty explaining their behaviors
- Seeking repeated reassurance about safety
- Attempts to be secretive about their obsessions or compulsions
- Feelings of shame about the compulsion
- Feeling they can't stop the obsessions or compulsions
- Thinking they might be "crazy" because of their thoughts

At school, the teacher might see:

- Difficulty concentrating
- Isolating or withdrawing from friends
- Low self-esteem socially or academically

Risk Factors

When a child has OCD, peer relationships, school functioning, and family functioning may all suffer. Depression, hair pulling, constantly feeling sick, anorexia or bulimia nervosa, panic disorder, GAD, or social anxiety disorder may develop. For some children, social isolation may increase because of extreme anxiety and a need to limit activities may result. Some children may have thoughts of self-harm.

Because your child may feel ashamed and embarrassed about his OCD, it might be hard for him to talk about. When it all stays in his head, it becomes even more difficult to stop his thinking and your child may even start to wonder if he is crazy. With OCD patience really is a virtue, and that means you will need to take care of yourself as well. See Appendix B of the book for a Web site that will connect you with other parents who also have children with OCD to gain the support you need.

Alert!

Environmental stressors such as abuse, changes in living situation, illness, occupational changes or problems, relationship concerns, and school-related problems can worsen OCD symptoms.

Post-Traumatic Stress Disorder

The diagnosis of post-traumatic stress disorder, or PTSD, was developed to help define the trauma experience of war veterans. What makes this disorder different from many of the other anxiety disorders discussed is that PTSD requires that a specific event occurred before the onset of symptoms. Many upsetting things can happen in your child's life, like a best friend moving or failing a test. While upsetting, these events generally do not develop into PTSD. On the contrary, PTSD is triggered by an event that was terrifying, threatening, and traumatizing for your child either physically or psychologically. Examples include physical, emotional, or sexual abuse, watching someone else being physically assaulted, or being in a disaster such as a flood, fire, or serious accident. Please note that just because your child had, or witnessed, a traumatic event, it does not mean she will develop PTSD. To the contrary, most do not.

Symptoms

To be diagnosed with post-traumatic stress disorder, your child must have symptoms from these three categories: re-experiencing the trauma, avoidance and emotional numbing, and increased arousal.

Symptoms include:

- Exposure to a traumatic event involving threat or actual injury
- Response involving intense fear, helplessness, or horror
- Re-experiencing the event with distressing memories, dreams, acting, or feeling as if the event is recurring
- Avoidance of reminders of the trauma
- Detachment from, loss of, or limited emotions
- Sleep issues, difficulty concentrating, irritability, guilt, intense panic, and/or angry outbursts

Defining the symptoms of PTSD is a little tricky for doctors and parents because PTSD has different age-specific features. Young children who are not verbal yet might develop stranger anxiety, have trouble sleeping, or regress developmentally. As they get older, some children will act out or engage in play that resembles what they went through. It is also common to see an adolescent express impulsive and aggressive behaviors as a way to deal with intense feelings.

Alert!

In a large national survey, 9 percent of high-school students reported having been raped at some point in their lives. It has also been reported that 1.7 million young people between the ages of twelve and nineteen have been a victim of a violent crime.

Risk Factors

The most important factors to consider when identifying how well a child will come through a trauma are the severity, how close physically she was to the situation, and how the parents acted in response. Research also suggests that when a child experiences a trauma where someone intentionally hurts another person, she is more likely to develop PTSD.

Depending on age, children with PTSD may have suicidal thoughts, argue with friends, develop stomach troubles, or have poor immune response. They may also engage in substance abuse or disruptive behaviors. The best place to start with your child, if she has experienced a trauma, is to communicate early and often. Allow her time to explore her feelings, allow her time to recover.

Question?

My twelve-year-old was assaulted on the bus eight months ago and everything has been fine. All of a sudden, he can't sleep and he is angry all the time. Could this still be from the assault?

Sometimes symptoms do not occur until months or even a year after an incident. This can be upsetting for parents because it seems like the symptoms have come out of nowhere. Delayed PTSD is diagnosed if the onset of symptoms occurs six months or more after the trauma. It is often triggered by an anniversary, or something that reminds the child of the original trauma, and it is very real. In this situation, it is best to see a counselor for an assessment.

Night Terrors

If your child wakes from sleep with a sudden episode of intense terror, bolting upright with his eyes wide open, a look of fear and panic, and lets out a scream, he just had a night terror.

Causes

Usually, within fifteen minutes of your child falling asleep, he will begin his deepest sleep of the night called slow wave sleep, or deep non-REM sleep. Typically this lasts from forty-five to seventy-five minutes. It is during this part of his sleep, just before the transition to lighter sleep, that your child becomes stuck. Caught between stages, your child will have a period of partial arousal. During this time your child will groan, cry, kick, hit, and scream. His eyes may be open or closed; he will look confused, upset, or even "possessed," as many parents have described it. Typically, night terrors last for about ten minutes, although it may be over in one minute, or last as long as thirty minutes.

Night terrors normally affect young children between the ages of three to five years old. Watching a child go through this is very emotional and frightening for most parents, so it is important to know that for the most part, it is a harmless situation. Guidelines to decrease the impact of night terrors include having a strict bedtime and waking time and dimming the lights one to two hours before sleep; avoiding naps, reading, and watching TV in bed; limiting soda pop, chocolate, or other stimulants; and eliminating physical exertion and heavy liquids like milkshakes prior to bedtime.

 Essential

In most cases, it is best not to hold or restrain your child while she is experiencing a night terror. Simply sit guard and tune into your child's cues. If your child responds positively to a comforting voice or rubbing his back, do it. If not, do not. Being there to offer comfort to him when he wakes up is critical, however. Most important is to protect your child from injury.

Several issues play a part in your child having night terrors. If you or your spouse had night terrors, studies suggest your child will, too. Being really tired can also play a part. Doctors suggest extra time for sleep and talking to your child to soothe his tendency to worry. If night terrors become frequent and using the guidelines listed previously does not work, then it is time to get professional advice.

CHAPTER 7

Parenting and Anxiety

Picture yourself as the trunk of a tree and your children as the branches. The strength of the roots you grow allows for safety and stability in those who count on you. If your child thinks something is wrong with the trunk, she will automatically think something is also wrong with the branch. If she sees that the trunk is unstable, she will feel unsafe, and if she feels the trunk could break, she will be scared that she too will break. As much as you might want that to be different, studies show that is the perception. Therefore, how you handle your life serves as a model for your child to handle hers.

The Parent's Role

Besides genetics, life experiences seem to play a part in why a child has an anxiety issue. As a role model for your children, your fears about either your own life, or theirs, will have an effect on your child's confidence and self-esteem. Through their relationship with you, and imitation, your child will make decisions about what life looks like, how she feels about herself in the world, and how capable she believes she is to manage that world. Letting your child see you experience some mild to moderate anxiety and resolving it effectively will be incredibly beneficial. Feelings of fear and anxiety are inevitable, and by watching you, when your child is faced with fear or anxiety, she will know she too can meet difficulties in life head on. However, if your fears for your child seem extreme or unmanageable, your child will perceive her own anxious moments this way as well. The message your child hears is, "I do not trust you to care for yourself or think you will make good decisions, so I must worry," and the child can then internalize beliefs like "I can't," or "I shouldn't."

 Essential

Of course you do not want your children put in harm's way. Within reason, though, "Kids need to feel badly sometimes," says child psychologist David Elkind, a professor at Tufts University. "We learn through experience and we learn through bad experiences. Through failure we learn how to cope."

Your Choices Can Affect a Child's Anxiety

You are a crucial element in your child's day-to-day functioning, so the choices you make can have a great deal to do with how anxious your child may feel. If you choose to divorce, separate, start a job, move, act abusively, try to be a perfect parent, use substances, or stress performance, you are shaping your child. You are also shaping your child by exercising to keep fit, getting together with friends, taking a class to feed your own soul, or sitting down to relax and read a book for enjoyment. Even the rules you make in the house have the power to create anxiety or reduce it. For example, if the rule is "you must get an A in school because you are smart enough to do it," or there is a consequence for not making the grade, your child will be anxious about his performance. That might actually decrease your child's ability to concentrate and cause what the child is most afraid of—an inability to remember what he studied, and your disappointment. If the rule is "you must do chores when you get home from school, and then do your homework before you can go out to play," and your child never finishes before dinner, you will have a frustrated, angry child. Because your child loves you and wants to be seen as good, he may internalize his anger and instead you will see an irritable, anxious, or depressed child.

Strong Parents Make Strong Children

Since you are the cornerstone for your children's emotional and social development, your capacity to understand them will be a gift to them as they grow. This is also true when you show compassion for, and know how to interpret, their needs. Those qualities have been cited in studies as crucial building blocks in your child's self-concept, ability to cope, and school readiness.

Your Behavior Is Important

A group of American and German researchers studied 1,000 teenage subjects, fourteen to seventeen years old, mostly middle class and attending school, and they found that more than genetics plays a part in a child developing an anxiety disorder. Children who had parents with social phobia, depression, other anxiety disorders, who abused alcohol, were overprotective, or rejected by their parents were at a significantly increased risk of developing social phobias. Other researchers concur that social fears may be learned, at least in part by parents who are shy and withdrawn. Granted, that is a lot of responsibility, but what about good parenting is not?

 **Alert!**

Fostering dependency in your child can inhibit his attempts to learn to do things by himself. When a child has the view that he is incompetent, without help from others he can become discouraged and see himself as stuck. This downward sense of self may then become part of his foundation throughout life.

Tips for Strong Parenting

Allowing your child to experience small degrees of control and mastery, even if she is timid or fearful, can produce less anxious children. Strong parenting uses "shaping," and encouragement to help an anxious child retrain or learn new responses or to circumvent a childhood with anxiety from the start. Here are some examples of how to foster confidence and independence.

- **Do not run to pick up a fussy, timid, or crying child.** Allow your child to experience her own feelings for at least a minute, and allow her a moment to cope with or fix the situation before you intervene. How quickly you intervene should be based on your child's age and developmental ability. For example, leaving a one-year-old to cry for more than a couple of minutes might have the opposite effect than you are trying to achieve; your child could feel overwhelmed by her feelings. On the other hand, an eight-year-old needs more than two or three minutes to grapple with his feelings before he will find his way through to a solution.

- **Do not burden your child with your problems.** Find a friend, write in a journal, or go scream in a field, but do not treat your child like a confidant. She does not need the pressure, and in fact a child who is "parentified" in this way may show increased anxiety.

- **Allow your child to learn personal management.** This includes how to dress appropriately or how to handle arguments with siblings or friends. Let your kids discover how to be responsible to and for each other.

- **It is best not to call parents of other children or make decisions about who your child can or can't play with, unless your child is put in danger.** Instead ask your child what options she sees she has, discuss tools to deal with the problem, and gently guide her to an appropriate response. In other words, be your child's problem "helper" versus problem "solver," with guidance and support.

- **Always allow your child the opportunity to prove he can be successful.** This is especially important even if he tried an activity before and it did not go well.
- **If your child is afraid to go somewhere or try something new, gently encourage or suggest small increments of engaging in the feared situation.** If she is afraid to sleep in her own bed, but you want her out of yours, set up an air mattress at the end of your bed to begin with. Each day move it slightly. First move the mattress toward the door, and after a night or two of success, into the hallway, and eventually, into your child's room. This type of "shaping" is a great way to help your child learn new behavior without overwhelming her.

When Parents Are Overprotective

Consider the following scenario: "Did you call Jimmy to play? Oh, okay, what time did you say you would be there? Don't forget to take your jacket just in case the weather turns cold, and don't forget to look both ways when you cross our street, and remember to say thank you to Mrs. Michael for inviting you, and if she offers you something to eat, remember to chew with your mouth closed, elbows off the table, and say thank you when you are done. And, oh, don't forget to call me before you leave so I know you are on your way and can look for you as you make your way across the street."

 Fact

In 1946, Dr. Spock came out with his bestselling "baby bible," *Baby and Child Care*. In it he encouraged parents to give their children appropriate amounts of increasing independence as a way to ready them for leaving home as healthy, secure young adults. Overprotectiveness, he said, just makes for anxious children.

Overparenting or being overprotective tends to have very negative consequences. The message your child will hear is, "I have to worry about you so much because you are not competent to deal with things on your own. You need my supervision and decision-making or this will end up badly." Commonly, your child will end up feeling angry and insulted to what will feel like a put-down. Alternately, a child may simply "quit trying" because she feels she has no control in the world. Basically, overparenting becomes the opposite of what a parent's most important job is, to encourage autonomy and foster a healthy self-concept.

What the Doctors Say

Harvard psychologist Jerome Kagan, researching temperament, has shown unequivocally that what creates anxious children is parents hovering and protecting them from stressful experiences. He found that infants who were born "overexcitable" tended to cope better with life, and had a more positive outlook, if their parents gave them freedom to do, think, and make mistakes on their own.

The author of *Worried All the Time: Rediscovering the Joy in Parenthood in an Age of Anxiety*, David Anderegg, feels that parents have equated worrying, or protecting, children with being devoted to them. He states that in the past parents understood once their child left the house "God took over." He also believes that years ago parents were clearer they could not be in control of what happened to their children once they left the home. Nowadays, parents talk to their kids by cell phone or text message them continuously while they are gone from the house. It is the new way to hover over your child.

Michael Liebowitz, clinical professor of psychiatry at Columbia University and head of the Anxiety Disorders Clinic at New York State Psychiatric Institute, believes parents can have well-adjusted children if they take the time to gently encourage their children to try new things, even if they are scared, so they can learn that nothing bad will happen. "They need gradual exposure to find that the world is not dangerous. Having overprotective parents is a risk factor for anxiety disorders because children do not have opportunities to master their innate shyness and become more comfortable in the world."

The general consensus is that when children are overprotected they never learn to modify or reshape the connections in their brain, as discussed in previous chapters. It is important to allow your child to change his perceptions, by continuous modification of the feared issue, so the anxiety does not follow her throughout her life.

When Parents Are Depressed

It has been said a good therapist understands that when a child is struggling or having trouble with daily life, if you look to the parents, you will often find one that is depressed. Psychologists have also learned that even though the parents come to therapy and identify the child as the source of their distress, often, it is actually more likely that the child has been reacting to the parent's depression.

 Fact

Studies show that 20 percent of the population is depressed. Not just the "I'm having a bad day, or week," depressed; the "I hate my life and do not want to get out of bed" kind of depression. That means, if you count every fifth person you see on the street—that's how many people in your community are suffering from depression.

How Your Depression Affects Your Child

Studies have found that depressed mothers have trouble with bonding, and are less sensitive to, and more inconsistent with, a baby's needs. This in turn creates anxious, unhappy children that are difficult to comfort, have behavioral issues, are difficult to feed, struggle to go to sleep, and can experience more isolation socially. As they grow into toddlers, they can be very hard to manage; they fight authority, including parental authority, and can be negative thinkers. The distress the parent feels in response reinforces a sense of failure, and more depression ensues. Research has also documented that a child brought up in a home with a depressed parent is at a high risk for depression, substance abuse, and antisocial activities.

When Parents Are Stressed

While periodic frustration with your child is inevitable, overall, your child is counting on you to learn how to cope with your own issues so you can concentrate on theirs. If you have difficulty dealing with stress, and your children experience you that way more days than not, they will most likely have difficulty also. In a study by the Institute of Education on life satisfaction, researchers found that, for children whose parents are stressed out, the child was significantly affected, especially if the father's distress level was high. They went further to claim that a parent's emotional health or lack thereof has a long-term impact on the child's emotional health.

 Essential

It is important to pay attention to your child's behavior to see if the stress you are experiencing in your life is manifesting in her. Look first for physical and emotional aches and pains. If your child has been complaining, then you can start asking gentle questions to find the source. Check your own barometer to see if your child's complaints mirror your own stress level.

How Your Stress Affects Your Child

It is easy to forget that your children have ears. Even if they are not in the room, that does not mean they are not listening. When children hear you argue or yell, they will internalize your experience and make it their own. Research shows they will carry negative feelings around inside of themselves. This can cause children to become depressed, anxious, withdrawn, mistrusting of people, or fearful. Children of stressed-out parents also feel the need to read their parents' moods and tone of voice as a way to judge how safe it is to be around them at that time, or to ask for what they need. Unfortunately, this behavior creates tremendous stress and anxiety internally for a child, altering what would have been his normal developmental process. Future consequences might cause him to lack assertiveness and fear confrontation.

 *Question?*

My child watches everything I do, and then imitates me. Is this normal?
Yes, and modeling healthy choices while under stress or during difficult times is an excellent way for your children to learn. Writing in a journal, taking a walk or bike riding, calling a good friend, or destressing in a hot bath is the ticket to teach your child that stress is, at times, a part of life, and does not have to have negative consequences.

It is also important to keep in mind the coping skills your children learn as they watch you handle stress. Do you unconsciously reach for food, a cigarette, a beer or glass of wine, or use foul language when you are under pressure? Studies have shown your child will internalize your choices as an appropriate coping method. It is also important to note that anxiety will be lessened, even if your child or the family is under stress, when your child does not have to take care of you emotionally.

How Is Your Marriage?

You probably will not be surprised at this point if you hear that the state of your marriage can have a deep and lasting effect on your children. Arguments and issues to resolve are normal, and in fact can teach your child how to handle conflict appropriately, as she grows. It is when yelling has no resolve, when you call each other names, and everyone walks away hurt, sad, or angry that the negative connections get made. Because you and your spouse are role models for how your child will feel and what she will come to expect from relationships, take a moment to ask yourself what you are really modeling.

Important Questions to Ask Yourself
Because of the value modeling has on the growth of your children, your relationship with your significant other will be something you want to think about, and/or make changes to. Here are a few questions to ask yourself, and think about, to determine if you child's anxiety could be decreased by some small adjustments on your part:

- Do you know how to forgive and be forgiven?
- Do you know when to let go of an argument?
- Do you know how to talk so others listen and listen so others talk?
- Do you know how to get over your past and your past wounds in the marriage?
- Do you know how to protect your children from your marital problems?
- Do you know how to restore honor and dignity to your relationship?
- Do you know how to say "I'm sorry" and "I was wrong"?
- Do you feel emotionally supported and encouraged?

When you get along and support your partner, your children will mirror you and will likely get along with each other better, and learn to be better friends and family members. If they do see you argue and fight, it is very important they also see you solve problems, make up, and hug and kiss, as well.

The Four Horsemen of the Apocalypse

Drs. John and Julie Gottman have been doing research and writing books on how to have a successful marriage for years. Through their extensive work in the field, they have come up with the "four horsemen of the apocalypse" which are four behaviors that they feel can cause a marriage to become a divorce. They are:

- **Criticism:** This will begin as a complaint that is then coupled with a global attack on your character. It frequently begins with "you always" or "you never."
- **Defensiveness:** This is the counterattack used to defend one's innocence, or deny responsibility. It frequently feels like your partner is whining and dodging.
- **Contempt:** This has a twist of hostility or disgust to it. It will often involve mocking or sarcasm.
- **Stonewalling:** This is what happens when your partner acts like they are not affected by what you are saying, almost as if they have withdrawn from the conversation or you, even though they are still there physically.

Separation, Divorce, and Blended Families

There is as much conflicting evidence about the effects of separation and divorce on children as there are studies. There are books that say children of divorce or separated parents will suffer more from depression and anxiety, have lower self-esteem, and tend to tolerate or exhibit more abuse and neglect in their own relationships. There are also books that tell you if you stay together in a high-conflict marriage that will cause exactly the same issues. Some researchers have said that low-conflict marriages where the parents just do not love each other anymore, and divorce anyway, cause the most anxiety and depression for a child. Other studies show that five- and six-year-olds from low-conflict marriages perceive their parents' marriage as high-conflict anyway! Research on blended families has also come in with lots of conflicting evidence.

 Essential

Some studies caution parents not to remarry until the children are gone from the house because it creates too much anxiety and stress on the children, and other researchers believe a family can be blended, but that it takes approximately three to five years to mold into a cohesive family unit, and not uncommonly up to seven years.

Researchers have found that adolescents find it the most difficult to adjust to the blended family arrangement. Although young children want to engage with a stepparent, if that parent is seen as warm, engaging, and available, they still have considerable anxiety over how to be loyal to their own parent. Adolescents, because of their age, developing sexuality, and establishing autonomy, can find the presence of a stranger in the house anxiety-provoking and disruptive. These studies have suggested that because of this anxiety, about one-third of adolescent boys and one-fourth of adolescent girls choose to disengage from their stepfamilies and spend their time with friends, outside of the house, instead.

Your Child's Age Makes a Difference

If your child is in preschool, research confirms he will miss the parent who has moved out of the home and have a greater need for safety and security. He might, because of his anxiety and fears, regress in his most recent developmental accomplishment. He might have difficulty sleeping, be fearful, irritable, aggressive, demanding, or depressed and withdrawn. It is suggested that children ages five to eight can be more self-blaming and verbal about their sadness, be scared you will find another family to love, have difficulty understanding what "permanent" means, may be forgetful, and seem to lose time, or seem to be in a dream state. Children ages nine through adolescence tend to be more vocal, angry, resentful, blaming, and often act out in a more hostile way.

 Fact

Over six million children are living in divorced families, with 50 percent of all first marriages ending in divorce, and 60 percent of all second marriages ending in divorce. Some studies have found the divorce rate for third marriages is 70 percent.

Warning Signs

If your child has several of the following symptoms persistently over time, either because you have divorced, separated, or blended your family with another, it is important to look into therapy:

- Does not want to go out and play or call friends
- Has become negative, fearful, anxious, or clingy
- Is unwilling to go to bed, has difficulty falling asleep, is waking up in the middle of the night, has nightmares, reoccurring bedwetting, refusal to wake up or go to school
- Is angry, fighting with friends or siblings, or yelling at you with greater frequency
- Experiments with tobacco, medications, household substances, drugs, or alcohol
- Inflicts physical pain, or takes excessive physical risks that could or have resulted in injury to herself
- Talks of suicide, or hating her life

Although children, tweens, and teens can be dramatic as a way to get you to hear them, if your child's behavior seems overly exaggerated following a change in the family dynamic, you should give it further consideration.

Parenting Tips While Divorced or Blending

To lessen the anxiety your child will feel during separation and divorce, here are some key points to remember: First, let your child be a child. The best you can do for him right now is to keep him out of your business, keep what happens between you and your partner private, and do not put him in a position of parenting, or emotionally caretaking you. Some kids may attempt to do this even when you try to prevent it. They are merely trying to have some sense of control over their situation. Give them some other way of having control, like choosing when they do their homework—either after school, or after dinner. Maybe you can let them choose how many books they want you to read them before bed, or allow them to decide which chores they feel they would be best at, instead of telling them which ones they will do.

 Essential

To lessen a child's anxiety, no matter what their age, it is very important during a time of change to keep your promises, be consistent, and have a routine. While blending families together the most important piece revolves around communication. That means you communicate to your children *and* allow them to communicate to you. Having a family meeting once a week is an excellent start.

Keep in mind that the new stepparents, and possibly stepsiblings, are *your* choice, not necessarily your child's. It is important to have compassion for how this might feel for them and realize it can take years to work out. That does not mean your kids are being difficult, or that something is wrong with your family. Lastly, to reduce both anxiety and conflict, it is best to let the biological parent remain primarily responsible for control and discipline of their own children until the children feel they have developed a strong bond with the stepparent. This often means after a few years, not after weeks or months. This rule is especially important for adolescents, who may already be struggling with authority and independence issues.

 Fact

Families come in all different shapes and sizes. According to the Census Bureau, over 1,300 stepfamilies are formed daily, and 6.4 million children live with one birth parent, and one stepparent.

So, the bottom line is this: As a parent, your child will look to you as a gauge for how he forms his perceptions about acting and being in his own life. If you are anxious, stressed, or depressed, your child will mostly likely be as well. When adjustments are going to occur for your child that are out of his control, help him feel he is being taken into account by communicating with compassion and by being your best self. This will allow him to feel safe as he is struggling to navigate through the change. Being your best self means taking an inventory of your ability to cope with stress, your emotional life, and your marriage. Looking for ways to find balance in these areas benefits both you and your child.

CHAPTER 8

What to Look for
in a Counselor

The first appointment you will want to schedule when you see your child struggling is with your family doctor. Because many physical illnesses are closely related to the symptoms of anxiety, you want a clean bill of physical health. Once that has been established your doctor should suggest, and if he does not you can ask for, a referral to a therapist. It is important to know that sometimes these referrals are not necessarily based on the doctor's knowledge of the therapist's ability or practice. Instead, the recommendation might be because of a personal friendship, a mutual referral arrangement, word of mouth, or geographic location. This chapter will focus on the information you will need when making such an important decision for your child.

Provider Credentials and Experience

The best referral is usually from a friend or family member who has had experience working with a therapist treating an anxiety disorder. If that is not possible, the next step is to call a professional you trust and get a suggestion of someone they know professionally, and are not involved with socially. Besides your family doctor, sources to ask for a referral from include your minister or rabbi, an employee assistance program at work, your child's school counselor, or your insurance company. Because cognitive behavioral therapy has been the most highly researched, and therefore the treatment most often recommended, you can consult the

AABT, the Association for the Advancement of Behavioral and Cognitive Therapies Web site's directory of providers (*www.aabt.org*). Many other therapies have been shown to be effective as well, so do not limit your child to one resource. Other professional Web sites to check include the American Psychological Association (*www.apa.org*), your state psychological association, or the American Association for Marriage and Family Therapy (*www.aamft.org*). Also, you could look at the Directory of Providers on the Anxiety Disorder Association of America Web site (*www.adaa.org*).

Credentials

You want to find a therapist who has either a master's or a doctorate degree in a mental health field like psychology, marriage and family therapy, social work, or counseling. A licensed professional who has an advanced degree and has taken an exam given by the state she is practicing in will often be more specialized. This is important when dealing with children. The following list contains the most common credentials you will bump into, and what they signify:

- **M.A., M.S., M.C.:** A master of arts, master of science, or master of counseling can be earned in counseling, psychology, or a related field. It usually requires two years of postcollegiate study. Therapists with these degrees could become independently licensed up to about a decade ago, but the laws governing psychology have changed, and now a Ph.D. or Psy.D. is required for private practice.
- **M.S.W.:** Is a master of social work. A social worker works with an individual in the context of the wider community. She may help with domestic violence, child abuse, and drug abuse or foster-care issues. Social workers can practice therapy on their own if they are licensed, or in settings such as schools, clinics, or government agencies. The M.S.W. typically requires two to four years of study.
- **Ph.D.:** Is a doctor of philosophy. This academic degree takes four to seven years to earn. Many Ph.D.s go on to work in

academic settings as researchers and professors. Psychologists with a Ph.D. are also fully trained in the assessment and treatment of most conditions, and may offer testing and evaluation services.

- **Psy.D.:** Is a doctor of psychology and focuses on therapy and counseling rather than research. The degree was developed in the late 1960s to address the need for practitioners. This degree takes four years of study post-college.

- **Ed.D.:** Is a doctor of education. Professionals with Ed.D.s practice therapy just as do those with Ph.D.s. Often they are trained in child development and education and can focus on educational planning and assessment. Some work as school superintendents, principals, or directors of nonprofit organizations. This degree usually takes a total of four years to earn after undergraduate school.

- **M.D.:** Is a medical doctor. Medical doctors can prescribe medication and those with the specialty of psychiatric medications are psychiatrists. They receive an additional four years of clinical training in a mental health specialty after completing medical school. Some also do therapy, but you want to make sure they have the coursework and experience to counsel, as well as provide medication.

- **L.P.C.:** Is a licensed professional counselor. A licensing qualification is granted to those who have advanced training, a graduate academic degree, clinical work experience, and have passed a state-certified licensing examination. Often, L.P.C. practitioners are supervised by psychologists with higher levels of training.

- **L.P.:** Stands for licensed psychologist. This signifies that a therapist has met the educational criteria and passed state examinations to practice independently. In most states, this level of certification requires a doctoral degree.

- **L.I.C.S.W.:** Is a licensed clinical social worker. They are required to have a master's degree or doctoral degree and pass a licensing exam for the state they work in.

- **L.M.F.T.:** Is a licensed marriage and family therapist. L.M.F.T.s are required to complete 1,000 hours of individual or family therapy with 100 hours of supervision and two years of additional coursework to obtain this certification.

Although psychiatrists hold medical degrees and psychologists hold a doctoral degree or master's degree, there are no governing bodies to regulate titles such as "psychotherapist" and "therapist," so be prepared to look into credentials for practitioners using these titles.

Experience

Once you have gathered some names from trusted sources, it is important to either spend a few minutes on the phone, or have a session with each candidate, so you can decide who might be best for your child. Treating an anxiety disorder can take months or longer, depending on the severity, so this relationship is not one to rush into. Take your time to find someone who meets the high standards you want as you will trust your child's well-being to them.

Questions you might want to ask include: What type of experience, training, and license do you have, and for how long? What training and experience do you have specifically in treating anxiety disorders? What is your basic approach to treatment for a child? Can you prescribe medication or refer me to someone who can, if that proves necessary? Have you ever had a license revoked or suspended or been disciplined by a state or professional ethics board? (You can call the clinician's state licensing board to check on license, credentials, and any ethical violations.)

 Fact

Taking the time to ask questions and find a therapist who seems to connect with you and your child naturally will increase the chance that your child will want to go to therapy and stay in therapy.

Therapeutic Style and Importance of Rapport

Rapport and comfort are essential elements in the therapeutic relationship, and have a lot to do with the outcome of therapy. Some studies have suggested that rapport is actually more important than the type of therapy provided. Because of that, initially you will want to think about whether a male or female therapist would be best for your child. Take into consideration whether your child's anxiety is related to a trauma, and who the key players were in the experience. After you have decided male or female, you will also want to have an idea about which type of approach and demeanor might be best. Some children feel more comfortable with a therapist who has a "down-to-earth" approach, wears jeans and sneakers, and loves to get on the floor to play games. Other children might feel best talking to someone who is more reserved, wears a suit or dresses up, and sits behind a desk, or in a chair in front of them. It might help to think about what teachers your child seems to like best, if she has already started school.

Alert!

Do not let anyone, not a doctor, therapist, friend, or family member tell you there is one single best way to deal with your child or his anxiety. The mind and body are complex structures, not an absolute science, and therefore many different approaches could be helpful.

Think about the children she has played with and any comments she might have made about the moms and dads she has met. Or, maybe she is on a sports team and feels really comfortable with a certain coach, or a dance teacher. Whoever it is, think about what qualities that person has seeing how comfortable your child has been around them, and keep that in mind as you look for a therapist. You may be able to read something about their style when listening to their answer in your initial phone conversation. Rapport can start as early as listening to a voicemail or gel as late as the third session. If you or your child are still not feeling a connection with the therapist after three sessions you may need to reconsider who you are seeing.

Do Not Limit Yourself

Trust yourself to know what might work best for your child. If what you come up with is, "I'm just not sure," then that is what you know; go with it. What that means is try a few different styles, both male and female, and let your child decide who felt the best and was the easiest to talk to. Finding a good therapist is a process, and there is no "one size fits all." Sometimes it takes a few tries before you and your child will feel comfortable and safe, and you know you have found the right place for your child to do her work. Your approach can be, "let's give a few people a try, and then pick who we liked best." Nevertheless, try to limit yourself to two or three to begin; you do not want to overwhelm your child with choices and you want to start making progress as soon as you can. There might not be an option as to whether or not your child goes to therapy, but that doesn't mean you can't take a collaborative approach to finding the right one.

What Collaboration Looks Like

After each initial appointment, on the way home, you and your child can openly rate how you each felt and make a game out of it. For example, you can make a chart that has certain factors listed on it, with a rating scale already made up and ready to go. Rate on a scale of 1–5:

1 = awful, no way   3 = okay, or maybe   5 = great, let's try it

How did the office feel when you walked in?   _____

Did the therapist seem to value your input?   _____

How caring did this therapist seem?   _____

Did you feel safe when you talked to him?   _____

Did she know how to talk with you about your feelings? _____

Does he have a good plan to help with your anxiety?   _____

Does she seem like someone you could talk to again?   _____

This kind of activity will help your child feel empowered and sup-ported, setting the stage for a more positive therapy relationship to develop. He will feel as if you are all in this together, and that you care about how he feels by allowing him to be a part of the process. For a child with anxiety, that can be invaluable.

Clinic or Private Practice?

Choosing between seeing a therapist at a mental health clinic or a private practice is an individual issue. Each setting has pros and cons, depending on the type of services your child needs. When making your decision, what is most important is how you and your child feel about the person and the services being provided.

Private Practice

In order for a therapist to work privately, and charge your insur-ance company for the visit, she must be licensed by the state she works in. Some psychologists in private practice do not take insur-ance at all, or only work with a select few insurance companies. Always ask what the fee is. Sometimes it can be more than in a clinic setting. Often with a private clinic or practitioner, you will pay the full cost of the services, less the amount paid by your insurer. If you need medication, group, or other services, you might be referred out to another provider. Some therapists in private practice run their own groups, but they are usually specialized. Examples include groups for eating disorders, anger, anxiety, or depression.

Services Offered by a Private Practice

Many private offices have specific times when the office is open and when the therapist will be available to return phone calls. When you see someone in a private practice, he may or may not be more accessible than a provider in a clinic setting. Some private practitioners answer the phone themselves and schedule their own appointments, and others use answering services. Some private offices have an after-hours answering service or offer emergency services. Sometimes you can get an appointment within a week or two of your first phone call, and can be seen regularly right away, but it may take weeks before you can get in for an appointment if the therapist is good. Many offer early morning, day, and evening hours, and sometimes see clients on Saturdays. Some offer a sliding fee based on your income. Often psychologists in private practice have an office and waiting room that is specially designed with the client in mind. They will create a space that feels comforting, warm, and relaxing, very much like a living room.

A Clinic

Unless you are calling for a specific person you might be given to the therapist who is next in line for a referral. However, many clinics use triage systems to determine the best fit between a client's needs and therapist availability. Always ask about the therapist you are scheduled with if someone has not given you a specific name. Therapists might be right out of school, be licensed or not, be receiving supervision or not, or be degreed in psychology or not. Often you can wait weeks to get an appointment, similar to private practice, and if the clinic is busy, your child might not be able to be seen again, by the same person, for another month. It can take awhile to get on a therapist's schedule with frequency. Often clinics offer a sliding fee scale and many try to become a provider for every insurance company possible, including medical assistance/Medicaid and Medicare. There are some clinics that have a psychiatrist and vocational counselor on staff, or can provide testing and assessment as well, providing you convenient access under one roof.

Services Offered at a Clinic

Usually you will find a multitude of options at a mental health clinic because of the number of counselors or mental health workers on staff. Most offer psychological and psychiatric evaluations, medication and medication management, psychological testing, individual, group, and family therapy, play or art therapy, crisis intervention, and twenty-four-hour emergency services. Most clinics have a larger waiting room, similar to a doctor's office, where you will sit with a number of people waiting for your appointment. A clinic will usually have a business office, several people who do your scheduling, and an office manager. A clinic normally offers evening hours for appointments and may also have weekend hours.

Things to Consider

Pay attention to the surroundings and the staff, noticing if they feel comfortable in the space and are respectful and warm to one another. Check to make sure client confidentiality is protected. Use your own instincts; knowing your child best, you can make a good determination of what would be a comfortable setting for him.

 Essential

If when you first meet the counselor she does not greet you warmly, with eye contact, seems distracted, rushed, or not able to find a sense of ease with your child, you might need to look for another therapist.

When you do choose a therapist or psychiatrist, find out who covers for her when she is not working, or is on vacation. Always ask who does the billing for insurance and how co-pays or the fee is collected.

Geographic and Scheduling Issues

Try to find a psychologist within a reasonable distance from your house or child's school; you do not want the drive to be a deterrent to your child getting the help he needs. You also do not want to say no to a recommended therapist just because he is not located in your town. Many therapists will tell you what appointments they have left and you will feel the need to take what you can get to begin with. Those who work with children know that taking a child out of school for an appointment is a bad idea. However, therapists who see mostly children may have no choice but to schedule some appointments during school hours. Taking your child out of class draws attention to him and can cause him to miss schoolwork, homework, and tests. This may upset your child, and cause him to feel therapy is only complicating his problems. For a child who has anxiety, therapy should feel as if it is a good and comforting opportunity, not one that brings shame and more anxiety with it. If you need to schedule appointments during school time, try to rotate the subjects or classes your child misses to avoid undue pressure in one area.

 Fact

According to Marilyn Atherley, a writer for "e-ssortment," "What a child needs in a therapist is similar to what the child needs from any adult, including the parent. He wants gentleness, not harsh words, a loving and caring attitude, not a threatening one, encouragement and praise, not rebuffs and invalidation, firmness not permissiveness, persistence and consistency, not randomness."

How Long Should You Wait?

There are two questions here. How long should you wait to get in to see a therapist, and how long should you wait before you decide if this therapist is the right one? If your child is having significant difficulty, waiting more than two weeks for your first appointment is not reasonable. When your child is hurting, two weeks can feel like forever. It is important to note that some insurance companies may offer "crisis appointments." However, the next available provider may not be located in an area that is convenient for you. Consider this carefully before agreeing to a stopgap measure that may not be practical in the end. If you decide your child seems to have a problem, but it is not damaging to his daily life yet, waiting two to three weeks for the first appointment is reasonable. After that first session, though, it is important to have your child seen weekly, at least until the flow of therapy is established. Not only has it been shown that weekly therapy helps establish rapport, it is also necessary so your child can get some quick symptom relief.

 Essential

> Here are a few questions that are important to ask when looking for a therapist: What is your experience and basic approach to treatment for a child? Can you prescribe medication or refer me to someone who can, if that proves necessary? How long before you have room in your schedule? How frequent are the sessions, and how long do they last? Do you include family members in therapy?

If a therapist tells you she is a month out on her calendar, you need to question whether this is the right person for your child. When a therapist is that heavily booked out of the gate, the time she can fit you in will likely be limited, and as noted earlier, taking children out of school brings with it a host of other issues.

Is This Therapist the Right One?

In regard to how long before you know whether you've found the right person to work with your child and family, give the therapist three to four sessions. By then you will know if your child has connected and can form a trusting, open relationship with this person. The therapist will have also had the time to decide on goals and should have discussed a plan with you. By all means, ask any questions and raise any concerns you might have; a therapist's ability and willingness to address these issues can say a lot about her as a professional.

Alert!

If after three months of therapy you have not noticed a difference in your child, and your child has not been given specific things she can do to help her when she is feeling anxious, then it is time to look for another therapist.

What If You Don't Have Insurance?

The high cost of managed health care has been a hot topic for years. Unfortunately, there has not been enough reform to the system, which continues to make treatment out of reach for more than 38 million Americans. Even for those that do have health insurance, which is discussed in Chapter 12, some insurance plans do not cover mental health.

Resources for the Uninsured

Many communities have Community Mental Health Centers. Usually, for a reduced or sliding fee scale determined by your income, you can receive mental health services at your local center, which may in some cases be a county agency. Sometimes these clinics require you to be a recipient of public assistance or have a private insurance plan through the state. Often, to receive a reduced rate, you must live in the city or county in which the clinic is located. Many such centers are nonprofit agencies.

Your church or synagogue is also an excellent place to call. Often they will have a rabbi or certified pastoral counselor available for appointments. Many have professional counseling experience and provide services on a sliding scale, or no fee basis. It is important to verify credentials when choosing clergy for counseling.

 Essential

Another option is to have your child join a self-help or support group in school or in the community. They are generally free and can be found in virtually every community in America. Many young people like the group process because it helps them realize they are not alone with their anxiety, and it gives them a sense of belonging.

Public Assistance is another place to look. Examples of such programs are Social Security, Medicare, and Medicaid. Some have specific requirements such as age and income limitations. It will be necessary to call your government office and find out eligibility requirements.

Parent Involvement

Parents are often eager to support their children's learning, but can feel at a loss when dealing with their child's anxiety. Increasing your communication with your child about feelings, goals, and tools can be helpful. In fact, studies confirm parent involvement has positive effects on a child's anxiety when it is seen as encouraging and loving.

Parent Involvement in Cognitive Behavioral Therapy

A well-known study in 1996 by Barrett, et. al., found that children who had parents who were involved in their therapy had success rates that were significantly higher, 84 percent, compared to 57 percent for children who did not. In 2001 Barrett and colleagues found that, five to seven years after their original study, the children were able to maintain their gains. These same children, whose parents were involved in their care, also were significantly less fearful at long-term follow-up. Researchers believe the children were successful in part because of the added component of giving parents the skills needed to improve their own anxious feelings.

Another positive aspect of having parents involved in their child's therapy is that support can be given for tasks, or "homework" the child will be requested to do in between sessions. When your child feels understood and supported in therapy, the gains are usually greater.

 *Alert!*

The number of people without health insurance rose for the second year in a row to 43.6 million people, according to statistics gathered in 2003 by the U.S. Census Bureau. The proportion of children who are uninsured remained the same at 8.5 million, or almost 12 percent of children.

Other Ways Parents Can Help or Hinder

You can facilitate treatment by providing invaluable information regarding your child's history, extended family history, how functional your child is on a daily basis, issues with school and peers, and what other factors might be causing anxiety. It is just as important to tell the clinician, in front of your child, what you enjoy about her, what other kids seem to like or admire about her, and what assets she brings to school, family, and fun. Sometimes a parent can unwittingly impede his child's treatment by overfunctioning or underfunctioning in the therapy session, or at home. If you try to rescue your child from an anxiety-provoking situation, she might not be able to challenge herself and move past her fears. When you have difficulty setting limits, your child might have difficulty setting her own boundaries. Also, your child might be confused about how to attach to the therapist without hurting your feelings. Last, even though it can feel hard to find the time to take care of yourself or your own anxiety, it is important to remember your child loves you and will want to model you. All of these issues can, and should, be addressed in therapy.

Expectations Regarding Privacy and Safety

As an adult, you have a right to expect absolute privacy and confidentiality in therapy. Without your explicit consent, the therapist is prevented by law from discussing with anyone else information you share during your sessions. State and federal case law defines the circumstances in which confidentiality can be breached. The most common circumstances include:

- Third-party insurance reimbursement
- Collection of debt
- Defense of malpractice or professional complaint
- Danger to self or others
- Abuse of children, elderly, or mentally or physically handicapped
- Abuse by a medical professional

For minor children, that same sense of privacy does not exist. As a parent, you legally have a right to know what is discussed in each session and to see your child's file if you want to. Clinically, especially if the child is older, it is important for the therapist to be able to develop a relationship that feels safe, trusting, and open, and will not be compromised by what the parents need, feel, and want. Some children, as they reach eight or nine years old, crave a sense of autonomy and independence from parents and will not talk unless they feel there is confidentiality and privacy. You might consider not asking for information about your child's therapy unless you have a specific concern. For example, if your child is not making progress or you believe she might be suicidal, definitely approach the clinician. In fact, you can confirm, up front, with your child's therapist that if your child reveals a potential threat to herself or someone else, the therapist will alert you immediately as required by the law. This way you do not need to wonder; you are assured your child's therapist is sharing the most important information as it comes up. Another example might be, you do not need to know that your son has a crush on the fourteen-year-old daughter of your best friend, but you do need to know if he feels anxious upon arriving at school because a group of bullies has been hanging out at the front door and intimidating him. As children move toward adolescence, this need increases. Few things carry such potential to disrupt treatment as an adolescent's feeling that what he discussed with his therapist in session is shared without his knowledge. Many therapists address this concern directly in the first session. A patient bill of rights should be posted in your doctor's office, and you will be given a confidentiality document, with your rights on it, to sign as well.

CHAPTER 9

Individual, Family, and Group Therapy

There may be almost as many types of therapy as there are settings that provide them. Choosing the right type of therapy for your child can be a bit challenging, so this chapter will serve as a guide. It is important to keep in mind that not all therapists are skilled in all types of therapy, and that the approach used will be based on your clinician's training and the setting in which she practices. In general, there are three basic types of therapy: individual, family, and group, and many of the therapies described in the following sections can be used in all three settings with a child with anxiety.

Individual Therapy

Individual, "one-to-one," or "talk therapy" is the most common psychological therapy for children and adults. Individual therapy is based on the premise that when a trusting relationship with a therapist is established, a client can increase self-awareness and change destructive or unhealthy patterns of thought, emotion, and behavior. A real-life example is when you feel relief from and resolution to an issue by talking it through with a supportive friend. Though theoretical approaches vary, most individual therapy is based on the concepts outlined below. However, it is important to keep in mind that some schools of thought, such as behaviorism, focus almost exclusively on behavior change and bypass the importance of the therapeutic relationship, and the need for emotional catharsis, or release.

"Name It, Claim It, and Tame It"

In a broad sense, name it, claim it, and tame it captures the essence of personal growth, both in therapy and in life. The ability to identify a problem or pattern such as anxiety, take ownership of the problem, and take steps to change it, are at the root of personal development. Individual therapy is designed to facilitate this process while offering support, suggestions, affirmation, and a compassionate ear.

Problem Patterns and Positive Psychology

Individual therapy usually begins with an assessment of "what's not working" for a client with respect to thinking, emotions, relationships, and behavior. A skilled therapist will help clients identify maladaptive or unhelpful patterns, and set measurable goals to decrease them while increasing more positive, productive patterns. Because of the inherent negativity in anxiety, a therapist who helps your child own and build on her strengths can be essential.

 Fact

For younger children, the use of play, art, or other child-centered techniques will almost always be incorporated into the session, and for adolescents, who are more verbal and reflective, "talk therapy" is more common. Tweens may do best with a combination of both approaches.

Catharsis and Release

Many schools of therapy are based on the idea that examining patterns of thought, emotion, and interaction can bring up strong feelings that a client can then release, or let go. Hidden or buried emotion may be discovered and integrated as well, and it is believed that this process leaves room for new, more effective patterns to emerge.

A child with anxiety or his parents, for example, might find that they have underlying grief or sadness about the limitations and losses associated with anxiety. Spending some time with these feelings may allow them to transform and dissolve, making way for empowerment and new hope for the future.

Creating Change

The crux of any successful therapy is the ability to which it is effective in creating lasting change. Usually, therapy continues until the changes are stable; that is, new patterns of thinking, acting, feeling, and interacting/socializing are used more often than not to meet life's challenges. Careful observation and goal setting at the beginning of therapy are crucial to being able to assess the extent to which a child has been successful in changing old, less functional patterns. It is exciting to see how each change your child is able to make creates opportunities for more learning and growth to occur.

Family Therapy

Historically, family therapy grew out of individual therapy as psychologists began to realize that family patterns, interactions, and wounds contribute to both the problem and the solution to emotional and behavioral troubles. There are several schools of thought that drive family therapy, but the overall premise is that families exist as systems, and that "the whole is greater than the sum of its parts." With younger children, parenting and/or family therapy may be preferred, as parents and siblings have the most direct impact on a child's world. Other components, such as individual play therapy or skill building, can be added to your child's plan of care based on his needs.

Family Dynamics

Family dynamics is a term used to describe the general pattern and functioning of your family. Family therapists look at patterns of communication, alliances, problem solving, and the assignment of power and resources, among other things, to determine a family's overall style and then assess what about that style is working and what is not. Family therapists also assess a family's adjustment to various transitions, coping, parenting styles, and marital stability to determine which areas might need to be addressed.

 Essential

In order to fully assess and treat a family, it is generally best for all family members to attend sessions. Children who are very young or older children who may not live full-time with the family may not be included, or included in specific sessions only.

Homeostasis

A primary theory in family therapy is the tendency of families to seek to maintain sameness, even in the face of extreme external changes. This is not unlike an automatic piloting system, which is set to maintain a certain course no matter what the weather or currents. An example of homeostasis is a child with anxiety who is learning to be more independent and spend more time away from home, whose parents may miss her company, or be afraid she will not do well, and subtly discourage her progress.

Enmeshment and Disengagement

Enmeshment and disengagement are classic terms used in certain forms of family therapy to describe how close (enmeshed) or distant (disengaged) family members are from one another. The goal in this aspect of family functioning is to seek a balance between these two polarities, and to enhance a family's ability to move, flexibly and adaptively, between the two extremes.

Families who are extremely disengaged may be more likely where there is depression or schizophrenia. An extremely disengaged family system can produce anxiety in children if they feel there is no one to connect with, or to protect them. This can be especially true for children who live in high-crime neighborhoods.

Alert!

In families in which one or more members have anxiety, the trouble is usually enmeshment, or too little "personal space" between family members. As you saw in Chapter 7, being overprotective can be one form of enmeshment, blocking children from establishing independent, confident selves.

Extended Family

Extended family, such as grandparents, aunts, and uncles may be included in family therapy for a number of reasons. This can be especially important if extended family provides care for your child or if the contact is especially close, so that your child's new skills and the techniques he's learning are supported and reinforced in as many settings as possible. If you have a strong relationship with your family already, and feel they can be team players, you will more than likely be able to enlist their support for your child without the assistance of a therapist.

Parent Coaching

Parent coaching can be offered individually or in groups, and is often woven into individual therapy when a therapist provides focused time for parents without the child present. It is typical for therapists who specialize in play therapy to offer parent coaching versus family therapy, as they see the child as the "primary patient," but still want to offer guidance to the parents. Parent coaching can be an essential tool in helping parents to ally with each other, and help their children by reducing anxiety created by mixed messages or approaches.

Group Therapy

Group therapy can be a powerful tool for decreasing isolation, increasing confidence, and practicing emotional expression and social skills. One of the primary benefits of group therapy occurs when a child realizes that he is not alone in his fears and struggles; that he is not as different from others as he may have come to believe.

 Fact

Although true for most children, teens and tweens, especially, can benefit from group therapy. This is because of their strong need to connect with, and be accepted by, peers. Groups are also excellent ways to help kids reduce feelings of isolation and alienation. This concept, in itself, can go a long way to reduce anxiety.

Behavioral Groups

Behavioral therapy in the group setting is designed to help people learn new skills and let go of old, ineffective ones. Training and practice in social skills and assertiveness can be especially helpful for children with social phobia, and teaching relaxation and other coping strategies can be done effectively in a group setting. The group itself allows for trial and error, direct feedback, support, and opportunities for immediate reinforcement of new skills.

Parenting Groups

Parenting groups that provide opportunities for both peer support and skills training are available in many communities. Systematic Training for Effective Parenting (STEP) is one such model. Though many parenting groups are based on childrearing and discipline, there may be specialty groups in your area that are suited to your particular needs. Your care providers, insurance company, or local hospital or clinic may be able to help you pinpoint resources. Early Childhood Family Education (ECFE) and places of worship may offer group-parenting therapy as well.

Supportive Approaches

Supportive therapy is a general term to describe any number of interventions that are intended to reduce discomfort and enhance the effectiveness of therapy for your child. Supportive therapy can be used together with individual, family, or group therapy, and may be recommended by your mental health provider if she feels it will be helpful for you and your child. Several types of supportive therapy are highlighted below.

Coordination with Other Providers
It is sometimes essential for a care provider to coordinate with others who support your child. For example, therapists often consult closely with pediatricians or psychiatrists to help monitor a child's response to medication. If your child shows school avoidance or refusal, contact with his teachers and other school staff can ensure that his transition back to school is the smoothest it can be.

Peer Counseling
As reflected in the section above, the intent behind peer counseling is to help your child build trust, gain support and confidence, and decrease isolation through her connection to a peer counselor. Peer counseling may be available at your child's school, either in groups or one-to-one, and community resources may offer similar opportunities for you or your extended family.

Mentors
A mentor is an older, more experienced person who can take you or your child "under his wing" for support and education. Good

mentors for children with anxiety might be older students, siblings, or family members who have tackled anxiety issues, or school personnel who have had similar experiences. Make sure that you know and trust your child's mentor(s) so that your own anxiety will not complicate your child's opportunity to benefit from the relationship.

Calming Animal Companions

Pets can be wonderfully supportive: They ask for little, are great listeners, and generally do not talk back. Companion animals and their therapeutic benefits have become more popular over the past decade, and there have even been specific "animal therapies" developed for special populations.

 Fact

Research shows that sitting with and stroking a cat or dog reduces muscle tension and blood pressure, and slows breathing and heart rate. As such, a child who may have trouble learning relaxation techniques may benefit just as much by sitting quietly with her pet.

To enhance your child's ability to achieve relaxation while connecting with a pet, you can encourage her to slow down, speak softly (or not at all), and breathe deeply. Finally, the responsibility of caring for a pet is a great way for an anxious or worried child to develop confidence and mastery.

Play Therapy

As you saw in Chapter 4, projective techniques are commonly used to assess underlying emotional issues, which drive anxiety, depression, and other conditions. Play therapy is a projective technique in which your child's conflicts and desires are revealed through her play and her interaction with the therapist. Generally, play therapy is the mode of choice for children under the age of ten to age twelve, as they are less verbal and abstract than older children. As children mature, their ability to "think about thinking" and work with their emotions directly increases, and play techniques give way to more traditional talk therapies, which focus directly on emotional expression, problem solving, and behavioral change. It is important to note that play that occurs in a professional setting is different from play that occurs outside of the office. Unless your child's therapist guides you, it is generally unwise to attempt to make free play "therapeutic."

The Symbolic Nature of Play

Play therapists work from the assumption that the symbols your child uses in his creative play are windows into the deeper recesses of his fears, desires, and motivations. When he expresses these through his play, they gradually become a part of his awareness; that is, he can learn about himself when guided by someone who is observant and responsive to his nonverbal messages. When your child feels fully understood, he is more likely to trust that he can manage his emotions and solve his problems.

 Essential

Unfortunately, the highly subjective nature of play therapy does not lend itself well to research, though specific techniques such as sand tray therapy do have some support in the literature.

The Cathartic Nature of Play

When your child expresses her inner nature through her play, a natural emotional release, or catharsis, occurs. This emotional response can also uncover other, related emotions. For example, a girl who re-enacts a fight with her father in play therapy may feel relief, or might move from anger to sadness as her role in the conflict becomes clearer. Your child can then use her insights to change her self-talk and behavior about the situation, and make future adjustments. When an anxious child expresses fears or worries in therapy, they lose some of their power to torment her in her daily life.

 Fact

Self-talk is a term coined from cognitive behavioral therapy. It refers to the things you say to yourself in your head about your experiences, like "She didn't say hello to me, so she must not like me." These powerful thoughts influence your core beliefs and your emotions, which in turn influence your behavior. Learning to change self-talk is essential in managing anxiety.

Learning New Behavior Through Play

Play therapists are trained to gently comment on and intervene in play to help your child learn new behavior. For example, in the situation just described, a therapist might model a father and daughter having a talk together or making up, or suggest that a child come up with a different, more satisfactory scenario. In addition, though much of play therapy itself is unstructured, there are multiple opportunities to teach social skills such as developing confidence, taking turns, following the rules of a game, and negotiating. Play therapists incorporate all of these skills to help a child with anxiety develop confidence, decrease his need for control, and tolerate anxiety.

Tools of the Trade

A therapist who uses play therapy with children will usually have an array of items at hand to meet your child's particular needs and concerns. The experience of play therapy includes not only the play itself, but also the opportunity to build trust and cooperation, which sets the stage for change. The most common props used in play therapy are described in the following paragraphs.

DOLLHOUSE

A dollhouse is a common tool. It is used in therapy to help your child express thoughts, feelings, and experiences about her family and other people in her world such as pets or neighbors.

GAMES

Games are used by many child therapists to help establish comfort and trust, to provide a window into a child's experiences, and to serve as a tool for skill building. There are many therapeutic games available to help children act spontaneously and express opinions and emotions in nonthreatening ways. Games may also be targeted toward specific objectives, such as making friends or expressing anger. Games provide a backdrop for children to express and work on issues of control and mastery, which are especially important for children with anxiety. In addition, playing games with children in therapy provides a perfect opportunity for therapists to help children improve their social skills.

 Essential

The practice of "acting as if" can encourage a child with anxiety to try on new ways of thinking and acting, which may bring relief from fear, worry, or withdrawal and lead to new ways of acting outside the therapy office. Storytelling and role-playing are also techniques that draw on "make believe."

PUPPETS, DOLLS, AND ANIMALS

Puppets can often convey feelings or thoughts a child is afraid to express because they let the child feel "once removed" from his direct experience. This emotional distance can allow a child to feel freer to fully express his needs and emotions. Dolls and animals serve a similar purpose, allowing your child to project his inner self without having to use more complicated means of expression. It is common for a child in therapy to choose a stuffed animal to "speak for him" or to say or do things he may feel he is unable to. Sometimes, therapeutic suggestions from "an older, wiser being" (like a well-worn teddy bear) are received on a deeper level than would be possible in simple "talk therapy."

SAND PLAY/SAND TRAY

Sand play incorporates specially designed trays of sand in which children can form menageries of animals, people, houses, and other symbols that represent their internal world. Sand tray therapists are trained to interpret the scenes your child creates in the sand and to use these to help your child in therapy. The therapist may also use your child's creations to help her tell "stories," to express strong needs and emotions in a nonthreatening way, and to point to recurring themes, which may indicate your child's concerns, strengths, or weaknesses.

Art and Music Therapy

The creative arts are a perfect medium for the expression of personal experiences, emotions, desires, and aspirations. Therapists skilled in these areas may use a variety of techniques to identify and address problem areas for a child. Opportunities for creative expression also allow children to build on strengths and increase confidence.

Music Therapy

Music therapy is commonly offered in a group setting, such as residential treatment, and is relatively uncommon in general practice. Music can be a great vehicle for eliciting and expressing emotion, such as fear or sadness. In fact, if you were to watch a movie without the music track, you might find the drama of the story far less compelling. A music therapist can play particular music to draw on certain emotions that your child can explore more fully. Conversely, a music therapist may suggest your child use various musical instruments to express a particular feeling or problem.

Art Therapy

Art therapy can use any medium to help your child explore and express his experiences and emotions. Drawing, as you have seen, can be a useful tool in both assessment and therapy. The use of paint, clay, chalk, and collage materials is also common in art therapy.

Do You Need a Specialist?

In many areas of the country, it may be hard to find specialized art and music therapy. However, therapists may incorporate art or music into sessions with your child, depending on their skill and interest. It is worth mentioning that building confidence through art, music, or performance can be extremely helpful for children with anxiety. However, if a child shows high levels of performance anxiety, this type of therapy may be too overwhelming and may not be appropriate.

 **Alert!**

There are many programs available through schools, libraries, community centers, and art centers from which you and your child might choose. If your child has anxiety, try to give her two or three options to choose from, and then help her stick to her commitment.

Cognitive-Behavioral Therapy

Cognitive-behavioral therapy (CBT) is probably the most widely researched of all types of therapy. It was developed in the 1970s as behavioral psychology began to push the field toward more specificity, effectiveness, and measurability. Cognitive therapy focuses primarily on how to change destructive thought patterns, and behavioral therapy helps people identify and change unhelpful behaviors, and replace them with new, more effective skills. Put the two together and you get CBT. CBT is offered in both group and individual therapy, and may be used as a component of family therapy as well. Cognitive therapy is useful for tweens and teens who are developing the ability to monitor and change their thinking, and behavioral therapy can be especially helpful for younger children who need their world to be manipulated more directly.

Thoughts Rule

The term "cognitive" refers to the thought processes, both positive and negative, which in turn drive our emotions and behavior. Cognitive statements include messages you give yourself about events in your life, messages you have internalized from and about your past, and messages about your future success or failure. The goal of cognitive therapy is to minimize negative, self-defeating thoughts, and to maximize positive, supportive, and growth-oriented thoughts. As you can see, cognitive therapy is one of the most crucial components of treatment for anxiety, no matter the age of the client.

Skills Training

Simply titled, skills training is used to help people learn new patterns of behavior and to replace older, less effective patterns. Skills training is crucial for children with anxiety so that they can gradually build small skill sets (like calling friends) to develop larger skill sets (like going on a sleepover). Skills training can be used along with behavioral management to increase the impact of practicing the new behavior. Other uses of skills training for children with anxiety include teaching a shy child to ask for help, or helping a teen learn to be more confident by building social skills.

Assertiveness as Antidote

Assertiveness has been well researched as an antidote to anxiety, and has been popular in both group and individual therapy for decades. Though many people feel anxious when they antici-pate having to assert themselves, the act of self-assertion actually decreases anxiety by producing a sense of mastery and control over the environment. Even small children can benefit from assertiveness training at very basic levels, by learning to identify and express their feelings, and to ask for help if they are worried or uncomfortable. This is particularly crucial for a child with anxiety, who may feel so overwhelmed by emotion that she can't soothe herself or garner support.

 *Question?*

Have you ever felt a sense of relief or elation after standing up for yourself?
If so, you may have experienced the "biochemistry of assertion." Some researchers believe that there may be specific neurobio-logical structures that produce pleasure when you assert yourself. Happily, this sense of well-being builds on itself, encouraging future assertion.

Behavioral Management

Though behavioral management is not always viewed as an aspect of CBT, it is a useful tool in helping children with anxiety. A typical use of behavioral management in therapy is for you, your child, and his therapist to develop a systematic plan to reinforce, or reward, his progress. For example, if a child who has been school-avoidant attends school for a full week, you might reward him with a special treat, outing, meal, or quality time together. As mentioned in Chapter 4, tracking change over time creates a sense of accom-plishment, and may even improve behavior on its own. More tips on behavioral management are available in Chapter 19.

CHAPTER 10

Additional Help

Once you find a trusted, knowledgeable therapist who has just the right mix of humor, empathy, and helpful tools he might also ask you to take your child to see a psychiatrist for an evaluation. A psychiatrist is simply a medical doctor who has special training in the field of psychiatric medicine. She can provide a diagnostic evaluation, consider physical factors that might suggest a physical diagnosis, or prescribe medications. Be sure to ask whether she specializes in treating children. This may seem like a common-sense question but you would be surprised how many people do not ask it.

How Can a Psychiatrist Help?

Because a psychiatrist is a specialist in how the body and brain work, she can assess the causes and potential treatments for your child's anxiety more fully. She will discuss with you whether medication could be helpful with your child's type and level of anxiety, and which medications might work best. She can also provide additional support, treatment options, and encouragement.

Why Was My Child Asked to See a Psychiatrist?

It could be your therapist wanted a second opinion about your child's diagnosis, level of functioning, or the treatment plan. Even though your child might benefit from medication, in most cases, a therapist cannot provide that (there is change coming, though; New

Mexico is the first state to allow psychologists with specialized train- ing to prescribe medications because of need in more rural areas). In addition, the psychiatrist can give a second opinion on possible medical factors suspected of contributing to the anxiety. Web sites, such as the American Medical Association and the Anxiety Disorder Association of America, that can be helpful as you look for a psychia- trist, are located in Appendix B.

What Happens When You See a Psychiatrist?

Just as with your family doctor and therapist, the psychiatrist will meet with you and your child to look at family history, address physi- cal symptoms, and discuss your child's general development. Often, the first time you meet will be longer because the psychiatrist will be gathering all the information needed to address the possibility of pre- scribing medication. Share any issues with sleep, appetite, or energy level. This will help your psychiatrist have a thorough understanding of the difficulty your child is experiencing. It is also essential that the doctor know about any current or past medications your child has been prescribed, as well as who prescribed them. Tell the doctor if your child has begun therapy and with whom as well.

Find the Right Psychiatrist for Your Child

Your HMO or insurance company usually has a list of pediatric psychiatrists who are in your network. Sometimes you need a referral, so when you contact your insurance company for the list, ask about the proper procedure. You can also talk with your therapist, family doctor, other mental health professionals, your child's school, family members, or friends. As with the referral to a therapist, you want to ask for a few names and call each one with a list of general questions.

Involving a Primary Care Physician

Primary care physicians are clinicians that are trained in general medicine, pediatrics, gynecology, or family practice. A PCP, as they are also known, establishes the first point of entry for a patient who is not feeling well and is not exactly sure why. The primary care provider can treat a wide range of health concerns and typically is well educated in a broad number of areas. Some will even be comfortable managing a child's psychiatric medications, particularly if your child has taken them and shown stability over time. You can think about the primary care provider as the doctor who has to know enough about every area of medicine to make the proper referrals to the appropriate specialists.

Alert!

Because of recent concerns with suicidal thinking and behavior in children taking antidepressant/antianxiety medication, it is recommended that your child receive regular follow-up, especially when starting or stopping a medication. Your PCP, NP, or GP may offer this option, though you may have to ask for it.

PCPs are considered the primary gatekeeper in health plans, authorizing referrals to specialists for more complex and time-intensive diagnostic procedures. After taking on a patient, they often will manage the long-term care of that person if the patient has a basic medical condition that is nonsurgical in nature.

Can My Regular Doctor Prescribe Antianxiety Medication?

If your child's anxiety is severe, and it has been decided that medication is the best route along with therapy, you might be wondering if your family doctor can write the prescription.

Many general practitioners are comfortable and competent prescribing medications for basic or uncomplicated anxiety and depression. Some are not, as they may feel that it is out of the scope of their practice. If your child has overlapping conditions such as ADHD and anxiety, or a more complex condition such as OCD, it is invaluable to have the input of a psychiatrist. Because your child's pediatrician typically can see your child immediately, start with her. The wait to see a psychiatrist, particularly one who sees children, can be anywhere from four to twelve weeks. If your child's pediatrician is comfortable prescribing for anxiety, she can get you help as soon as possible. In the meantime, schedule an appointment with the psychiatrist, and by the time you have your first appointment, you will have weeks of data to share about your child's mood and behavior, and how the medication is working. The psychiatrist is in the best position at that point to evaluate what to do next.

 Fact

According to the American Academy of Family Physicians and the American College of Physicians (January 2006), there is an ever-growing shortage of primary care physicians. They found "the number of medical students entering family practice training dropped by 50 percent between 1997 and 2005." Moreover, "in 1998, half of internal medicine residents chose primary care, but by 2006, over 80 percent became specialists or hospitalists."

Help from a Nurse Practitioner

A nurse practitioner (NP) is a registered nurse (RN) who provides high-quality medical care similar to a doctor. They have a minimum of a master's degree and are trained to diagnose and manage common medical conditions, focus on health education, and provide counsel to you about your child's illness. Like a PCP, they will educate you and your child on how actions and lifestyle can affect your well-being. A nurse practitioner can be a patient's regular health care provider, and in most states, many nurse practitioners have a DEA registration number so they can write prescriptions for "controlled" medications.

Why Choose a Nurse Practitioner?

An NP is an excellent point of entry into the medical system because she may provide services for an entire family, is easily accessible, treats the mind and body, can fill prescriptions, and bills insurance for services performed. With an NP you get the full package, from diagnosing, treating, evaluating, and managing non–life-threatening acute and chronic illness and diseases, to providing primary and specialty care services, performing minor surgeries and procedures, and collaborating with physicians and other health professionals as needed. She can order, perform, and interpret basic diagnostic studies as well.

 Essential

Because anxiety can be due to a poor or inadequate diet, a health professional might recommend a visit to a dietitian or nutritionist who will create a food and meal plan specifically with your child's physical and mental health needs in mind.

Questions to Ask a Psychiatrist

When looking for a psychiatrist, you might find the following list helpful. These questions are similar to the ones you want to ask when you look for a therapist:

- What experience does she have with children and anxiety disorders?

- What insurance does she take and who files the insurance?

  _____

- Can she offer your child before- or after-school appointments?

  _____

- What are the possible side effects of the medication she is prescribing?

  _____

- How long will it take the medication to work?

  _____

Also, ask if your child should avoid other medications or certain foods while she takes the medication, what to do if the medication does not work, and how to stop the medication when it is time.

 **Question?**

What is a psychiatric nurse, and how can she help?
In many clinic and hospital settings, a psychiatric nurse acts as "the right hand" of the psychiatrist. Psychiatric nurses often gather history and background information at your visits with the psychiatrist. They will often be your first point of contact, and will interface with the doctor about your concerns. Some psychiatric nurses can even recommend an increase or decrease in your child's dosage as well.

Developing a Treatment Plan

Your focus, which is probably in part why you picked up this book, lies in helping your child find symptom relief. As discussed previously, being a part of the evaluative process and treatment can bring better results. Creating a treatment plan with the therapist is the first step to ensure you and your child get your needs met. At the end of the day, helping your child by working with the school, doctor, therapist, and psychiatrist will mean you are actually your child's case manager.

Treatment Plan for Anxiety

It is helpful that everyone who is involved in your child's care is a specialist in anxiety if possible. You want to be assured they understand the complex and pervasive impact anxiety can have, or has had, on him. When making the treatment plan, discuss a combination of therapy, skill building (personal and social), assertiveness training, relaxation skills, and self-esteem building. Also, include in your plan an educational component so you and your child can understand how anxiety affects the mind and body. It is also helpful to include your ideas about whether medication will be considered, at what point, and how. Part of the plan also needs to include how and with whom information will be shared, and who will be included in the support system. For example, many families choose to share the treatment plan with the counselor, nurse, and teachers at school, and family members who live at home, too.

 **Alert!**

It is always best if everyone is moving in the same direction, so as your child takes baby steps to facilitate change, others throughout his day can provide support and understanding. Having a clear, written plan will assist you in this.

Building on Your Child's Strengths

When you are discussing with the therapist or psychiatrist treatment choices and selection it is essential to consider how to positively reinforce your child's strengths. It is best to create a treatment plan that includes strategies to manage the negative symptoms accompanying anxiety, but also includes opportunities to build on what's right, enhance your child's self-concept, level of confidence, autonomy, resilience, and a sense of self-efficacy.

An important reminder for every parent: More often than not, it is the strengths your children acquire, sometimes through adversity, that bring with them a vision of what their lives can be and what their true potential is. It is there that they find hope and the inspiration to proceed through difficulty. With that in mind, building a well-balanced, strength-based treatment plan so your child has a sense of building, instead of tearing apart, can be the foundation for long-term change. A quote by Dr. Bob Brooks may say it best: "If one has a bigger sea of dysfunction to swim through, then one must possess larger islands of competence to rest upon."

CHAPTER 11

To Medicate or Not

The use of psychiatric medication, especially in children, has been under close scrutiny for over a decade. Reports of antidepressants causing suicidal behavior in children, and outcry against the over-medication of children for ADHD have raised both public and professional concern. A concern about the "quick fix" mentality of the pharmaceutical industry has made many potential consumers skeptical about the rationale and safety behind the use of psychiatric medications. This chapter will help you to consider all the facts and make a decision about medication that you will be comfortable with. If you are uncomfortable with the idea of medication, use the other resources offered throughout the book as your first line of defense.

Is My Child's Condition Simple or Complex?

As previously mentioned, determining whether your child's condition is straightforward or more complicated is important in helping you to decide whether and what type of professional help will be most beneficial to your child. If your child's condition is relatively simple, such as trouble going to bed at night or playing at other children's houses, you may opt to address the issues at home. If, however, your child's anxiety interferes with many areas of her functioning and prevents her from living her life fully, or if her anxiety overlaps with other conditions, this increases the need to seek professional help, including considering medication. As discussed in Chapter 10, as a general rule, the more complex your child's condition, the wiser it is to see a psychiatrist, versus a general practitioner.

 Essential

> The decision about whether to use medications in treating children with anxiety is one that is highly personal, and often complex. It is best to make the decision with solid education and support from professionals whom you trust, and who know your child well.

Nature Versus Nurture

A classic debate in psychology is the degree to which innate biological characteristics (nature) or environmental influences (nurture) cause disturbances in thinking, emotions, and behavior. Research has certainly demonstrated a strong biological component in conditions such as schizophrenia, bipolar disorder, major depression, and to a certain extent, anxiety. For milder conditions, however, like panic attacks and adjustment problems, the waters are a bit murkier.

If you feel that your child has both nature and nurture in her way, that is, if there is a family history of anxiety, and your child experiences one or more of the issues discussed in this chapter, your best course of action may be to consult with a psychiatrist.

Dual Diagnosis

Dual diagnosis is a psychiatric and medical term used to describe a situation in which a person has two, often overlapping, conditions. Medically, this might include someone who has diabetes and obesity, or asthma and allergies. As you have learned, it is common for psychological conditions like depression and anxiety to overlap, and for chemical dependency to overlap with anxiety and other conditions. In children, it is common for anxiety and ADHD to produce mild depression. Children with persistent medical conditions like asthma or diabetes may experience both depression and anxiety, and as you've seen, anxiety and depression can result from loss and trauma. For example, consider a child who has separation anxiety. If she has trouble being away from home, she may feel sad about not having many friends and feel even more isolated. As you can see, the anxiety and depression spiral in on themselves, making the situation more and more difficult to unravel.

 Essential

In teens, anxiety and depression can overlap with, and even cause, substance abuse. This often occurs as a teen self-medicates social anxiety or internal feelings of hopelessness or chaos by using drugs or alcohol.

Family History

If you or anyone in your extended family has suffered from anxiety or related conditions, it can be especially important to seek evaluation for medication. Studies show that children of parents with anxiety disorders are more likely to have difficulty with anxiety, and it is clear that early intervention improves your child's ability to recover fully from anxiety. If you are not sure about whether your family members have had troublesome anxiety, consider gently asking, for the benefit of your child. The good news is that if you are alert to patterns that already exist in your family, you are in prime position to intervene early and ensure the best care for your child, regardless of whether you choose medication as an option.

Medical Complications

Children with medical conditions such as diabetes, asthma, or cerebral palsy, among others, may be at risk for increased anxiety or depression due to the chronic nature of these ailments. Other complicating factors might include serious illness such as leukemia, growth or hormonal deficiencies, or serious injuries or accidents. The anxiety may be a side effect of a treatment, an aspect of the illness itself, or simply a psychological reaction to coping with such an illness.

Types of Medication

Though there is good evidence to support the benefits of medication in treating adult anxiety, the long-term research needed to validate safety, effectiveness, and developmental effects in children is ongoing. Due to the tightening FDA regulations, those who prescribe medication for children may only have a few options to work with, especially if they practice in a managed-care setting. Following is a list of typical types of medication that your child's doctor may prescribe. Some newer medications are formulated so they need only be taken once a day. They may have the designations CR (controlled release), SR (sustained release), ER or XR (extended release), or LA (long-acting).

 Fact

Remember, if you've responded well to a medication yourself, your child's physician may want to consider the same medication as a first course for your child. Be sure to let your child's doctor know if you've responded well to a medication for anxiety or depression.

Antidepressants

Antidepressant medications have been used for decades to reduce anxiety, whether or not depression is present. There are three basic types of medications, and they are grouped based upon the neurotransmitters they act upon. In general, antidepressants work by helping the brain to restore the optimal chemical functioning that it needs to improve mood, thinking, and physical troubles such as sleep, appetite, and energy. In addition, the overall support of brain chemistry by antidepressants can help stop negative, unproductive thinking and behavior. Following are examples of selective serotonin reuptake inhibitors (SSRIs), which are among the most commonly prescribed for both children and adults with anxiety. For convenience, the name of the chemical agent is given first, and the brand name is shown in parentheses: fluoxetine (Prozac), sertraline, (Zoloft), paroxetine (Paxil), fluvoxamine (Luvox), venlafaxine (Effexor), citalopram (Celexa), and escitalopram (Lexapro). Examples of atypical (alternative) antidepressants include: bupropion (Wellbutrin), nefazodone (Serzone), trazodone (Desyrel), and mirtazapine (Remeron). Tricyclic antidepressants (TCAs) were most commonly prescribed before SSRIs came on the market. They include amitriptyline (Elavil), clomipramine (Anafranil), imipramine (Tofranil), and nortriptyline (Pamelor). Monoamine oxidase inhibitors (MAOIs) are older medications that typically require changes in diet. They include phenelzine (Nardil) and tranylcypromine (Parnate).

Antianxiety Medications

These medications are generally used to treat severe cases of anxiety, and include three classes of medications: benzodiazepines, antihistamines, and atypical antianxiety medications. Examples of benzodiazepines include: alprazolam (Xanax), lorazepam (Ativan), diazepam (Valium), and clonazepam (Klonopin). Because Benadryl and Vistaril may cause dependency and are considered controlled substances, they are used sparingly to treat children's anxiety except in extreme circumstances such as acute trauma.

Sleep Aids

Your child's doctor may prescribe this type of medication for a short time if your child is having trouble falling or staying asleep. Examples include: trazodone (Desyrel), zolpidem (Ambien), zaleplon (Sonata), and diphenhydramine (Benadryl).

Alert!

Though diphenhydramine, or Benadryl, is available over the counter, you should check with your child's physician before using it to make sure that it will be safe for your child. It is also very important to check your child's dosage based on age and weight.

Is Medication Safe?

When taken as prescribed by a doctor skilled in treating children and adolescents, medication can be extremely helpful in reducing or eliminating symptoms that interfere with your child's daily functioning. Unfortunately, the long-term effects of such medications on a child's development and health are little understood due to the lack of research. Be sure to ask your child's doctor about any FDA warnings associated with your child's medication, and if you research medication online, be careful to make sure your sources are valid and reputable. Often, your pharmacist can provide education and support as you investigate your child's medication.

Special Considerations with Children

Because children's brains and bodies are still developing, most practitioners use caution in prescribing psychiatric medication, especially for children under twelve. In addition, longitudinal studies on the way medication may affect children's development are only recently coming available, and are nonexistent for newer medications. Because there is an indication that antidepressant medication may increase suicidal thinking and behavior in adolescents, it is especially important to monitor your teen carefully, especially during the initiation, change, or cessation of a medication. For example, do not be fooled if your teen seems to have more energy after beginning a medication. This might actually be a risk factor for suicide if he continues to have suicidal thoughts along with increased energy.

Allergic and Toxic Reactions

Rarely, a child may have an allergic or toxic reaction to medication. This is different than a side effect and may require IMMEDIATE MEDICAL ATTENTION. Typical signs of an allergic reaction might include disorientation, extreme lethargy or agitation, bizarre physical sensations (tingling, numbness, buzzing), debilitating headache, vomiting, skin rash/mottling or hives, difficulty breathing, or trouble with coordination.

Alert!

If your child experiences any allergic reaction symptoms while on a medication, it is important to speak with your care provider without delay. If your child becomes unresponsive, unconscious, or if she can't breathe, call 911 immediately!

Off-Label Prescribing

Because the FDA has increased regulations and warnings for medications used for children, doctors may choose to override the warnings and prescribe "off-label." For example, a child younger than is approved by the FDA may use a medication, or at a different dosage. Be cautious about off-label prescribing; there is a reason the FDA has approved drugs in the manner they have. Ask your child's physician directly about any concerns you might have.

Generics

Generic brands of medication become available after the original patent for the pharmaceutical agent runs out. This allows for competition in the marketplace, which reduces the cost to the consumer as companies compete for their business. Many larger chain stores offer generic prescriptions for low cost to those who do not have insurance coverage, and some insurance companies will not pay for anything but the generic. Because some of the medications used for children with anxiety are still under patent, they are not available generically. Occasionally, a generic medication will not work as well because of small changes in the makeup of the tablet or capsule.

Monitor Responses to Medication

All of the warnings and precautions in this chapter may cause many of you to feel skittish about considering medication as a part of your child's treatment plan. For some children this is an essential component in their care, and the benefits far and away outweigh any risks. Remember that if you choose to have your child evaluated by a psychiatrist, you are not obligated to accept or fill a prescription. In some cases, a psychiatrist will determine that your child may in fact not need medication, but would be better served by another therapy.

Starting a Medication

Medication is often started at a low dose. After the body becomes reregulated with the medication, it is then increased. If your child has bothersome side effects, a dose can often be reduced until his body adjusts. Make sure to have all your questions answered, and see that your child takes his medication at about the same time every day. Be sure to ask the doctor or pharmacist about any interactions that might occur with other medications your child is taking.

 Fact

Some children may have no side effects at all, but others may be troubled either by side effects or by how a medication makes them feel. In general, antidepressants reach full effect about four to six weeks after the full dose is reached. Some patients may respond after a week or two, and for some it may take longer.

Side Effects

You and your child will no doubt be concerned with potential side effects of the medication your doctor prescribes. Depending on the individual and the medication, these side effects can be mild or more serious. You should be given clear information about what to expect, and when to be concerned enough to call the doctor. In general, the side effects of a medication should subside within several weeks of starting it, and should not outweigh the benefit of taking the medication. Because side effects vary by medication, a comprehensive list of all possible side effects is outside the scope of this book. Here is a list of the most common side effects to monitor:

- Nausea, diarrhea, or constipation
- Dizziness or headache
- Disrupted sleep, including strange or intense dreams
- Restlessness or fatigue
- Increase or decrease in appetite
- Dry mouth

Changing Medications

Cautions are in order when changing a medication, which may produce new side effects. There may be an additive effect if the new medication is to be used along with one your child is already taking. There may be effects from decreasing or discontinuing a medication, as the new one is added. Normally, your doctor will have a standard protocol for changing medications, and if your child is changing medications within the same class, side effects can be minimal or nonexistent.

Going off Medication

There has been recent press about the problems associated with discontinuing medication, particularly SSRIs. The adverse effects, though rare, are referred to as SSRI discontinuation (or) cessation syndrome. This syndrome is caused by what is referred to as the "half-life" of a medication, which refers to the extent to which it remains in the body after being discontinued. Symptoms can include dizziness, vertigo, lightheadedness, a whooshing or shocking sensation in the head, flashes of pain or discomfort, sweating, headaches, irritability, lethargy, nausea, diarrhea or vomiting, disrupted sleep, and general malaise. The best defense against these effects is to decrease a medication slowly, taking breaks until symptoms abate. Sometimes another medication is prescribed at a low dose to alleviate withdrawal symptoms, and many of the complementary and alternative therapies included in this book may be able to help. It is never advisable to stop a medication "cold turkey" unless there is a toxic or allergic reaction to it. Make sure you receive clear instructions and precautions from your doctor if your child will be stopping a medication.

Team Approach

It is true that "it takes a village to raise a child." The more resources you are able to use, the more powerful the intervention will be for your child. The sections below highlight areas you may wish to consider as your child begins taking medication for anxiety.

 *Question?*

What if you are uncomfortable with the recommendations?
If you are uncomfortable with any recommendations you receive from a care provider, discuss them first with your provider and then seek a second opinion if you feel it is warranted. Often people are concerned they will offend a doctor if they seek a second opinion; if your doctor is offended, get a different one. You do not need your doctor's ego getting in the way of your child's well-being.

Coordination of Providers

As previously mentioned, it is ideal if your child's care providers consult and coordinate with each other regarding your child's care. You will need to sign consent forms for this to occur, and you may have to advocate for coordination if your child's care providers do not normally work in this way. These days, providers can use phone, fax, e-mail, and regular mail to contact each other. In more complex cases, scheduling a team meeting involving all of the players may be essential to ensure everyone is working toward the same goal.

Combining Therapy and Medication

Combining therapy and medication has often been shown to be more effective than either therapy or medication alone. In fact, it is recommended by the AACAP and other professional organizations that if a child takes medication, she is seen by a therapist as well. For example, your child may find that medication decreases her anxiety even a little, which helps her tolerate distress as she is learning or retrieving skills. The new skills, once cemented by practice in and out of therapy, should remain once the medication is discontinued.

School

Your child should not need to take anxiety medications at school as they are administered once or twice daily and can be taken at home. However, some shorter acting medications for acute anxiety may be given at school. Your child's doctor will need to contact the school (often by fax) with the pertinent information.

 Fact

You will likely need to sign a consent form for your child to take medication at school, and may need to develop a protocol together with the doctor and school nurse for when and how a prn (as needed) medication should be taken.

Decide together with your child and care professionals how and who to inform about your child's medications. For example, some families may be comfortable informing a school nurse and social worker, but not the primary teacher.

Dealing with Friends

It is not uncommon for children who are anxious to worry about what their friends and other important people in their lives will think about their treatment. Unfortunately, there is still a great deal of stigma associated with mental health care, and even your extended family may question your choice to seek treatment for your child. You yourself may be confused about what to share about your child's troubles, and with whom. In fact, these issues are great topics for discussion in therapy, and can help your child "own" his condition and take some pride in the fact that he is taking control of his problems. The best rule of thumb is for you and your child to decide, with the help of a therapist if you wish, "the story" you'd like to present publicly. Developing a list of "pat" responses such as "I am getting help because I worry too much," or "I need to see a doctor to help my brain from working overtime" can afford you and your child some confidence in managing others' curiosity.

 Essential

At times, you may find yourself wanting to act as an advocate and educator for other parents and children with anxiety. Remember, though, that some children are more private than others, and unless you feel it is detrimental, try to respect your child's wishes regarding privacy.

All in the Family

There are many reasons and ways to involve family in your child's care, which are discussed in other chapters of this book. The focus of this section will be on how to help your family understand and support you and your child's choice to include medication in your child's care plan.

Getting Everyone on the Same Page

As previously mentioned, this issue is especially important in families with joint custody arrangements. It is equally as important in blended families, where there may be two sets of parents to consider and siblings as well. Honesty, education, and opportunities to ask questions and communicate about medications will help in your child's recovery. Make sure those closest to your child, especially if they will be caring for him, know the name, dosage, and reason for any medications your child is taking. This is especially important during any start, change, decrease, or discontinuation of medication so that others can help you watch for any signs of trouble. Do not hesitate to use resources like NIMH (*www.nimh.nih.gov*), NAMI (*www .nami.org*), or ADAA (*www.adaa.org*) to help those in your child's life to learn more about anxiety and its treatment.

Involving Siblings

Often, siblings are either a great source of comfort or a great source of distress. With regard to medication, it is probably most important for your child's siblings to be supportive of your choice, and encouraging to your child with anxiety. Remember to keep in mind the age of your child when educating her about her sibling's care, and do not let an older child be responsible for ensuring her sibling takes her medication.

When to Seek Help for Yourself

It sometimes happens that a child's diagnosis with anxiety, depression, or ADHD causes a parent to feel an eerie sense of familiarity and recognize that he may have a condition similar to that of his child, and to consider medications for himself. If this is true for you, you too can discuss this with your child's doctor, your doctor, or the therapist.

Question?

Should I tell my child's doctor about my own anxiety?
It is important to discuss your own anxiety with your child's doctor or therapist. Your child may have a sense of "not being so alone in the world" if she sees that you have struggled, too. As previously mentioned, a family history of anxiety may increase the likelihood your child could need medication. Also, there are many benefits to learning and practicing anxiety management with your child.

Working with Extended Family

Your child's grandparents, aunts and uncles, and cousins may need to be informed about your child's medications for several reasons. Letting the family at large know that your child's condition is serious enough to warrant medication will help them to understand that your child is not just "going through a phase," or "being difficult." Sharing information about your child's condition and care may also help your extended family reflect on potential problems they might have with anxiety, and this could make big changes for the better for everyone.

CHAPTER 12

Managing Managed Care Plans

Many families today have their health care costs covered by a managed care plan, also referred to as a Preferred Provider Organization (PPO) or Health Maintenance Organization (HMO). These plans have arrangements with doctors, hospitals, and other providers who have contracted to accept lower fees for their services from the insurer.

Because these systems are quite large, navigating them can be a bit of a challenge. This chapter will help you learn what to expect and how to proceed with your insurance. Those who do not have insurance coverage will find information on alternatives for covering health care costs.

Contacting Your Insurance Company

If you feel your child could benefit from therapy and/or psychiatric medication management, your first step should be to contact your insurance company to find out how to proceed. The telephone number for member services is generally found on the back of your insurance card, in member materials you received when you enrolled, or on your insurance company's Web site. If you have trouble knowing who to contact, check with your employer's Human Resources (HR) representative.

Determine Your Benefits

First, you will want to make sure you have mental health benefits, and you need to find out what the limits of coverage are. In some cases, your primary insurance company will have contracted with an agency that manages mental health benefits, so you may have to make a second call. Important questions to ask are:

- Am I restricted to a list of providers "in network," or am I free to use any provider?

  _____

- If I have out-of-network benefits, how do they work?

  _____

- Do I have a co-pay, deductible, or co-insurance cost for services?

  _____

- Is there a limit on the number of visits, and if so, what is it?

  _____

- Do I need a certification or prior authorization to proceed?

  _____

- Do you have a list of providers in my area?

  _____

Finding a Provider

As you've learned, finding a provider by word-of-mouth referral may be the best way to ensure that you will have a good therapy experience for your child. However, trusted friends or family may not have the same insurance coverage, and the provider they recommend may not be in your network. If you have a specific clinic or provider name, by all means, call your insurance company to check on coverage. The clinic or provider should be able to answer this question directly as well. If the provider does not accept insurance, she should be able to give you a receipt for services so you can submit this to your insurance company. In this case, if you have "out-of-network benefits" you should get some reimbursement. Chapters 8, 9, and 10 offer additional resources for locating providers.

What Is Mental Health Parity?

President Bill Clinton signed the Mental Health Parity Act (MHPA) into law in 1996. It is considered a landmark in health reform, and it received unprecedented bipartisan support. The MHPA eliminated a longstanding practice for insurance companies to offer lower rates of reimbursement for mental health as compared to physical health. It requires that annual or lifetime dollars spent on mental health benefits be no lower than dollar limits for medical or surgical coverage offered by group health plans. The mandate covers employers with fifty or more employees, and does not include coverage for substance abuse. It does not require your insurance provider to offer mental health benefits if they are not already part of the plan.

 Fact

The MHPA has been extended six times since its inception. In some cases, more liberal state law may "trump" the federal mandate. Check with your state insurance commissioner if you are concerned that your plan does not provide mental health parity.

What If You Don't Have Insurance?

Most providers are happy to accept clients who pay out of pocket, and some may negotiate with you for a reduced rate because your direct payment reduces their billing costs. In many areas, there are larger clinics that receive local, state, or federal funding, which allows them to offer clients a sliding fee scale based on financial need. Although federal funding and standards are limited, there are many state and some local programs regarding insurance coverage for children. Examples include tax credits for individuals and employers to cover health care, increasing the age of dependent coverage, expanded options for covering children, and premium assistance for lower-income families. For more information, ask the school social worker for information, or call your state or county human services department for guidance on this issue.

 Essential

Social Security Disability Insurance (SSDI) is federal funding that is available for people who meet the criteria to be classified as disabled. Though the benefits are generally thought of as supplementary income for adults who are unable to work, children can also receive SSDI. In most cases, to qualify for SSDI, a child's physical and/or emotional disability must be considered lifelong and will prevent future gainful employment. Some states may also have funding sources for children whose daily functioning is severely limited.

Referrals and Recommendations

In some cases, you may need a referral from your child's medical doctor in order to access mental health care. Usually, this means you will have to schedule a visit with your child's regular doctor. If your child does not have a regular physician, you can usually schedule a referral visit with a family practice doctor or a pediatrician if you prefer. This may be a good time to consider engaging a regular physician, so that your child can receive focused care and good follow-up.

Special Services

If your child will need psychological testing, alternative health care, or certain other specialty services such as music or art therapy, your insurance company may require a referral from a care provider. These may be denied, and in some cases may be appealed. Specialized services or special requests regarding the treatment plan (such as longer sessions or offsite visits) may require prior authorization, which is discussed in the following text.

EAP Programs

Many larger employers offer Employee Assistance Programs (EAP). Generally, an EAP can provide help for the employee and family members for mental health, substance abuse, and life transition issues. The services available vary by plan, and may include phone consultation, referral, and coverage for sessions with a counselor or therapist. Keep in mind that in some instances, your employer may be made aware that you have used EAP services. Unless an employee is referred to an EAP as a part of a disciplinary plan, the standard protection of confidentiality applies.

 Essential

If your child's therapist or doctor refers you for additional services, ask for a recommendation in your network. When you contact the referral, ask questions from your list and verify financial details. Otherwise, your insurance company can walk you through the process. Remember to weigh geography and expertise in following up on a referral.

Prior Authorization

In some cases, professionals caring for your child will need to contact your insurance company to request additional benefits. This usually happens when a specific number of sessions are used, or when a new or different service is being requested.

What Is a Prior Authorization?

A prior authorization (PA) is a request for services your provider submits to your insurance company. In some cases, a PA is necessary after the first two to three sessions with a provider. In other cases, your provider will submit one after a designated number of sessions have occurred so that your insurance company can review your child's care and ensure payment for appropriate service. The PA will give your insurance company information about your child's diagnosis, treatment plan, progress, and any complicating factors. You may be asked to review and sign the plan, which may also be shared with your child. A reviewer will then use the information to decide whether to authorize the requested services.

Medical Necessity

Insurance coverage for mental health is usually based on the concept of medical necessity. Medical necessity refers to the degree to which your child's symptoms impact her daily functioning and interfere with what is considered a normal quality of life. If the symptoms are severe enough, the services your child receives to reduce the symptoms are considered medically necessary. Most care providers are trained to evaluate medical necessity and to use standards of measurement such as the *DSM-IV* to document your child's symptoms and his response to treatment. The requirement of medical necessity can cause particular problems for a child's treatment. Therapy with children generally proceeds more slowly because of its more subjective nature.

 Fact

Often, even though a child's symptoms are reduced, she will need ongoing follow-up to make sure the symptoms stay at bay. In some cases, insurance plans may not cover in these situations, and you may need to be prepared to advocate for your child's continued care.

Denial and Appeal

If your insurance company deems that a PA does not meet the criteria for medical necessity, or if there is information that is missing or needs to be clarified, there is usually a standard appeal process. Sometimes a provider will be asked to send in case notes or other supporting information. Because there may be timelines associated with filing an appeal, you may need to keep in close contact with your provider and/or insurer.

Co-Pays

Many insurance plans require that you submit a co-pay to the provider. The reason a co-pay is required is to offset the amount your insurance company pays directly to the provider, which is almost always less than the fee he or she charges. There has been much debate about the intent of co-pays and deductibles, and potential negative effects on access to care, especially for low-income families. Conversely, there is a clear indication that making a financial contribution at the time of service may increase motivation and follow-through. Philosophical and ethical considerations aside, the co-pay is a fact of life in the current system.

 *Alert!*

In October of 2007, The American Academy of Child and Adolescent Psychiatry petitioned Congress to override President Bush's veto of H.R. 976, the State Children's Health Insurance Program (S-Chip) act, but the override failed. The veto is a terrible blow to the six million children who depend on S-Chip for basic health care needs.

Deductibles

A deductible is an out-of-pocket cost you must meet before your insurance company begins to pay out benefits. Amounts of deductibles vary, and you may have separate deductibles for in- and out-of-network services. Many families use flexible spending accounts or cafeteria plans to help cover them. These health coverage options are discussed below. Check your plan to see if alternative health care such as massage, chiropractic, acupuncture, or homeopathy, as well as prescription costs can be used to meet your deductible.

Co-Insurance

Co-insurance is similar to a co-pay, but it is usually based on a percentage of the fee your provider charges. Sometimes the rate is based on what is considered "usual and customary practice" in your area. In some cases, the percentage of the co-insurance varies slightly from session to session. You may be asked to pay your co-insurance after your provider has received an explanation of benefits showing the portion you owe.

When and How to Pay

After your deductible has been met, you will likely begin making co-pays or co-insurance payments. Most providers request that you make your co-pay at each session. This decreases billing and accounting costs, and ensures that you aren't left with a large balance at the end of treatment. Larger clinics may be able to set up payment plans or bill your charge account for services. They can also help you track your deductible, and make sure your insurance is billed in a timely fashion.

Physicals

The importance of getting your child a physical to rule out underlying medical issues that might cause anxiety symptoms has been highlighted throughout the book. Following are some additional tips to help you coordinate your child's medical and mental health needs with your health insurance benefits.

Clean Bill of Health

Using your insurance benefits to ensure that your child is physically healthy before you pursue mental health care can save time and expense in the long run. Many therapists and physicians request that their patients obtain a full physical to rule out any medical complications that might cause anxiety or affect recovery. The recent upsurge in theory, research, and practice in mind-body interaction points to the importance of taking a holistic approach to overall health. In addition, many insurance companies encourage mental health professionals to consult with a patient's primary care physician so that they can coordinate care.

Tests for Baseline Functions

If your child is taking certain types of medication, his physician may request baseline (initial) and follow-up testing as a part of treatment. These tests ensure that your child's physical systems are intact, and aren't being harmed by the medication. Typical tests include bloodwork (including tests of liver and kidney function, and heart monitoring [EKG]). In general, your insurance company should cover these tests when requested by the doctor, but you will still have to meet deductibles, and cover co-pay or co-insurance costs. If you are unsure if a test is covered, call the member services department for your health plan, or ask your provider or clinic to assist you.

CHAPTER 13

Alternative Therapies:
The Case for Natural Healing

Alternative opportunities for healing are actually abundant, can be very helpful, and may also be used in conjunction with traditional medicine. An added bonus for some of these therapies is that they can teach your child self-help skills that can relieve or prevent their anxiety. Knowing your child has those tools can also give you, the parent, a sense of relief and confidence that your child can move more easily through her day.

Massage

The ancient art of massage as a healing agent has come a long way. Its humble beginning of artistic hand strokes on the body to restore the soul, rejuvenate the body, and decrease stress has now become a nationally certified health care option. Traditional health care systems are recognizing the therapeutic effects of massage in the healing process. Employers, doctors, chiropractors, even hospitals recommend and offer massage for wellness as a viable and beneficial therapy.

The type of touch used on a baby or child does differ from that used on an adult. The massage will be more gentle and tender, and the length is determined by your child's age and sensitivity to stimulation. So, when choosing a massage therapist it is very important to make sure the practitioner is certified and has expertise working with children.

When using massage on a child, remember to create a quiet time free from interruptions and work in the direction of blood flow. It is also important to avoid sensitive or injured areas, stay away from massage with a child who is ill or has a fever, and avoid the stomach area for at least twenty minutes after your child eats.

Benefits

Massage has been found to decrease anxiety and slow down the heart rate. It can also increase attachment and bonding in the parent-child relationship when it is the parent who is giving the massage. Because massage can help children feel a sense of letting go, warmth, and care, your child's experience with massage may help her be more open to therapy. It may increase her ability to discuss issues related to why she feels anxious and increase the ability to trust in the helping profession. Physical advantages of massage include lowered blood pressure, slowed breathing rate, increased sense of comfort, improved circulation, and enhanced digestive functioning.

 Fact

The belief is that touch reduces anxiety because it promotes the growth of myelin. Myelin is the insulating material around nerves that makes nerve impulses travel faster, causing babies to handle themselves better, be less fussy, and feel calmer.

What the Research Shows

In separate studies at the Touch Research Institute, University of Miami School of Medicine, adolescents who received two chair massages over a month's time had decreased aggression; those with ADHD had reduced anxiety levels, improved behavior, and rated themselves as happier. Massage therapy reduced anxiety and depression in children who were diagnosed with post-traumatic stress disorder after Hurricane Andrew. Infants whose parents gave them a massage before they went to bed slept better throughout the night and fell asleep more peaceably. Because massage stimulates all of an infant's or child's body, studies show it stabilizes heart rate and respiration and increases the ability to cope with stress. Researchers also found that the level of cortisol, a stress-related hormone, decreased after a massage. Other research has shown that massage releases oxytocin in both the giver and receiver. The release of this hormone creates a "warm, fuzzy" feeling and may in part explain why bonding is strengthened during massage.

 **Alert!**

According to AskDrSears.com, a study was done with premature infants in a "grower nursery." A grower nursery is a specialized hospital setting designed to help babies gain weight. This study showed that premature babies who were massaged had 47 percent more weight gain than those who did not receive extra touch.

Chinese Pediatric Massage

This type of massage is also call Pediatric Tui Na. It is said to influence a child's energy flow, much like acupuncture. The difference is that Tui Na uses gentle massage to activate energy meridians or blockages instead of needles. Treatment can start at birth and is quick and effective until age six. After age six, regular acupuncture can be used. In most cases treatment only takes one to two sessions for symptoms to abate.

How to Find a Massage Therapist

Web sites to check out include the American Massage Therapy Association (AMTA) at *www.amtamassage.org*, or The International Association of Infant Massage (IAIM) at *www.iaim.net*, which is a nonprofit national directory of Certified Infant Massage Instructors.

They can help you find a massage therapist in your area, help you make decisions about what to look for in a massage therapist, and connect you with journals and research. A few questions IAIM suggests you ask when looking for a massage therapist are if the therapist is certified or licensed, how much training she has done with children, and what the treatment method will be.

 Fact

> The AMTA feels that at least 500 hours of training is a minimum requirement for a massage therapist. Because adult massage therapy does differ from massage for children, be sure to choose a practitioner with training specifically for working with children.

Acupuncture

This ancient system of healing was developed over 3,000 years ago in China and has, over the years, become recognized as an effective healing agent by Western health professionals. Today, acupuncture involves the use of fine needles placed in carefully chosen points, or meridians, once the practitioner has identified the disharmony within a person's body and mind. Most people associate needles with the pain of injections or having blood drawn. The needles used in acupuncture have no resemblance to that though; they are much finer, solid and not hollow, and tiny. Treatment can be one or two sessions or take a few months, depending on the target condition. As with all treatment options discussed, make sure you or your child are treated by a licensed acupuncturist (LAc).

Benefits
The Chinese believe that there is an energy flow called "Qi" (pronounced chee) running throughout the body, and that acupuncture

restores the balance of this energy flow, therefore eliminating symptoms of a disorder. With children and teenagers acupuncture seems to be helpful in reducing anxiety, attention deficit disorder, addictions such as smoking, alcohol, food, or drugs, arthritis, asthma, circulatory problems, depression, general aches and pains, menstrual problems, sciatica, and skin conditions.

How Pediatric Acupuncture Works

This form of treatment can be a safe and noninvasive option as compared to the possible side effects of medication for anxiety. Julian Scott, a pediatric acupuncturist, suggests using four to six body points for young children and a few more if the child is older. The technique should be one of gentle tapping and light stroking, which will most likely take from seconds to minutes. Because it can be so quick, many parents find that a helpful solution to a squirmy or fussy child. Usually your child can sit in your lap during treatment, which enables you to be a part of the healing process, and helps your child feel safe and supported.

 Essential

Traditional Chinese medicine includes herbs, and many acupuncturists may include herbs as a part of your child's treatment. Although the needling techniques have resulted in very few negative side effects, some herbs have been connected to more serious and frequent side effects.

Shonishin

Shonishin originated in Japan in the seventeenth century. It is literally translated as "children's acupuncture," or "acupuncture for children." It differs from standard acupuncture because the practitioner does not pierce the skin but instead uses an assortment of metal implements to gently stimulate the meridians and acupuncture points to move qi. This form of acupuncture, as with the standard kind, moves energy to unblock and to strengthen the qi where it is weak, creating balance in the child's body and a sense of calm. It is most useful for children from infancy through age five, although older children up to age twelve can benefit from this technique.

Aromatherapy

The use of essential oils and aromatic plants to affect mood or health dates back thousands of years to cultures including China, India, and Egypt and in fact receives several mentions in the Bible. Interestingly, up until the twenty-first century, thyme and rosemary were burned by many Western hospitals as a means of medically disinfecting the air and some dental offices still use essence of clove for its calming effects. The use of incense in Catholic and other religious services is also an example of aromatherapy.

 Fact

By the time Dr. Edward Bach died in 1936, using his intuition, natural gifts as a healer, and the energy in nature he had thirty-eight wildflower remedies. He created most of these remedies by testing them on himself first. What he created over seventy years ago began a system of medicine that is used for healing all over the world today.

Two men are primarily responsible for bringing flower and oil essence into the twenty-first century. French chemist Rene-Maurice Gattefosse, who coined the term "aromatherapie" in the 1920s, was convinced that oils had antiseptic properties and began working with them in his laboratory. Edward Bach, who was a medical doctor and homeopathic physician in London, left a lucrative practice and went on to develop the Bach flower remedies.

How Aromatherapy Works

Although there are very few empirical studies on aromatherapy many believe essential oils can enhance the mood, alleviate fatigue, reduce anxiety, and promote relaxation. It is believed that when inhaled, the essence works on the brain and nervous system through stimulation of the olfactory nerves. Basically, when a child breathes in an essential oil, electrochemical messages are sent to the emotion center of the brain, the limbic system. The limbic system then triggers memory and emotional responses, which send messages to the brain and body. This seems to produce a euphoric, relaxing, sedative reaction.

 Fact

Peppermint oil is useful for nausea and upset stomachs, and has been used to alleviate the effects of chemotherapy in children. To use, place two or three drops on a tissue, hankie, or natural cotton ball, or under the pillow. Avoid getting the oil on the skin.

Because children are delicate and sensitive, you must be very careful when using essential oils with them. Although some practitioners agree that essential oils are not recommended for use on children at all, some believe that children over the age of six can use a short list of oil blends that are one-third to one-half as potent as what is recommended for adults.

Lavender, chamomile, and mandarin are generally considered safe for children. Chamomile and lavender both calm anxiety. Chamomile has the added bonus of soothing digestion and is great with babies who struggle with colic. Lavender has the dual effect of not only helping alleviate anxiety; it also lifts the spirits and is great for insomnia. In addition, lavender is known to have antiseptic properties and may help with headaches.

Question?

How do you use aromatherapy with children?
You can spray or dip a cotton ball, a tissue, or use the essential oil on a pillowcase (for a really good night's sleep), and allow your child to breathe it in. A diffuser is a great way to fill the air with an aroma in your child's room. You can also massage your child with commercially prepared lotions, or use oils in her bath. Be careful to use only essential oils; synthetic blends can cause allergic reactions and are unlikely to provide the same benefits as the original source.

Cautions for Children

You should also be aware that many "carrier oils," which are what the scent is blended into, are nut-based, such as almond, macadamia, or hazelnut. So be aware that if your child has a nut allergy, these should absolutely be avoided. Many parents do not know that even baby oil contains almond. Nut-free oil alternatives include olive, sunflower, grapeseed, and avocado. It is best not to use aromatherapy on babies. Always consult with an expert, and never try to blend a potion on your own.

Biofeedback

Biofeedback evolved out of laboratory research in the 1940s to become one of the earliest known behavioral medicine treatments. The word *biofeedback* comes from *bio*, which means life, and *feedback*, which means "returning to the source." Originally considered an alternative medicine option that fuses the mind-body, thirty years later biofeedback is commonly practiced by physicians, nurses, psychologists, physical therapists, dentists, and other professionals in private and hospital settings to treat adults and children with anxiety, and to address chronic physical conditions like pain.

How Biofeedback Works

Biofeedback is a painless, noninvasive technique that monitors the body's functions such as muscle tension, blood pressure, or heart rate, and "feeds back" the information to the patient. During a biofeedback session, your child will sit in front of a computer monitor with sensors on his skin that will measure one or more of the bodily functions above. This will happen as he looks at animated games, cartoons, or stories, or listens to tones or melodies. The images and sounds on the screen change as your child learns to change his physical state and the associated feelings. As he becomes more relaxed, opening up a channel of communication between himself and his body, he is learning to regulate his anxiety and stress. The doctor or therapist will monitor the results on a separate screen, and give you and your child feedback on how he is progressing.

 Fact

Deepak Chopra, M.D., and Dean Ornish, M.D., created a software program called The Journey to Wild Divine, a biofeedback "game." Children can use this game at home to help learn about deep breathing and guided imagery in order to reduce anxiety.

Biofeedback can be an excellent self-help discipline, with each session lasting between thirty to sixty minutes.

EEG Biofeedback

EEG biofeedback, also referred to as neurobiofeedback, uses an electroencephalograph (EEG). This is a device that detects, monitors, and records the electrical activity in the brain, called brainwaves. Through the biofeedback machine, your child will learn how to increase or decrease brainwave levels. In general, the focus is on slowing brain waves to foster greater focus and calm attention. The most typical application for this technique is in treating ADHD, and it has also been found useful in treating anxiety and addiction.

What Biofeedback Can Help

Biofeedback treatments can help a variety of medical problems in children such as headaches, panic disorder, asthma, abdominal pain, sleep disorder, ADHD, stress, and addictions. As you can see, many of the conditions for which biofeedback is helpful also have anxiety as a component.

Biofeedback has two sides; it can help your child become calmer and alleviate anxiety, chronic pain, insomnia, or muscle spasms. On the other hand, it can help your child become more alert, focused, and energetic, improving attention, concentration, schoolwork, or athletic performance. Biofeedback can enhance creativity as well as mental flexibility and emotional resilience.

Alert!

Providers, even if they have advanced degrees such as M.D., Ph.D. or RN, must still get additional training to use biofeedback. Providers are not required to be licensed to administer biofeedback, although there are certification programs available. That means you will want to specifically ask about training and experience, and about whether the type of biofeedback your child is receiving will be effective.

Energy Work

Many people, when hearing the words "energy work," will immediately feel put off as if they are delving into something mystical, or on the edge of reason. What they do not realize is that they already use energy therapy every day. Think about it—your child can't sleep, so you go into her room, sit down next to her, and gently talk to her, rubbing her back—that's energy therapy. Or, your child falls off his bike and you go to him, hold him in your arms, kiss his hurt knee and hug him until the tears are gone—that's energy therapy. In each of those instances, you have passed your calm, loving energy to your child. That is also why you are the first person your child wants when he is hurt, you are the one he gives the harshest attitudes to, and you are the one he calls when he is scared. Your energy is what your children are seeking. It is unconditional, safe, and gives them comfort and strength.

History

In the early 1800s, Phineas Quimby was considered the intellectual father of New Thought. He posited a link between the body and mind's natural, internal powers and the ability to heal oneself. Since then many have used his basic tenets to form their own types of energy healing.

 Fact

Quimby's theory: "the trouble is in the mind, for the body is only the house for the mind to dwell in. . . . If your mind has been deceived by some invisible enemy into a belief, you have put it into the form of a disease, with or without your knowledge. By my theory or truth I come in contact with your enemy and restore you to health and happiness." —Page 208 of Quimby's *The Complete Writings, Volume 3*

What Is It and How Can It Help?

Energy therapy is a healing process that creates environments, philosophies, and therapies to support children who hurt inside. Much like acupuncture, it is done by correcting the imbalances in their internal energy. Most of the techniques are easy to learn and can be self-administered. Some examples of practices involving the use of energy to heal include:

- **Reiki and Johrei** are Japanese techniques for stress reduction and relaxation that many believe can promote healing. These are based on the idea that an unseen "life force energy" flows through all people and if it is low, then you are more susceptible to feeling anxious or getting sick, and if it is high, you can attain a sense of well-being.
- **Qigong** is based on the Chinese principle of "qi," energy. It is believed that different breathing patterns, when accompanied by certain motions and postures of the body, can enhance and create a sense of balance and calm, and release emotional and physical blocks.
- **Healing touch** occurs when a massage therapist identifies imbalances in your child's body and then corrects the energy. To accomplish this, the practitioner passes his hands over your child, without actually touching her.
- **Intercessory prayer** involves a person or group who intervenes through prayer on behalf of another.
- **EFT, energy field therapy, or TFT, through field therapy**, occurs when certain meridians on the body are touched to release an emotional or physical problem. EFT and TFT can be done anywhere and self-administered, are portable and efficient ways to calm the mind, and give a person a greater sense of control over anxious or distressing feelings.

Energy healing is a process that requires you to look beyond a symptom of illness, like the fact that your child is afraid to leave your side after a trauma, and instead look into your child's inner being to quiet her mind. The intent is to release the fear that created a blockage so your child can feel free again.

Question?

My child was bullied at school. We have talked to him many times since the incident. He cried, we came up with a game plan for future incidences, and he seems happy again— isn't that enough?

No, because he has not released the trauma internally. It is believed that energy blocks can remain with you for years or a lifetime if they are not treated. In this belief system your child can become susceptible to disease, emotional or mental disorders, and spiritual disconnection because he is internalizing his fear.

Blocks in energy are viewed as an attempt by the body and spirit to protect itself. Essentially, once your child stores the trauma or fear, she internalizes it, takes on the negative energy associated with it, and establishes a "new normal" so she can go on with life. Energy therapy can be used alone, or as a complement to any traditional or holistic treatment methods. Many believe it can reduce stress and anxiety, increase energy, improve physical health and wellness, and help your child feel more content.

Meditation

A reality in today's world, unfortunately, is that many children are under as much stress as adults. It used to be that if a child knew how to tie her shoelaces by first grade parents were happy, and so was the teacher. Nowadays some children take entrance exams at age five or six, read, and have to know how to write their name in script by kindergarten. Divorce is everywhere, with children living for a few days in one house and then shifting to another. Bullying, school shootings, drugs, alcohol, and sex can start as early as elementary school. Our children live in a fast-paced society full of difficult choices. Meditation is one way to help restore balance.

What Is Meditation?

Teaching your child to meditate is an opportunity to teach her how to become conscious of and present with herself. It is the ability to listen to her breathing, finding quiet time to shut out the world for a few minutes, and restore balance inside herself. It is kind of like a waking nap, or time-out. Connecting with her internal self can create a sense of deep relaxation and acceptance. Relaxation and acceptance are antithetical to anxiety, so meditation can be an essential tool when helping your child let go of anxiety.

 Fact

Children can learn to start meditating by the age of five, and sessions can take as little as two minutes. Children do not need special equipment and can meditate with others or practice alone.

Your child can meditate sitting up in a chair, lying down, or sitting cross-legged on the floor. Because your child can meditate with her eyes open, she can even meditate for a few minutes before a school exam to clear her thoughts and relax without anyone knowing she is doing it. Mindfulness meditation is simply being present here and now with the self, and often focuses on the breath. Other forms of meditation may be more focused, such as the use of guided imagery or soothing self-statements. For example, you and your child can write down positive thoughts and phrases that he can repeat to himself when meditating. Or you or your child could make a tape of the phrases that can be played back while he is meditating. Sometimes just listening to positive statements helps children connect with their hearts and calms them down.

The Benefits

There are very few studies on the benefits of meditation to date, although there is a general belief it has been helpful for children with anxiety, ADHD, and behavioral problems. The Discovery Project in England introduced meditation to their primary schools for study. The consensus by the teachers was that it did reduce the amount of anxiety, anger, and negativity in the children. Meditation seems to help children become more attentive, improve athletic skills and academic skills, and make them emotionally calmer. They learn how to think before reacting, and it seems to strengthen self-esteem. The concept of meditation has attracted prestigious attention and is still growing. Over the last decade it has gained entrance into school programs through funding by organizations such as the American Heart Association, the National Institutes of Health, and Chrysler and General Motors.

 Essential

If meditation piques your interest, check out the book *Sensational Meditation for Children*, by Sarah Wood. This friendly and comprehensive guide looks at the many advantages of children learning to meditate, and has numerous guided meditation scripts for you to use with your children.

Yoga

This is an ancient meditation practice with Eastern roots that involves quieting the mind and using various body postures to attain a greater sense of balance and control and create a sense of well-being. Yoga integrates mind and body, and is said to be helpful because it works through not only the conscious self, but the subconscious as well.

You can model good self-care and foster togetherness by doing yoga with your child or as a family activity. Basic yoga techniques are readily available at *yogasite.com*, *childrensyoga.com*, and *karmakidsyoga.com*. Many communities have yoga centers that offer classes for children and/or families. Check these sites or your local bookstore or library for children's yoga tapes, CDs, and DVDs.

CHAPTER 14

Home Is Where the Heart Is

As discussed previously, your home is the foundation of your child's physical, emotional, and spiritual well-being. The attitudes and influences you provide as parents are the basis for your child's identity, self-esteem, coping, and worldview. These influences begin in your child's early years and are combined with your child's experiences outside of your home. Together, they form the values and expectations that will guide your child throughout her life. To decrease anxiety as much as possible, the following are some suggestions that can easily be in your control.

Open Communication with Your Child

Communication is the basis of all relationships. When it becomes derailed, you can become confused, frustrated, and isolated from one another, which for a child with anxiety can spell disaster. Because of that, having clear and open communication with your child who is worried is best. It will create an island of security, possibly minimizing the internal chaos and helplessness he might feel.

Reciprocity

There are two aspects to communication: what is being said (transmission) and how it is understood (reception). If either of these dimensions is unclear, a communication breakdown will occur. Have you ever made a comment that wasn't received in the way you intended? That is an example of what can happen when your intention is misread. Speaking clearly and listening intently are the two most important aspects of communication with a child who is panicky. To enhance your skills, try some of the techniques in the following sections.

Using "I-Messages"

Although this term sounds like something from digital electronics, it is actually one of the most basic skills in communicating assertively. Therapists across the country regularly teach this technique to clients, and it is widely used in chemical health, management, and other fields.

 Fact

The goal of I-messages is to focus on what you experience, rather than laying blame on another for making you feel or act in a certain way. When you focus on your own thoughts, feelings, and behavior as you communicate a concern, the person on the receiving end may be less likely to become defensive, and may be more likely to fully hear your point.

Here is an example: Imagine that your child has asked you for the third time to stay up later because he is anxious about going to bed. Instead of saying something like "you always do this, it makes me so angry," consider the following:

- **I NOTICE THAT** . . . you seem to be having trouble going to bed tonight.
- **I FEEL** . . . frustrated.
- **I WOULD LIKE** . . . to figure out a way we can manage this better.

Although this technique feels awkward at first, with practice it becomes second nature. In some cases, you do not need to use all of the steps to make your point. What is most important is that you focus on your feelings, make a nonjudgmental statement about the other person's behavior, and clearly state your desire and/or intention. Your nonverbal messages are essential here. The most beautifully crafted I-statement will fall to waste if you deliver it with sarcasm, anger in your voice, or other negative nonverbals such as a clenched jaw or tightly crossed arms.

 *Fact*

Research and theory support the concept that there are five to seven basic human emotions: anger, sadness, happiness, fear, disgust, surprise, and shame. Shame is more complex than the other feelings, as it can contain more than one of the basic emotions. To help your child learn to communicate more effectively, it can be helpful to reference a list of "feeling words."

If you or your child with anxiety struggles with communicating effectively you might consider practicing direct communication into a recorder or video camera and then listen to and/or watch yourself to see how you are coming across. By enhancing these skills you will be less inclined to be caught up in your own emotions, and your child will be more likely to be able to problem-solve, rather than become anxious, defensive, or have a meltdown.

Reflective Listening

Reflective listening occurs when a person acts as a sort of mirror for another, reflecting back what they observe, with just a bit of interpretation. This type of listening is actually the basis of most forms of psychotherapy, and recent research indicates that it can foster the development of new brain structures that mitigate depression and anxiety. Reflective listening validates the other person's experience and communicates empathy and understanding. It also opens the door for more and deeper communication, which is especially important with a child with anxiety. Therefore, if your child says in a trembling voice, "I do not want to go to school today," you might say, "I see you are anxious about school. Is it because of your math test?"

 Fact

> When you use reflective listening, by mirroring your child's experience, you are teaching her how to stop and acknowledge her feelings. This builds identity, confidence, and self-esteem.

It's a Family Affair

Anxiety tends to cluster in families. This means your child can be affected by someone in the family who has anxiety, or your child's anxiety can have an effect on the family. Therefore, this section will highlight key elements in family involvement, which are important in your child's overall care.

Look for Patterns

As you learned in Chapters 7 and 11, it will be important for you and your spouse (or your child's other biological parent) to look into the possibility you may have traits of anxiety. There is a "trickle-down effect" with respect to mental health in parents, so it can never hurt to improve your own levels of adjustment and coping.

Share Information

If you suspect that there are family patterns that point to anxiety, gently explore them with your family members. Be aware of any chemical abuse issues in your family, as these can be a coping mechanism for anxiety and depression, and can be hereditary.

Ask for Support

You and your child may also need support from your family. In addition to encouragement and emotional support, your family may be able to help you with the nuts and bolts of your child's care plan. Maybe your child could practice sleepovers or learn to be away from the immediate family for brief periods by spending time with aunts, uncles, or cousins. Perhaps a family member can visit your child's school for lunch, or bring her a treat as a show of support. Spending special time with grandparents may be comforting for your child, and might even afford you and your spouse a night out together. Sometimes family can be helpful in taking your child to and from appointments, but be sure to check with your child's doctor or therapist to make sure that this is okay. In most cases, you will need to be present for any medical appointments your child has, to give consent for medications, tests, or any other procedures.

Alert!

Teens, especially, will need to know about possible chemical health issues in the family as they mature and make choices about alcohol or drugs. You might not want to have this conversation, but it is important. It is also a great time to set expectations and consequences regarding chemical use.

Create a Support Team

Throughout the book, you have been encouraged to form a support team to best care for your child with anxiety. The sections that follow will revisit the players, and show how they might participate in your child's plan of care.

Medical

Your child's doctor or nurse practitioner, together with her psychiatrist and/or psychiatric nurse, comprises your child's medical team. Alternative care providers like chiropractors or homeopaths can also be considered part of the medical team. Be sure to sign any releases of information so that they can communicate with one another, and to the school if necessary. It is especially important that your child's therapist and psychiatrist agree on the best plan of care, and you may have to work at this issue a bit if the providers do not practice in the same location.

Mental Health

Your child's therapist, other providers such as marital and family therapists, and specialty providers should also be on the same page regarding your child's issues. As previously mentioned, you may wish to request a brief written summary of your child's condition and care plan, which can be shared with other providers. Many providers will furnish you with "walking papers" you can share with other support persons at your discretion, but you may have to sign a release for them. Other providers may prefer to contact team members directly.

Alert!

Many children find great support in knowing that they can ask to see the social worker or nurse if they are having a particularly difficult day at school. Also, if your child is taking medication, you may want to inform the school nurse so that she can be on alert to any potential side effects or interactions.

Spiritual Resources

A place of worship may be a source of support and encouragement for both you and your child. Spiritual concerns are more common in older children, and can be especially troublesome for teens. Sometimes children are angry with God because they are suffering, or can't make sense of their experience from a spiritual perspective. If you feel your child is struggling in this area, ask him if he would like to speak with someone of your faith. Some places of worship offer counseling. Be aware that the spiritual community does not always view mental health issues in the same way that the medical system does. You may need to seek support if the two appear to be in conflict.

Community Resources and School

Community resources include community education, ECFE, after-school programs, park and recreation programs, libraries, and even local businesses. For example, if your child is anxious about leaving home, but old enough to do so safely, you might consider working with a local shop owner to assist your child in expanding her range. Perhaps your child could call you from the store or restaurant, or you could prepay for a treat she can collect when she arrives. Dance, music, theater, gymnastics, and martial arts can also provide great opportunities to practice social skills, build mastery, and learn self-reliance.

Tell the Truth

Your ability to be clear and honest about what you and your child are experiencing can go a long way in combating anxiety. Knowledge is power, and honesty about what you and your child observe, think, and feel will give both of you a sense of solidity as you move through the troubled waters of anxiety. Remember, though, to keep the focus on your child and avoid at all costs making him feel responsible for your reactions to the situation.

Tread Carefully

Being truthful may require tact and some self-restraint. Children with anxiety can demand excessive time and attention, causing frustration and resentment to parents. Though you may need to express your feelings in order to set limits and help your child change her behavior, it is important to avoid shame or blame, because this will only magnify your child's worry and anxiety. Expressing the attitude that "we are all in this together" can help minimize the possibility that your child will internalize blame for her condition or for your frustration.

 Fact

The classic work on assertiveness, called *Stand Up, Speak Out, Talk Back*, by Alberti and Emmons is an easy-to-read primer on being assertive. There are many other resources available, including books, Internet resources, classes, and groups, which focus on assertiveness.

Age Appropriateness

When you face the need to share information, such as explaining anxiety or prepping your child for a visit to a doctor or therapist, keep your child's age in mind. Younger children need clear, concrete descriptions, and may respond to a "story" about another child with similar experiences. Older children do well if they are able to ask you questions based on their fears or worries about what is happening to them. You may wish to check a local bookstore for resources specifically geared toward your child's age level. Your doctor or therapist should also be able to help you make sure that your child has the facts he needs, at a level he understands, to combat his anxiety.

Effects on Siblings

Siblings of children with anxiety may have a wide range of emotional and behavioral reactions, and may not always be able to express resentment or disappointment directly. It is important to be honest, observant, reflective, and supportive. At times, it may be helpful to give a disenfranchised sibling a direct role in your child's care, such as a daily in-school check-in, homework helper, or companion on outings. Make sure, though, that you have a willing participant so you are helping siblings to feel involved, but not responsible for your child's care. The goal here is to provide an opportunity for a sibling to feel like a valued participant, rather than an outsider in the recovery of the child with anxiety.

Jealousy

It is actually quite common for siblings of children receiving care for anxiety or other conditions to feel jealous of the amount of time and care spent by parents on their sibling. They may feel their sibling is favored and receiving special treatment they are not entitled to. Sometimes involving a sibling in therapy sessions can help create a sense of inclusion and teamwork. It may help to remind your child of times you went the extra mile for him, and to reassure him how loved and appreciated he is. It is also helpful to tell your child that the love you feel for him is just as much as for his sibling with anxiety.

 Essential

Siblings may need reassurance that they will not necessarily face the same issues with being anxious, but that if they do, you will be there to care for them as well. It is also important to let siblings know that, in time, the child with anxiety will be better and things will get back to normal.

Frustration

Siblings of a child with anxiety can become frustrated for a number of reasons. For example, if one child has trouble attending school, her sibling might resent that you are more lenient with her about staying home from school, even if there is a clear plan established to return to regular attendance. Your child's siblings might be frustrated if it is difficult for her to attend family gatherings or go on family vacations because of her anxiety. Clear, honest communication can go a long way to decrease frustration. A good sympathetic ear, without defensive responses, is necessary when supporting a frustrated sibling. Be honest, and try to emphasize the hope and expectation that your family can help the child with anxiety and the whole family to be even better than before.

Isolation

Sometimes siblings will withdraw in response to their feeling that all of the attention in the family goes to the child with anxiety. This may be especially apparent with teens or with children who are quieter and more introverted to begin with. Watch out for long periods spent alone or for changes in the amount of time a sibling spends with his friends or activities. Because a sustained decreased interest in what used to be pleasurable for a child may indicate depression, you may want to watch out for the possibility that siblings of a child with anxiety may be having adjustment issues that need attention. If your compassionate attempts to communicate clearly and reach out to your child do not seem to be helping, you may wish to consider family therapy, or ask your care provider how siblings might be included in the treatment plan.

You Are Special, Too!

As you can see, having a child with anxiety can be difficult on her siblings as well. It is extremely important to support other children at the same time you are focusing your attention on your child with anxiety. This may seem overwhelming at times, but there are often relatively simple options. For example, consider taking a sibling out for a soda or ice cream after practice or game, or "just because." You can schedule one-to-one time with each of your children, even if it is a few minutes homework support, a ride-along to the grocery store, an extra bedtime story, or a quick game of cards. Take care to let all of your children know that they are special and loved, even if their anxious sibling needs extra time and attention at the current time.

Effects on Your Marriage

Research shows an increased percentage of marital dissatisfaction in families with children who experience emotional disturbances. Because parents have varying levels of distress tolerance and coping, individual differences can be magnified when a couple is under stress. For example, an introverted spouse may become even more withdrawn when under stress, leading the other parent to feel unsupported or neglected. As you read the sections below, you may wish to identify talking points to share with your spouse.

Alert!

Increasing your ability to see eye-to-eye and stand shoulder-to-shoulder with your partner, spouse, or co-parent will strengthen your marriage and family, and optimize your child's recovery.

Receiving the Diagnosis

Any time a family member receives a mental health diagnosis there is a natural sense of grief and loss that occurs. Some parents may experience a sort of "kicked in the gut" feeling, others may be sad and withdrawn, and still others, angry with themselves, the child, the situation, or God. In fact, theory and research on the grieving process indicate that parents may have any or all of these reactions, and may alternate between emotional states. Regarding your marriage, the most important factor is that you are able to communicate with each other about what you are experiencing individually and as a couple, and that you allow each other the space and time to process whatever feelings you experience in response to your child's condition.

Fact

Elisabeth Kübler-Ross identified five stages of grief: shock, denial, anger, bargaining, and acceptance. Developmental psychologists have learned that not everyone experiences all of the stages in response to loss, and that they can alternate, and even overlap. Overall, the goal is to accept and move through the changeable process, not to "finish grieving."

Parenting Style

Because a large part of your child's recovery will involve reassurance that his world is safe and manageable, it will be important for you and your spouse to assess your parenting styles. Diana Baumrind, in her classic work, identifies three different parenting styles: Authoritarian, Permissive, and Authoritative. Authoritarian parents take the reins of control fully, and adhere to strict rules and expectations for their children. This style can create submissiveness or resentment, and is reflective of attitudes in the 1940s and 1950s. By contrast, Permissive parents exert little control, generally allow children to do as they wish, and give lots of room for children to explore and learn from their own mistakes. If extreme, this style can create confusion, and possibly even a feeling of neglect. It mirrors the focus on self-expression and self-esteem prevalent in the 60s and 70s. Authoritative parents are able to strike a balance between these two extremes and share control and decision-making with their children. Because the child is given some power to make decisions, but has consistent parental input, this style tends to foster self-reliance and self-control. Other family patterns that influence parenting styles include the degree of emotional closeness versus distance, flexibility versus rigidity regarding rules and expectations, and variations in the amount of supervision and advice parents provide to their children.

Standing Together

Because children with anxiety often experience an inner sense that things are out of control, it is especially important that parents be on the same page whether or not they live under the same roof. Although it is typical for parents to differ in their approaches to childrearing, you can create a unified front by ensuring consistency in the following elements of family life:

- Establish clear rules about activities and curfew
- Be clear about bottom-line expectations for behavior
- Agree to consequences for breaking the rules
- Determine how you will positively reinforce progress
- Brainstorm and arrange fun outings as a team

Streamlining your parenting styles can go a long way to creating a sense of cohesion in your marriage, and in the family as a whole. You may wish to attend a parenting group or class to learn a new approach together to enhance your child's recovery.

CHAPTER 15

Parenting Pointers

Being the caregiver of an anxious child can be at times frustrating, demanding, and stressful. That is not necessarily your child's intent, but when children are acting out of fear the mere irrationality of their symptoms can feel overwhelming for those around them. You know the saying "Misery loves miserable company"? Well, when you have a child with an anxiety disorder the saying could instead be, "Anxiety creates anxious company." This chapter, as well as Chapters 16 and 19, are all about pointers, strategies, and tools to help you and your child.

Consistency and Follow-Through

To a child with anxiety, missing the ball at a soccer game or having a homework assignment due at school can be opportunities for disaster; the final proving ground for how ineffective she feels in her life. Providing stability, security, and consistency can increase your child's sense of self worth and calm negative thoughts. When life feels tenuous and out of control, having clear rules, consequences, and order are best.

Consistency

Being reliable and predictable is crucial to effective parenting with an anxious child. Children need to know what and whom they can count on—and that needs to be you. They do not do well with a spontaneous, disorganized lifestyle. Creating a routine so your child knows what to expect is a good way to minimize worry. This can easily be done by placing a calendar on your refrigerator or in an area that your child goes to every day, with everyone's schedule spelled out.

Alert!

If the day includes a new activity, or a change in time for pick up or drop off, explain beforehand why the pattern is different. If your child is too young to read, use pictures on the calendar so he can see where he is going or what he is doing that day.

To foster consistency the rules you make for the household need to remain constant until you have a family meeting, or an opportunity to sit down with your child and identify the new expectation and related consequence. Because children with anxiety can become overwhelmed easily, anticipating and averting unnecessary triggers is helpful. With that in mind, it might be important to set a specific time to do homework, have a set time for meals, plan and organize projects for school with a timeline, and consistently reward your child if he sets a goal and accomplishes it. For children with anxiety, consistency can equal stability. Therefore, when you think about how to bring consistency into your family, you can also ask, "What can we implement to make life feel more stable?"

It is best to have clear rules early on, with you, the parent, making the decision about what is best, while honoring your child's desires and changing abilities. As children grow older you can offer small choices and see how they do with them, limiting their choices to two specific options at first. If they struggle too much, you know you took this step too early. That's fine. Stop for now and try again in six months.

Follow-Through

Like consistency, follow-through for children can translate to security and trust. So, creating an environment at home that optimizes your child's ability to count on you doing what you told them you would do, even if it means a consequence for their behavior, is important for anxiety reduction. The foundation parents instill with follow-through in the home can increase a child's ability to have trust, and decrease worry in relationships outside the home.

 **Question?**

I thought the right way to parent was to give my child options, letting her have more control in her life, yet she seems more anxious and irritable now. Why?
When parents give choices, the child then has to make a decision. That is a big task for kids with anxiety who do not trust themselves. They end up agitated out of fear, seem to be procrastinating and actually are unable to make a choice, and they then feel worse about themselves.

The same holds for building an environment where children feel they can work through a hurtful communication with a parent or sibling, and in creating a home where they feel accepted exactly as they are. Telling your child you care that he is struggling with anxiety is one thing, showing him by helping him succeed is how he will know you care. Follow-through also means keeping your commitments. A child with anxiety already has enough questions about life and people, and when parents or caregivers do not keep their word, or use threats to manage situations, the world is reflected as unstable, and the parent loses credibility in a child's eyes.

Changing your mind, breaking a promise, or being arbitrary with siblings and rules gives a child mixed messages. Besides undermining trust and security, these events might create anger and resentments. Not just with you and your child, but between the anxious child and his siblings as well.

Being Active and Proactive

Most children, especially when young, usually do not plan ahead for a situation that creates anxiety. That means your child will likely approach an issue in the same ineffective way time after time. Understandably, this can perpetuate a sense of failure and an inability to trust herself. If you know from experience that allowing your child to be in charge of herself in the morning creates havoc and anxiety—step in and change it. Do not hope she will figure it out.

Better yet, if you know that time and organizational skills have been problem spots, be proactive. Identify a potential issue and set up a plan to create success without everyone having to go through the stress of failure first. For example, say your son is invited to a birthday sleepover party. He is especially excited because it means some of the boys at school like him enough to want him there. However, when you get there he freezes at the door, grabs your leg, and refuses to go inside. At first you gently encourage and coax. When that does not work, you plead. Finally, you scold him and shake him off of you with embarrassment and irritation as the other boys and moms watch. Walking away, you are frustrated and perplexed that an exciting, fun event turned into a disaster and feel terrible for how you left him. This situation gives you and your son an opportunity to develop a plan, proactively, for the future. Next time a new situation comes up you two can sit down the day before to discuss it. You can talk about how he feels about being invited, what the most fun parts of the party might be, what he thinks they might all do, what he might be nervous about, and what his greatest fears might be. You also might suggest that you do not mind staying for a few extra minutes until he is settled in with his friends, or picking him up early if the sleeping over part feels the most scary. Most kids will agree to go to a party if they know they have a way out of what they fear most, and when the scary part comes they often are having so much fun they do not want to leave after all.

Build a Plan

Part of being active and proactive is knowing how to build a plan. In the book *Worried No More* by Aureen Pinto Wagner, Ph.D., the author has created a clear, solution-focused, and parent-friendly treatment plan to put you and your child on the positive side of handling anxious behavior. The book is an excellent resource, chock-full of easy-to-read and -follow suggestions.

Breaking her plan down, this is what is most important for you to know:

- First define the problem or behaviors you believe need to change.
- Prioritize your list.
- Make one goal for each issue on the list.
- Brainstorm possible interventions and write down any possibility you can think of that might help.
- Cultivate readiness by asking your child her thoughts about what she feels might work best for her.

After you have taken the steps above, apply the interventions, and then evaluate how effective they were. This process can be done at home or in the school setting, putting you and your child on the road to recovery. It is okay to be creative—this is your child, your family, your life. When you are brainstorming, it is helpful to think about the intervention in three parts: the thinking side, the active side, and the physiological side.

Here is an example of addressing the cognitive, behavioral, and physiological features of anxiety:

Let's return to the example of the little boy who was invited to the sleepover birthday party. Once home you will sit down with him and first discuss the fearful thoughts that went through his head. If he can't remember, that is okay. Instead, ask, "What do you *think* you were afraid of?" Then help him see the realistic side of his fears. In other words, remind him he was invited because they wanted him to come, that he plays with them after school and has a great time, and so on. You also want to create positive thoughts about what he can do if he becomes scared, like talk to his friend's parents or bring his favorite stuffed animal or blanket. That's the cognitive piece. Next, you want to set up exposure to the same event again so he can confront his fears. Call and make a sleepover first at your house and if that goes well, then at a friend's. It is crucial the first exposure to another sleepover is at your house, his home turf where he feels safe. Talk to your child about what went well at home to encourage him to do it at the friend's house too. That is the behavioral part of the intervention. And lastly, address the physiological—teach your child how to use relaxation and deep breathing skills to reduce what he is feeling inside of his body so he can calm himself down and be more successful next time.

 Fact

By proactively cultivating readiness in your child, you gain active participation, hopefully motivation, and your child can also see how committed you are to help. This allows her to feel a sense of control with support and safety.

Patience Really Is a Virtue

Although a few treatments can be quick like the medication Xanax or hypnosis, often there is not a quick fix for anxiety sufferers and treatment could be a slow process. A large component of anxiety is fear based and personal, so there is no one right answer that works with every child. As a caregiver to a child with anxiety it will not be uncommon to have some very intense feelings yourself. Remember though, reacting in an angry, impulsive, frustrated, or coercive way to a child who is hesitant and fearful is unlikely to have a positive outcome. Usually it causes the child to retreat further into their hopelessness about how it feels to be who they are. A thoughtful approach with a plan may take longer to set in place and execute, but will probably be a lot more effective and helpful than any "quick fix." This means you will need patience.

Don't Overfunction

It is important to be patient, even if it means a job will not be done timely or completely, and allow your child to have the experience of doing it for himself. Some children need to feel the reality of their anxiety, without parental intervention. This can help your child see that he, too, needs and wants to manage it better. This creates the internal motivation discussed previously. For example, say your daughter tells you she has a project due at school in three days. You have already helped a number of times with setting up a plan, establishing a timeline, and seeing her accomplish the project. Out of your own fear because of how projects have gone in the past, and the irritability it caused for both of you, you might want to jump right in and say, "Okay, let's get started; first, why don't you . . . . " Try instead, "I trust you have all the tools needed to do a great job with that. You did such a terrific job on the last one. Why don't you get started and I'll be by after the dishes to check it out." When you go to see how far she has gotten, be patient with whatever situation you walk into. Encourage, but do not take over, even if it took her an hour to get her materials together. Ask what she has decided her next step should be and gently guide her if she is off track. It can be a slow process, but necessary if you ever want her to be able to have a healthy sense of self-confidence and to work on her own. Your being anxious about how long she is taking or the well-intentioned rescue just sets you up to have to rescue her again next time. Your job as a parent is to help your child learn how to help herself.

It's Not about You

It helps to realize that most children with anxiety do procrastinate, can have a hard time thinking things through, and that if they are stuck in a ritual, they will not get very far with whatever their task was. Personalizing your child's inability to get on top of her anxiety will not be helpful. It is not a reflection of you. It is about her anxiety.

 Essential

If you get discouraged or upset with your child, remember the saying "What do you get when you put two fires together? A larger fire." Your job as a parent is to encourage and support, not to become part of the problem.

It is common to have strong feelings when your children are having difficulty, or are not what you envisioned, so talk with a friend, your spouse, or a therapist instead of directing frustration at your child.

Calm in Calamity

Much like patience, handling yourself in a steady, composed way is what will be most helpful to your child with anxiety. Even if you get stressed or feel overwhelmed, modeling how to collect yourself and work through a tough spot shows your child that she can learn to do the same thing.

Be a Model

This is what modeling looks like. First learn the breathing techniques in Chapter 16. Then when your child is flustered and starting to have a meltdown, whether you are as upset, or not, look directly into her eyes and start counting, out loud, and do some deep breathing.

Just keep doing it, with an encouraging smile, and after a minute say, "Hey, that felt good, let's try it together." Take your child gently by the hand and find a place to sit. Look into each other's eyes and breathe together. If she refuses because she is too far into the meltdown, you do it anyway. As hard as it might feel, pay no attention to her protests, and close your eyes if you need to. When you feel calmer, or after a few minutes have passed, just walk away and say, "When you are ready, come find me." This is no different from when your child has a temper tantrum; you do not want to become part of the problem. In this case, you are modeling a solution. Realizing that sometimes your child's meltdown will occur at inopportune times, you need to keep the end result in mind as you breathe your way through not reacting with anger.

 *Question?*

How can I take the time to do the breathing thing, I will be late for work!
Yes, it is true this will take a few minutes, but a meltdown is going to take the same amount of time anyway, so what do you have to lose? Your best bet is to stay calm, matter-of-fact, and sympathetic: "I know you are struggling because you do not want to get ready to go, but I need to go to work and you need to go to daycare. Let's try some of the breathing we practiced earlier."

With a teen, gently remind him about the breathing techniques learned, and start doing it yourself as you look directly at him, coaxing him with your eyes. You can also ask him if he needs to have a minute to himself or go into his room and scream into a pillow to get his frustration out. Again, do not join into the craziness by yelling back or telling him "This is ridiculous, all I asked was that you get your gym bag ready, and you are screaming at me." Teens may sometimes admit they don't know why they are yelling or crying. Many times they may just want to say "okay mom," but they yell instead because they feel so out of control. Remember when parents yell back, they are not helping. Whichever tools you remind your child about, give him a chance to implement them. Use positive statements to help, like "I see how frustrating being rushed is for you, but I know you want to go and will calm yourself down to make that happen."

Confidence

Part of being calm is to exude an air of knowing, or confidence. Verbalizing statements like "I know you are upset, I trust you can do this," or "I know this feels hard for you, you are strong though, I've seen it," can be very calming and helpful. Your children need to feel your confidence in them. They count on you when their emotions are too big and logic is lost to them. If your child is misbehaving, it is best not to argue or debate with her. Quietly remind her of the rules and consequences of acting out behavior and ask if she would like to do some calming behaviors, or take the consequence. If your child chooses to use tools to de-escalate, praise her with confidence: "I knew you could do this, I am so proud of you," or, "Wow, look at you, I love your strength."

 Essential

If your child has a meltdown instead, do not assume falling apart was her choice, because sometimes, just as with a tantrum, the anxiety is so big your child cannot figure out how to get on top of it anymore.

Express your confidence by practicing the rule of "No shame, no blame." Instead, after a struggle or meltdown, ask your child to think about why it went too far and use the plan outlined previously to be proactive about eliminating that particular stressor, if possible, in the future.

Routine Is King

Regular patterns and routines tend to reduce anxiety in much the same way as consistency and follow-through. Children or adults with anxiety feel calmer in daily life when it is predictable, they know what is expected of them, and they are on a schedule. As you've seen, it is best to set specific times for meals, playtime, homework, quiet time, and bedtime, but you will want to avoid rigidity so that your child can practice flexibility from time to time.

Bedtime Routine

Help your child establish a bedtime routine. This means you do the same things, in the same order, and at the same time every night. For example, at 7:30 P.M. your child takes a warm bath, then brushes his teeth and combs his hair. By 8:00 P.M., he is in his bed and it is story time until 8:15 P.M. He then gets to choose to read for an additional fifteen minutes by himself, or chat with you about his day. Lights are out at 8:30 P.M. If you have a child who finds it difficult to fall asleep, quiet music or a story or relaxation tape works great. It is important to keep in mind that new routines can take several weeks to establish, so hang in there. More information about sleep routines and rituals are available in Chapter 18.

Co-Parenting

It is especially important, no matter if you are living together, blended, separated, or divorced from your child's other parent that you engage in healthy conversations about parenting and managing your child's anxiety. Agreement can give your child one less thing to be anxious about and the consistency of your approach gives your child the structure he needs. For example, bedtime schedules and routine need to be the same even if one parent is not at home for the evening. If you live separately and choose different routines, that is okay, but you still need consistency. Each house has a particular routine your child can count on when she is at that house.

Question?

Am I a bad parent if I just want a break?
Absolutely not. An overnight retreat is an excellent way to replenish the relationship with your partner and get a new perspective on an old issue. Every now and then you need some distance to see possibilities, and the space to discuss them. Besides, a night away can also give you an opportunity to miss the kids.

If you find that your partner is not following through on an agreement, it is best to let the other know without doing it in front of the children. Maybe a tap on the shoulder as you walk by, or a squeeze of the hand could be just the reminder your partner needs. It is best not to discuss frustrations or react angrily in front of a child with anxiety. The guilt and esteem issues they have already will only be complicated if they believe you are upset with each other because of them. You can be honest with your children and let them know that it is okay to disagree; how you resolve the issue is what is most important.

What Affects You

Be as honest as you can with yourself and your partner or co-parent about your own childhood and how it might be influencing you now as a parent. Rather than judge or criticize yourself or feel guilt because you are struggling, be open about your issues so you can get support. For example, if you were taught that "good" children were seen and not heard and now you have a child who breaks down emotionally, you might react negatively, or even overreact to your child. If the co-parent knows this and your child starts to act up, he can take over and give support to both of you. It does not mean you are entitled not to grow in that area; it does mean, though, that your child's emotional health is important and you both recognize you still have work to do in that area. That is what collaborating is about.

Parenting Tips

Good tips to follow are to create one voice when parenting and to openly listen to your co-parent. Listening does not mean you agree, it just means you respect that the other parent has a thought or opinion they want to share. In addition, watch what you say, talk over disagreements in private, and make your home a safe haven.

 Essential

Most divorced couples find that the issues they had while married follow them into the divorce. Therefore, if you had communication issues, you likely will still have these. Divorce does not change the problems you experienced in the relationship, so you will have to work on communication if you want your kids to flourish.

Educate Yourself

Creating a resource of information about anxiety and the professionals in the community who specialize in this field is a great first defense to a complex issue. Not only can it supply you with tips, tools, advocacy, support, and validation, it also creates a feeling of empowerment and control.

Be in the Driver's Seat

The more you understand, the less fear you have; knowledge then equals power and movement. Also keep in mind that learning a new tool, like how to breathe when anxiety begins, might be just what your child needs to help him get on top of his anxiety without having to see a doctor or take medication. The worst feeling in the world is not to know what to do, or how to help your own child. Packing your toolbox with skills and knowledge when dealing with a child with anxiety is half the journey.

Helping Yourself

You can find information on the Web, at bookstores, the library, at your child's school, doctor, and through friends and family. Although there are hundreds of Web sites about anxiety, some are better and more complete than others are. There is a list of recommended resources for you in Appendix B. If you go to a bookstore, look in the self-help section and the children's section for books on anxiety and mental health. When visiting your local library you can talk with a librarian or use the computerized card catalog to find books, journals, tapes, and magazine articles. Finding a support group online or in your community is also a great asset. You need to know that you are normal, even when you are upset with your child with anxiety, and that will happen when you find others with similar issues and struggles.

CHAPTER 16

Sanity Strategies for Parent and Child

Finding ways to balance your child's anxiety with your own and their overall emotional well-being can be a challenge. The mere fact that anxiety can manifest in so many different ways and has a multitude of possible symptoms, from obvious to obscure, means you will need a variety of strategies to draw on. This chapter is addressed to parents and children to help you both with the balancing act.

The Relaxation Response

This technique, developed by Dr. Herbert Benson in the 1970s has been extensively studied and tested for managing stress. He also wrote a book with the same name, *The Relaxation Response.* He studied transcendental meditation and decided relaxation was a physical state of deep rest that changes how the body responds when stressed, and when practiced, allows people to have control over the fight-or-flight response. You or your child will get the most from this simple technique when you do it in a quiet space, free from distractions. The basic technique involves silently repeating a word, phrase, or sound for ten to twenty minutes. Typical words or sounds used are "om" (I Am), "one," or "peace." You can substitute other words or short phrases, as long as they are positive and have personal meaning. Do this exercise sitting, rather than lying down, so you do not fall asleep.

Using the Method

The best part about this technique is its simplicity, which means even young children can use this strategy.

1. Sit comfortably and close your eyes.
2. Allow yourself to pay attention to your breathing and repeat a word or phrase silently to yourself, as you release your breath.
3. Your mind might wander; just notice it and refocus on your breathing.
4. Practice for ten to twenty minutes each day if possible, or better yet, twice a day.

Benefits

This technique will decrease stress, pulse rate, blood pressure, metabolism, and muscle tension while enhancing mood and helping you feel more peaceful. You will become more in touch with your body so you can be more in control of how anxious and stressed you become. Because you and your child might need to repeatedly bring yourself back to the meditation, your concentration may also improve. Finally, the relaxation response has the added benefit of showing you how to overcome what you think about because you will continually have to quiet your mind to practice this technique.

Breathing Calms the Mind

Breath work is an excellent and effective technique that you can practice anywhere and at any time. These exercises are wonderful for children of all ages once they are able to follow along, because they can be learned in a matter of a few minutes and create immediate benefits. There is also an interesting dual nature to breath work: on the one hand breathing is automatic, and on the other hand, you can control it. For people who have anxiety this is important because their anxiety creates a tendency to freeze, or hold one's breath, increasing the feeling that things are out of control. This easy technique is a great tool and breathing quickly becomes a way to self-manage and control outcomes.

Breathing Basics

Studies show a very effective way to calm oneself is to prolong your out-breath in a slow, controlled manner. So, when practicing the exercises that follow, keep that in mind. Here is an example of breath work. It can be done for two to ten minutes.

- Sit cross-legged with your back straight. If you are on the floor, or outside, you might want to sit on a pillow for comfort. If you and your child would rather sit on a chair, it is best to keep your feet on the floor in front of you.
- Allow your hands to rest comfortably on your lap and let your thumb touch your middle fingertip.
- Close your eyes if you would like, or focus on one point.
- Begin to breathe easily and evenly, in and out, prolonging the out-breath.
- Silently count each breath in as one count, and each breath out as one count, until twenty counts, or another even number. For example: Count 1—breathe in; count 2—breathe out; count 3—breathe in; count 4—breathe out.
- To finish the meditation, take a deep breath in, and release. Stand up and stretch.

Counted or Rhythmic Breathing

Rhythmic breathing can increase oxygen supply and help the body feel as if it has re-established its own natural rhythm again. It is timed to the rhythm of your heartbeat. This can be a very short meditation to help in those stressful moments so you or your child can feel relaxed and calm again in short order. Here is how to do it:

- Sit comfortably and put the second, third, and fourth fingers of your right hand on your left wrist to find your pulse.

- Feel the pulse beat and when you and your child feel like you can connect your breath with the beat, start counting 1-2-3-4.
- Continue mentally counting 1-2-3-4, 1-2-3-4 until you fall into a rhythm and can follow it without holding your pulse.
- Then you can put your hands on your knees and continue.

You can also do this exercise without counting the pulse. Just a few moments of even breathing can give your child or you a chance to relax and get back in control of the situation again. This technique is great for your child especially before a test, trying out for a sports team, or when standing up in front of the class. It's also great for both of you when you are starting to feel anxiety. Taking a minute to concentrate on breathing evenly can stop those racing thoughts of "I can't take this one more minute." This short time-out is an easy way to calm both your body and mind. It interrupts negative thoughts long enough for you to choose different thoughts, giving you control in a moment's notice.

 Fact

Besides keeping you alive, breathing is restorative for the body. It can calm your nerves, slow your heart rate, and help your body clear toxins, release fear and tension, and, some believe, alleviate symptoms of illness.

The benefits of breathing fully and deeply in daily life are essential. The only caution is the possibility of hyperventilation. If, when you are breathing, you or your child feel lightheaded from taking in air, just stop for a minute, breathe regularly, and then continue.

Progressive Muscle Relaxation

This widely used technique has been around since the 1930s. Progressive muscle relaxation, or PMR, is a two-step process of deliberately applying tension to certain muscle groups, contracting them, and then releasing the muscle and noticing it relax. The object of this technique is to help you and your child quickly learn to recognize what a tensed muscle and a completely relaxed muscle feel like. Then you both will be able to have more control over the first signs of tension that often accompany anxiety, and control it through noticing and releasing your muscles. Combining deep breathing with PMR achieves even better results.

How to Perform PMR

It is best to practice PMR in a quiet, comfortable place, wearing loose-fitting clothes and removing your shoes. You can lie down, but as is common with these types of exercises, it increases the chance that you or your child may fall asleep. Therefore, unless that is the goal, it may be better to sit in a comfortable chair. This is the process:

1. Starting with your toes, tighten the muscles in your toes and hold for a count of five. Then let go, and notice and enjoy the release of tension for a count of thirty.
2. Then, tighten the muscles in your feet and hold for a count of five. Again, relax through the release for a count of thirty.
3. Continue by moving slowly up through your body; contracting and releasing each leg, your abdomen, back, neck, face, and eyes.
4. With each body part, breathe through the muscle work deeply and slowly.

After you have finished with your entire body, relax with your eyes closed for a few seconds, then get up slowly and stretch.

Be Creative with Children

There are many fun ways to present breathing techniques to children. A simple way is to get a bottle of bubbles from a toy store or have your child pretend to blow bubbles. The breathing required is the same as for the calm breathing technique, but you can have fun trying to see who can blow the biggest bubble. This takes long, slow, steady breath, which increases relaxation. You can then tell her anytime she feels anxious she can say to herself, "I do not need to worry, I can do bubble blowing and make it go away!" Alternatively, for progressive muscle relaxation, you might suggest your child pretend she has a half of an orange or lemon in her hand. Ask her to squeeze it as hard as she can to get all the juice out. Tell her to feel how tight her hand and arm feels as she squeezes. Now ask her to pretend to drop the lemon and notice how her muscles feel when they are relaxed. Then do the process with her again. Tell her to take the other half of the orange in the other hand and squeeze, this time squeezing harder than she did the first time. Then ask her to drop the imaginary fruit and notice how her hand feels over a few seconds' time. Help her notice how much better her hand and arm feel when she lets go.

 **Question?**

My daughter is five and gets very anxious before she goes to sleep. What can I do?
Lori Lite wrote a wonderful book called *A Boy and a Bear: The Children's Relaxation Book* for just that type of issue. Reading before bedtime is very calming to begin with, and your daughter can learn and practice the diaphragmatic/belly breathing discussed in the book. Surprisingly, the boy in the story teaches the bear how to calm down. This twist helps your child to internalize mastery and empowerment.

Imagery as a Tool

Using visual imagery can feel like a journey toward a place of peace and calm that you cannot get to in your everyday life. When it is in the dead of winter or you are overwhelmed with work and home, how many times have you fantasized in your head that you were on a vacation? Or, how many times has your child imagined he finally grew that head taller that he always wanted, or got an "A" on an upcoming test? The use of imagery in anxiety reduction is an opportunity for you and your child to use your imagination to capture a time or experience that is, or would feel, calming.

 Fact

According to Guided Imagery, Inc., research has concluded that stimulating the brain through imagery may directly affect both the endocrine and nervous systems. They feel this can lead to changes in how the immune system functions, can decrease pain, and reduce anxiety by 65 percent.

How Imagery Works

This technique is based on the same concepts discussed previously; that your mind and body are connected, and if you use all your senses, your body can respond as if what you imagine is real. The more deeply you fantasize about the imagined place, the more relaxing the experience can be. Here's an example of how imagery works: Imagine you are holding an orange. Visualize the brightness of the color; feel the texture of the peel against your fingers, and now imagine you are pulling the peel away from the fruit. It is squirting you, and stings an open cut you have on your hand. Wow, that really burns. Now, bring it up to your mouth and take a bite. You can feel the juices squirting into your mouth and dripping down the corner of your lips. Many people salivate when they do this, or lick their lips. This demonstrates how your body can respond to your imagination.

What Is Guided Imagery?

Guided imagery uses a more formal method to direct your thoughts and get suggestions that guide your imagination toward relaxation. Tapes, CDs, a script, or an instructor can help you with this process. Imagery works well for children because they do not have to think, they can just sit back, close their eyes, and let a soothing voice take them to a calm, relaxing place, through a gentle story. Guided imagery has also been useful with children who have difficulty falling asleep, or staying asleep because of anxiety. It allows children and teens to turn off their minds and fall into a deep and peaceful sleep while listening to beautiful music, the sounds of nature, and a calming, affirming story.

 Essential

Imagery may aid in healing, increase learning and creativity, and enhance performance. By using imagery, your child can feel more in control of his emotions and the thoughts in his head, increasing self-efficacy.

Imagery as Rehearsal

You might find this is a great tool for yourself and your child. Rehearsing before a big event allows you to mentally prepare and practice in advance how to handle a situation, especially if you or your child has anticipatory anxiety. This is a great way to help problem solve, remember tools like when and how to breathe, and to verbally work through not just fears, but to also see yourselves as successful because you have taken the time to rehearse. Athletes, performers, and anyone who has to be in front of an audience use this technique as a way to build self-confidence. Chapter 17 will offer tips on rehearsing imagery to help with test anxiety.

Self-Talk

The internal dialogue you or your child has is called self-talk. It is important to identify that internal conversation because how you respond to your worries is largely determined by that self-talk. Cognitive therapists, among others like Buddhists, believe that anxious self-talk leads to anxious thoughts, which lead to anxious feelings, which lead to anxious behaviors. Yes, this internal companion that you have created talks to you continuously, literally nonstop; even subconsciously when you are sleeping! You can choose to guide yourself, criticize yourself, make fun of yourself, support yourself, be relaxed, lost, happy, sad, or anxious. You are what you believe yourself to be . . . what you tell yourself you are.

Worrywarts

Children or adults with anxiety are sometimes called worrywarts. Worrywarts have a tendency to talk to themselves in ways that can bring on anxiety and leave them feeling scared and unable to trust themselves. Small mistakes become big mistakes and everything can get picked apart relentlessly. Unfortunately, uncertainty and self-doubt rule a worrywart's thought process and can create a constant state of anxiety and dread. The key is to stop the thoughts that lead to anxiety and replace them with thoughts that are more rational, realistic, and self-supportive.

Thought-Stopping for Older Children, Teens, and Adults

You or your child might have difficulty controlling your negative self-talk and worry, so thought-stopping may be a good technique to use to end that vicious cycle. It works because it interrupts the worry response before it turns into high anxiety, giving you an opportunity to recover with positive self-talk. The idea is that as soon as you notice the first negative thought in your head silently yell "Stop, stop thinking about that," or, "Stop, I am not going to do this," and then replace the negative worrisome comment with a more positive one. Some people find visualizing a stop sign or red light helpful. You may need to tell yourself to stop multiple times in a situation, and each time you need to follow up with a positive statement. Augment this technique by using deep breathing.

 Fact

> According to the Web site AnxietyBC (*www.anxietybc.com*), for an older child or teen it may work well to ask these three questions when you notice your child has been struggling: What is making you scared? What do you worry will happen? and What bad things do you expect will happen? By doing this you help your child break the fear into more manageable elements.

Armed with positive coping statements, you have an opportunity to deal with the worry before it becomes anxiety, and help your child be successful. Each time you or your child uses thought-stopping and makes a rational, realistic, positive statement instead, you are rewiring and reworking your brain, and these positive changes have an additive effect.

Positive Self-Statements

First say, "Stop." Then add a positive coping statement that you want to believe, such as:

- I expect to feel some worry over this, but I know I will cope though it.
- This may seem hard now, but it will become easier and easier over time.

- When this is over, I will be glad that I did it.
- I have more control over these thoughts and feelings than I once imagined.
- Right now, I have feelings I do not like. They will be over with soon and I will be fine.
- I have stopped my negative thoughts before and I am going to do it again. I am better and better at challenging my worry and anxiety.

Remember, when you or your child are deciding about the list of positive coping statements, keep in mind that these statements are like affirmations. The objective is to reprogram the computer in your head to fit the life you want, and create the momentum needed to be the person you know is hiding inside.

Who Am I?

If you or your child are not sure who that person is, make a list of what you "wish" you could be, or look at someone you respect and make a list of his or her personality traits you would like to incorporate into your own life. Then, "fake it until you make it" and gear your positive statements toward your list. However, beware: If you try to incorporate positive statements that you could not believe in a million years, it won't work. This approach will be most effective when you choose statements that are reasonable and believable. Saying "I know I will sing the song perfectly tonight," is unrealistic if 1) you have never sung it perfectly in the past and/or 2) you are like most people and make mistakes at times. A more realistic positive statement, such as "I'm going to give it my best and feel good about my effort" will have a much better result.

Thought-Stopping with Young Children

Young children may find it hard to understand what you mean by "creating your own anxious thoughts," and therefore will not be able to understand how to use thought-stopping. A fun approach to try would be to play "the question game." As you read a book with pictures together, stop and ask with each picture, "Humm, I wonder what he is thinking, what would be your guess?" If your child struggles at the beginning, help her work it through like this "Well, let's see if we can tell by her eyes, or her face," then move to her body, "what do you think her arms are saying crossed like that?" This allows you the opportunity to help your child identify possibilities, positive ones as well, in an effort to understand his own feelings better. Then talk about how to say "Stop" and replace the thought with something like this: "Yes, her eyes do looked worried, do you think she is worried her dad will miss her game? Maybe she can say "Stop" to herself and remember that he has never missed a game yet and he helps her practice all the time, so he either is on his way or has a very good reason if he does not show. What else do you think she can say to herself?" This approach is also a great way to help children identify feelings and separate out the difference between a thought and a feeling, which can be difficult for younger children. Another option would be to have your child say "Stop" and then imagine locking up her fears or worry in an imaginary box. She might actually feel better if she knows she can come back to it at another time when it does not interfere with moving forward.

 Essential

It is difficult for a young child to understand the difference between a thought and a feeling. An explanation of that difference might sound like: "A thought is something that happens in your head, like all of a sudden when you see your toothbrush and you are thinking 'Oh, mommy said to brush my teeth!' A feeling is something that might happen in your stomach or heart. That would be like the feeling of butterflies in your belly because you forgot, and you think I will be upset."

Questions You Can Ask Yourself

When addressing your negative self-talk or that of your child, it is important to refute the automatic negative mindset, as noted earlier. A great way to make this happen is to ask these questions when you start to worry:

- What makes me think this is true?
- If a friend told me this what would I say to them?
- How many times has this happened before?
- What is the worst that could happen if it were true?
- If it happened, how would I cope through it?

Another trick to stop old patterns or negative talk is to concentrate on what you say about the worrisome situation and how you say it. You can use this approach yourself, or with older children. Imagine telling this worry to your best friend. Notice the exact words you use. What would that friend say to be caring and validating? What might this person say to help you feel better about yourself, and how would she say it? What you imagine this friend would say or do for you is what you need to do for yourself; that is, to be compassionate with yourself, which increases confidence and decreases the impact of negative thinking.

Self-Soothing Strategies

As discussed previously, it is essential you and your child learn how to care for yourselves with techniques that can calm your anxiety. Meditation, breathing exercises, physical exercise, a warm bath, getting involved in a hobby you enjoy, getting together with friends, and using thought-stopping can be helpful.

Creating an Action Plan

For some, creating a written plan, something that can be referred back to, put in a pocket, or hung up where they will see it all the time, can be soothing. Your plan can include reminders of how to breathe, so you can bring your heart rate down first. Then add a few positive statements to counteract the anxious thoughts, followed by a list of reminders of what you want to believe about yourself, or that you are now finding is truer of you, and one thing you will do differently to get a different result.

Taking Time-Outs

Do not be afraid to take time for yourself and to disengage from the situation or people you feel anxious around. Yes, there are times when you want to challenge yourself to hang in there and prove you can cope, but there are also times when you need to care for yourself by walking away. You can tell yourself and others, "I am going to my room for an hour; I need some me-time." Or, "I am going to take a walk or a bath." As you do this, you are modeling self-management for your child.

 Essential

If you find that you or your child is feeling overwhelmed, it is okay to let go of the anxiety rope, and go back to the situation when you feel more able to cope through it. Often, taking a time-out can have the effect of "hitting the reset button" and, in the end, can lead to better results for all.

Connecting with Other Parents

When your child is struggling, staying connected will help you ward off the constant worry and isolation, which can sometimes happen especially at the beginning of a diagnosis. Finding the time to gain support, resources, and have a place to blow off steam is a way to show yourself you are still important. How many times have you told a best friend or partner something that was bothering you, or you were confused about, and even though they did not answer it for you, you felt better when the conversation was over? Sometimes just by hearing yourself talk, or journaling a feeling, it becomes clear what you need to do. Or, just the fact that you got to discuss an upset allowed the intensity of your feelings to dissipate. Be careful that after talk follows action; do not use "venting" to avoid issues.

Where to Connect

Here are some examples of ways to stay connected, which can be helpful to reduce your own feelings of stress, sadness, confusion, anxiety, or frustration. Your connection with others also gives you an outlet to share your joy when your child is coping better. You might connect with other families from school, religious affiliations, community offerings, or your neighborhood through classes, activities, and outings. Widen your base of support by using technology-based programs like online communities through specialized anxiety Web sites.

Parent Pals

When you do connect with another parent who has a child with an anxiety disorder the two of you can agree to be each other's "parent pal." What this means is that when you have that especially hard day, or are confused about how to handle a situation, you specifically have each other for encouragement and support. Agree to connect through e-mails, phone calls, and visits, if you live in the same community. Realizing your partner, close friends, and family might have the best of intentions, and they can not be your "everything," this will provide another avenue to be supported by someone who also knows what it is like to walk in your shoes. Appendix B lists resources that can help you connect with parents of other children with anxiety.

CHAPTER 17

School Days

Because a large percentage of your child's time is spent in school, her anxiety will affect her school experience. Similarly, her experiences at school will also affect her anxiety. Children can have school-related anxiety for a number of reasons, and it can take some detective work to figure out the particulars of your child's concerns. Anticipatory anxiety and the avoidance that results can cause school troubles to spiral rapidly into unmanageability, and missed classes can create an overwhelming avalanche of catch-up. As such, it is important that you address anxiety about school as quickly and directly as possible.

Anxiety about School

A certain amount of anxiety about school is normal and expected. Making new friends, completing homework, taking tests, completing projects, athletic or performance schedules, and the demands of "fitting it all in" can tax even the most confident child. If your support and encouragement do not seem to help your child gain a sense of mastery, and if she loses sleep, avoids school, or worries more than you think she should, you will want to pay special attention to this chapter.

She Doth Protest Too Much

As you saw in Chapter 3, the most common tactic children use to avoid school is to complain about physical symptoms such as headaches, stomachaches, or general malaise. Children with anxiety may make frantic and repeated calls to be picked up from school early, or may be mysteriously ill after a long weekend or extended break. The child with anxiety may complain of overwhelming social pressures and push you to let her have a "mental health day," or she may repeatedly miss the bus. Other signs that anxiety may be a problem include difficulty getting up in the morning, prolonged dawdling, or a pattern of missing school on days when tests or class presentations are scheduled.

 *Question?*

Does your child often try to avoid going to school by complaining of illness?
After a medical checkup to rule out any true physical problems, follow the school's guidelines for illness so you do not become a part of the problem. If your child ultimately does stay home, avoid making the day an opportunity for playtime. That is, limit television, videogames, and the like. If a child is truly ill, the best medicine is a restful day in bed, of course, with a little TLC thrown in.

Communicate Your Expectations

Clearly communicate your expectations that your child can and will go to school regularly as adults go to work every day whether they want to or not. Encourage your child by letting her know that you have confidence in her capabilities, and that with effort and support, you know she can succeed. When a child is working on building new skills and confidence, your support is invaluable. You can also ask her if there is anything you can do as a parent to help, or if she would like you to speak with someone at the school who might be able to help. Teaching your child that it is okay to not be perfect, and normalizing her struggle can be very comforting.

Homework Hassles

If your child becomes anxious over doing homework, you will need to help him create structure in order to increase his sense of control and empowerment. First, help your child learn to keep track of assignments, projects, and tests. Most schools use planners or a folder system to help parents stay abreast of their child's assignments, and may require you to sign off when tasks are reviewed or completed. Your child's school Web site may list and track homework requirements online. Using a calendar to plan daily work or set deadlines for projects can be helpful for managing anxiety.

 Fact

A good tool for building social connections is to encourage your child to call a classmate with a question, or to get details on a missing assignment. It is a great way to open up a friendship. As your child gets older, study groups might be an option.

Anticipatory Anxiety

Anticipatory anxiety occurs when your child imagines a future event that he believes is outside his safe zone, and fears he will not be able to handle the situation without panic. Sometimes referred to as the fear of fear, the overall goal is really to avoid distressing feelings. The anxiety your child feels when thinking about the feared event increases his tendency to avoid it, and magnifies feelings of distress if the situation actually does occur. Anticipatory anxiety is indiscriminate; that is, it can involve negative thoughts about performance, panic, peers, perfection, or just about anything else and can be lifelong. The next section on test anxiety will offer possible solutions.

Test Anxiety

It has been said that almost all children will experience test anxiety at some time in their school careers. In fact, small to moderate levels of anxiety actually increase performance, while more severe amounts cause performance to drop off. Test anxiety occurs when strong or unpleasant emotions interfere with your child's ability to absorb, retain, and recall information. Anxiety creates a kind of "mental static" in the brain, which interferes with learning, memory, and the ability to reason and think clearly, as discussed in Chapter 2. Feelings such as worry, fear, and frustration actually derail the central nervous system, causing the SNS and PNS to get out of rhythm, thereby disrupting mental processes. Conversely, positive feelings like hope and appreciation lead to increased balance and harmony in the nervous system. This enhances performance and creates positive emotional pathways to build on success. The remainder of this chapter offers strategies to manage both general and test anxiety.

Be Prepared

One of the most basic approaches to managing test anxiety is to help your child maximize her sense of competence and control by ensuring preparation for an exam. You may wish to help by using practice questions or by encouraging her to review with friends. The younger your child is, the easier it may be to make a game out of this. A good night's sleep is essential to enhancing performance on an exam. Some children do well getting up just a few minutes early on a test day so they can make a final review of the subject material. Finally, make sure your child has had a good breakfast and adequate hydration on a test day. Even the best-prepared student can have trouble with testing if not properly nourished, because if the tank is empty, the engine just will not run.

Cognitive Rehearsal

Negative rehearsal or mental repetition of negative thoughts and fears is actually what drives anticipatory anxiety. The repeated negative thoughts about the feared event cement in the anxiety, creating an endless loop and making the situation seem unbearable. Using cognitive rehearsal constructively combats the negative rehearsal of anticipatory anxiety. To help your child replace self-defeating thoughts, first encourage him to relax by breathing deeply and/or using progressive muscle relaxation. Then ask him to imagine getting up, going to school, entering the classroom where the test will occur, taking, and finishing the test. As your child imagines these scenes, cue him to relax continually, and to imagine feeling confident and succeeding at his goal. Make sure to give positive messages about his ability to breathe, center, and succeed. If your child is a bit older, it can be very effective to record a "session" on a tape or DVR so that he can use it independently.

 **Question?**

I heard it is good to have your child tape his own voice, or the voice of someone he knows and feels loved by. Is that really helpful?
Yes. It is often helpful if your child uses his own voice or that of a parent or therapist on the recording so that he can more easily internalize positive messages. If your child is younger, you may wish to make up a short, silly song or familiar tune to help him flip the switch to positive self-talk.

Touchstones

Have you ever found yourself toying with change or keys in your pocket, or twisting a ring on your finger? If so, you are using a touchstone to calm yourself. A touchstone is an object that your child carries with her that she can touch or hold that becomes grounding and comforting for her. It should be small enough to be worn or carried, and should be an object that has a symbolic or emotional meaning for your child. Examples include smooth stones, coins, amulets or figurines, jewelry, or key rings. Help your child to find an object she can carry with her to use when anxious or upset. Dollar aisles, bead stores, craft stores, and nature are great sources for finding touchstones. Encourage your child to use her touchstone while she practices other skills such as breathing or imagery to reduce both testing and general anxiety.

Managing School Refusal

As explained in Chapter 3, one of the most pernicious problems for children with anxiety, and one of the most frustrating for parents, is the refusal to attend or stay at school. In a comprehensive article on the American Academy of Family Physicians Web site (*www.aafp.org*), Wanda Fremont, M.D., states that researchers have found that approximately 1 to 5 percent of all school-aged children, regardless of socioeconomic status, have school refusal, and that the rate is similar between boys and girls. Although school refusal occurs at all ages, it is more common in children five, six, ten, and eleven years of age. The article differentiates school refusal from truancy in that children who are truant usually do not feel anxious about school, may show a lack of interest in schoolwork, and may engage in antisocial behavior when away from school. Conversely, children with anxiety show a preference to be at home where they feel safe and secure, and may be quite interested in doing schoolwork.

 *Alert!*

Separation anxiety, detailed in Chapter 6, is a common culprit that drives school refusal. Generalized anxiety, social fears, and peer issues also contribute to school avoidance, as does test anxiety.

The following section will help you develop a game plan for addressing school avoidance and refusal.

Nurse Your Child Back to Health

If you feel your child attempts to stay home from school more than he should, you can use several approaches, depending on your child's particular pattern. If your child calls repeatedly to be picked up from school saying he is ill, your best ally is often the school nurse. Let the nurse know that you are concerned about school avoidance, and that you need to be certain that your child is truly ill before you will pick him up. Usually, school personnel are alert to school avoidance and will collaborate with you to ensure your child's best interest. You may wish to make a plan for how long your child can stay at the nurse's office, and at what point you should be called.

Behavioral Planning

In order to develop an effective behavior plan, you will need to identify a list of short- and long-term goals you and your child will attack. Keep the goals concrete and measurable so that you can easily track progress. It is best to attack only one or two key behaviors at a time to avoid confusion and the possibility you or your child might become overwhelmed. Use shorter-term goals to attain longer-term goals, reinforcing each accomplishment as you go along.

 **Fact**

Systematic Desensitization is a cognitive behavioral technique, usually carried out by a qualified mental health professional. It incorporates cognitive rehearsal by breaking down aspects of a feared situation, from least to most anxiety-provoking. The steps are then imagined in a relaxed state, and care is taken to ensure that each scene can be imagined comfortably before moving on to the next.

It helps to know what your child is already capable of doing, for example, how many hours he is able to stay in school. As you plan your goals, use the baseline to focus on increasing time at school by small increments, such as hours, days, weeks, and so on. For example, if you determine that your child misses school an average of one day a week, you might set a goal of increasing attendance by a half-day, offering an incentive after this happens once or twice. Then increase the goal to a full day's attendance with continued reinforcement.

Managing Anxiety at School

Just as children can have anticipatory anxiety even thinking about school, they can also have anxiety during various parts of the school day. The anxiety may simply be an annoyance, which your child can shrug off or manage with some basic relaxation techniques. Conversely, the anxiety may be so great that it makes it nearly impossible for your child to learn and concentrate, let alone make friends or have fun. Social anxiety disorder, separation anxiety disorder, generalized anxiety disorder, and OCD can make your child's day excruciating, and can all have devastating consequences for your child's school experience.

Lunchtime Laments

The social melting pot of your child's lunchroom can be overwhelming if he is especially sensitive, introverted, or has social phobia. If your child is unable to eat around others, a common feature of social phobia, you will want to address this early. Enlist school personnel and a therapist who can help with a plan of gradual exposure so that your child can fight fear and build confidence bit by bit. Other tips include helping your child to find a regular lunch partner or table, preparing a list of conversation topics and practicing basic conversational skills, and sending your child with a lunch from home if this is comforting for him. If your child makes progress in this arena, it might be fitting for you to make a lunchtime visit.

Essential

A younger child may delight in your presence at his lunch table, especially if you bring a small treat to share. An older child might appreciate you dropping off a special take-out lunch for him or a treat to share, but for tweens and teens who need more space, if you stay you may make them feel awkward.

Staying in Class

If your child has trouble staying in class and has frequent urges to leave, you will need to help her create a plan to manage the impulse to escape. First, make sure she has some tools such as relaxation, distraction, or self-soothing, which she can use to manage anxious thoughts and feelings. The use of a touchstone may be especially helpful here. Next, help your child practice staying "two more minutes" when she feels the urge to leave. The goal, of course, is to stay with and manage the anxiety, because running from it only increases its power. Your child can practice "two more minutes" for as long as she is able, and can increase the increment to five or more minutes as she gains confidence. If your child's anxiety is unbearable, make a plan for her to leave class in a structured and controlled fashion, rather than impulsively escaping. She may wish to develop a signal for her teacher, who can give her the nod to retreat to a predetermined "safe place." Examples might include the office of the nurse or social worker, the library, or restroom. After a specific period of "time-out," your child should return to class, and repeat the cycle as necessary. Use cognitive rehearsal to increase your child's sense of hopefulness and mastery.

Transition Troubles

Many children have special trouble during times of transition, where structure and expectations are unclear. You may want to help your child identify points in his day that he feels are stressful or difficult, and then come up with a plan to manage them. Talk with your child about which tools might be most helpful (breathing, touchstone, mindfulness); support and encourage him when he follows through. It may help to encourage your child's teacher to casually remind your child to use his skills.

Peers and Peer Pressure

The demands of social interaction can be especially traumatic for children with anxiety, who worry more and can be exceedingly shy or self-conscious. In fact, a common presenting concern for children coming to therapy is troublemaking, keeping, and interacting with friends.

Best Friends Forever

Your child's first best friend is truly a friend forever, because the experience of having a person outside of your family who mirrors your fears, fancies, and foibles creates a base or template for all of your child's future relationships. The developmental push to find and keep a best friend is greatest between the ages of about eight to eleven. Developmental psychologists see this as a crucial step, because the best friend or "chum" helps your child begin to fine-tune his identity and strengthen attachment. A child with anxiety will most likely have difficulty with this task and will need your help.

Peer Pressure

You have no doubt had firsthand experience with peer pressure, especially during your adolescent years. Peer pressure can add to insecurity and undermine self-confidence. As your child grows older, family influences take a backseat to those of his peer group. His circle of friends influences what he wears, watches, listens to, eats, believes in, and aspires to. Because children are trying to fit in at the same time they are learning to express themselves, the pressure to conform can become an easy solution to identity confusion. For socially anxious children, peer pressure may be especially powerful, with its promise of "safety in numbers." You can support your child by helping him talk about peer pressure, and especially, any influences he finds confusing or distasteful. It may help to ask, "How would you feel about a person who _____? Would you want that person as a friend?"

The Importance of Anchoring

For your child with anxiety to feel connected and supported, she will need a social anchor. Sports, dance, scouts, martial arts, drama, choir or band, and church youth groups can all provide your child with a base sense of security in the social world. They are ready-made opportunities for finding friends who share similar interests and schedules. Hopefully, other children in these specialized peer groups will be a positive influence on her attitudes and behavior, encouraging her to stretch socially. You might try carpooling or host a small gathering for her group to encourage your child to use new skills. Take pride and show interest in her choices by attending events or performances or by volunteering to help if you can.

Bullies and Gossip

Estimates are that as many as 20 to 30 percent of children either bully, or are bullied, at some time, and that bullying is most common in the middle-school years. The effects of bullying and gossip can even be harmful to those merely observing it. It was previously believed that bullies lacked self-esteem and put others down to gain self-confidence. However, recent findings show that bullies are more confident than previously thought, but they tend to lack empathy, are poor communicators, and may be raised in homes where aggression is an acceptable response to conflict.

Gossip is verbal bullying to which girls often resort. It can include name-calling, rumors, and lies, and can have devastating effects, particularly for a child who is already anxious socially. A child who struggles with anxiety may feel she has no recourse, and the powerlessness may lead to avoidance, isolation, and depression. If you suspect your child is the victim of bullying or gossip, listen supportively and try the following:

- Encourage your child to practice "safety in numbers."
- Help your child to widen her social circle.
- Role-play ways to ignore and walk away from teasing or pestering.
- Role-play saying no and being assertive.
- Involve the school if violence, racial slurs, or serious threats of harm occur.

Alert!

If your child is passive, especially introverted, or socially awkward, he may be an especially susceptible target for bullies. It is easy to dismiss complaints about bullying as a child being too sensitive or dramatic, so please take the time to listen to what your child is saying. Your support can provide the impetus your child needs to address the problem.

Middle-School Meltdowns

Middle-school (grades six through eight or nine) can be one of the most tumultuous times for children socially. Brains are rewiring and hormones are surging, and children at this age compete for social status, which can sometimes change rapidly. If your child is already having difficulty with worry and panic, this developmental transition can be extremely painful, and making sure therapy is available is important.

A hallmark of this age is the clique, a social group that is highly exclusive and demands strict conformity. The clique usually has a "ringleader" or "queen bee" and members see themselves as superior to others outside the group. Those who do not belong can feel inferior, and even threatened, as the clique can have great social power.

 Essential

> When children feel snubbed by members of a clique, they may struggle with self-doubt, anxiety, anger, and even depression. Check for meltdowns or moodiness after school, and help your child to talk about social struggles and celebrate her unique strengths to help her to cope. Use the ideas on anchoring above to help your child shift focus and find alternative social outlets.

Social Support

Many elementary and middle schools offer "friendship groups" for children who are awkward or have social anxiety, or who are new to the school. Usually, a school social worker leads the groups, in addition to providing individual support to children in the school district. Groups usually meet weekly or bimonthly, and most children look forward to the time-out from class and opportunity to build friendship skills. Other social connections at school may be available through mentoring, student government, peer support, or tutoring. Check with your child's school if you think he might benefit from some of these opportunities.

Staying Connected and Getting Involved

Throughout the book, you have been encouraged to form a support team to help manage your child's anxiety. If your child has school-based anxiety, it will be especially important to make and keep regular contact with various professionals at her school, and to support her by becoming more active in her educational experience.

Where Do You Start?

If your child is experiencing anxiety related concerns at school, the once or twice yearly conference will likely be inadequate to address his emotional needs. Your concerns for your child are important, and no doubt feel urgent. However, it is important to remember that the teacher has many students to attend to, and to respect the teacher's needs with regard to communication. Some teachers prefer to use e-mail; others may have reserved times to speak with parents about concerns over the phone. Many are happy to schedule meetings before or after school.

 Essential

If you feel your child's teacher is not receptive to your child's needs or your requests, respectfully involve other support people, such as the nurse, social worker, psychologist, or principal. You know your child best; trust what you feel and advocate when needed.

Classroom Volunteering

Many schools depend on volunteers to increase cooperation between families and schools, and to help things run smoothly. Volunteer opportunities vary from heading the Parent Teacher Organization to coordinating fund drives to correcting weekly spelling tests. If you become involved and interested in your child's school experience, her investment and motivation in school may improve as well. However, if you are concerned that your child might be clingy or tearful if you are there, or if your own anxiety causes you to hover or be overprotective, your child might do better without your presence. If you are unsure, talk over the options with your child's teacher or therapist to see what they might recommend.

Field Trips

Chaperoning one of your child's field trips can be a great way to learn more about your child's social world and about his daily struggles with anxiety. You may want to volunteer for field trips if your child has trouble managing them without you. However, you will also need to have a plan to decrease your participation so that your child can eventually experience independence. If volunteerism is especially popular in your child's school, you may have to compete with other parents for a spot. If joining a field trip is therapeutically necessary for your child, you may have to travel separately, or arrange to share parts of the field trip with other parents.

Special Events

Most schools have dances, all-school parties, fairs, or other events for fundraising and community building. These can be great opportunities to watch your child in action, support her, and connect with other parents and children to strengthen your support network. In-school stores, book fairs, and assemblies may provide similar opportunities. Scouting, which is often affiliated with the school district, and after-school, homework, athletic, and drama programs usually depend on volunteers for support. Be kind to yourself; don't feel guilty if you can't fit volunteering into your schedule, or if it's too overwhelming.

CHAPTER 18

Naturally Speaking: Exercise, Nutrition, and Sleep

Proper nutrition, sleep, and adequate physical activity create the foundation for overall health and emotional well-being. If your child has anxiety, it is especially important to address these issues so he has the best chance at managing emotional difficulties. Because one of the most common concerns for children with anxiety is sleep, the end of this chapter specifically addresses sleep routines and insomnia.

Quick Fixes for Anxiety

There are several easy antidotes for minor or temporary anxiety, which are effective for children at almost any age. These remedies, many based on traditional systems of healing, are noninvasive, largely inexpensive, and easy to implement. Also, note that yoga, massage, and aromatherapy are excellent quick fixes that are described in detail in Chapter 13.

The Turkey Sandwich Cure

Many people are familiar with the post-Thanksgiving "crash" which most attribute to overeating. It is more likely that the urge to snooze is a direct result of the turkey and mashed potatoes, which are often the centerpiece of the meal. Turkey is high in tryptophan, a naturally occurring amino acid that boosts serotonin and has a calming effect. Milk, especially when warmed, also contains high amounts of tryptophan. Eating these foods with a carbohydrate, such as pota-toes, bread, or rice, increases the body's ability to use tryptophan. Therefore, in a pinch, a turkey sandwich and a glass of warm milk can quickly help your child to calm down. Other kid-friendly foods that contain tryptophan include peanuts and peanut butter, apricots, bananas, cottage cheese, and other low-fat dairy products.

Tea and Sympathy

Tea has long been used worldwide as an herbal and social rem-edy for calming, digestive, and other effects on the body. Chamomile is one of the most well known for sleep, and passion flower, lemon balm, and jasmine are also purported to have soothing effects. Vale-rian can also be used as a tea, though some experts warn that it should be used cautiously. The warming sensation of the tea, along with some quiet, supportive attention, may soothe both you and your child and allow you to wind down in times of anxiety. Even the ritual of preparing the tea can be grounding, if it is done mindfully. Just remember to check that it does not contain caffeine!

The Bath

Bathing has been used for millennia in many cultures to promote health, hygiene, and spiritual purification, and even socialization. The calming effect of the warm water, especially when combined with aromatic soaps and oils, music, and soft lighting, can alleviate anxiety and help with insomnia. Many parents use bathing as a part of the bedtime ritual. For younger children especially, bath time can be excellent for bonding, and a time to incorporate massage, or even breathing and visualization. Use your intuition, though, to make sure combining more than one approach at a time is not over-stimulating. You can encourage older children to use bathing independently for calming and also insomnia.

Shake and Dance

This technique, taken from the health realization approach, uses the body's activity to help the mind let go of tension, anxiety, and worry. All it requires is music, a few minutes, and the ability to let go of self-consciousness. To start, find some lively music with a good beat that you think your child would enjoy, or, depending on age, ask your child to pick a piece of music to "get the jitters out." Play the music, and begin to very deliberately shake your body (do this with your child). Shake your hands, feet, arms, legs, head, torso, eyes, tongue, hair, and anything else you can! Do this for at least a minute or two; it's okay if you can't do the whole song. After shaking, if you like, you can then switch the music to something soaring, happy, uplifting, or calming. You and your child will both be surprised at how different you feel after this exercise, and the laughter that can result is good medicine in itself!

Finding Balance Through Food

Recent concerns about childhood obesity and diabetes have increased awareness of the importance of balanced nutrition in children. Many experts feel that if your child has a balanced diet, he should not need dietary supplements, or even a multivitamin. Other experts disagree, but all concur that a healthy, balanced diet providing a wide variety of foods, especially fresh, is the best building block for overall health. Supplementation can then be used, based on your child's particular needs, at the advice of your child's physician or naturopath.

 *Question?*

Is there a fun way to show healthy eating choices?
At *MyPyramid.gov*, you can access a special MyPyramid for kids, targeting those ages six to eleven. The interactive model includes online the MyPyramid Blast Off Game, which challenges children to fuel a rocket to "Planet Power" by making healthy food and exercise choices.

Sweets and Stimulants

Just as a healthy diet can relieve symptoms of anxiety, some foods can worsen mood symptoms because of their effects on the body's biochemistry. If your child has anxiety, you may wish to restrict or eliminate sugar, caffeine, some starches, and processed foods.

Caffeine

Most people know that caffeine, as a stimulant, can cause jitteriness, irritability, and anxiety, but many do not know about hidden sources of caffeine. Many sodas other than cola contain caffeine. Energy drinks, even if advertised as natural, may also contain caffeine. Caffeine is also present in cocoa, chocolate, and some teas. If your child has trouble sleeping, be sure to limit sources of caffeine at least four hours before bedtime. You may wish to eliminate caffeine entirely from your child's diet when anxiety is a concern.

Sugar

Many parents are familiar with the hyperactivity, and possible energy and emotional crash, which result from your child's excessive sugar consumption at Halloween, Valentine's Day, parties, or other occasions when sweets are center stage. Sugar, in and of itself, has no nutritional value other than simple calories. When ingested, it can cause a quick surge in energy, which can then be followed by a "crash," marked by tiredness, lethargy, or even emotionality and irritability.

 Essential

MSG is common in processed foods like soups, boxed or frozen dinners, and side dishes, fast food, and other restaurant food. It can cause gastric distress, headache, nervousness, and general malaise, so read nutritional labeling carefully, especially if your child has anxiety with tummy troubles.

For some, the energy surge can mimic a panic attack. You may wish to limit your child's sugar intake to help with anxiety. To sweeten foods more naturally, with a more gentle effect on mood and energy, consider fruit juice, stevia, (an herbal sweetener available at most health food stores), or honey, if your child is over two. Remember that fresh fruit is a natural, healthy, and satisfying option for dessert. Be alert to "disguised sugar" in the form of high fructose corn syrup and sucrose, which are common in many processed foods. Also, be aware of added sugar in nonsweet foods like breads, crackers, and spaghetti or other sauces.

Carbohydrates

Carbohydrates are essential for the production of energy, and all people need some carbs to be healthy. Carbohydrates can be increased when physical demands increase; take, for example, the athlete who eats a huge spaghetti dinner or pancake breakfast before a competition. However, if your child's diet is too high in carbohydrates, he may experience extreme fluctuations in mood and energy, and may be prone to periods of anxiety. This is because carbohydrates quickly metabolize into sugars (glucose) the body uses for energy. When the sugar burns off, a crash in energy, with accompanying malaise, distress, irritability, "spaciness," or moodiness, can occur. Conditions like hypoglycemia or diabetes are dependent on good management of carbohydrate intake, so check with your health professional if you are concerned carbohydrates affect your child's mood.

Protein Power

Increasing the amount of high-protein foods in the diet has been found to stabilize and elevate mood, and increase energy. Remember to use lean sources of protein such as fish, turkey, and chicken, and avoid meats high in fat, sodium, nitrates, or other additives. Adding protein to a meal or snack heavy in carbohydrates slows the metabolism of glucose, and prevents a "crash." If your child has trouble staying asleep, this may occur if a carb crash signals her body that she needs more calories. Try offering a small serving of protein (nuts or nut butters, meat, cheese, yogurt) before bed to see if this helps.

Vitamins and Nutritional Supplements

There is much recent controversy about the safety and efficacy of vitamins, herbs, enzymes, and nutritional supplements. The Dietary Supplement Health and Education Act (DSHEA), passed in 1994, restricts the FDA's authority over supplements, provided companies do not claim their products treat, prevent, or cure disease. As such, the FDA views nutritional supplements as foods that contain ingredients intended to augment the diet. As a result, the level of standardization for supplements is far less than that required for pharmaceutical drugs, and it is important to use caution when choosing these products. Most studies available use adult populations, and with rare exceptions, (such as teen girls with low calcium intake or those eating large amounts of fast food) many professionals, including the American Association of Pediatrics, warn against using supplements in children, as well as women who are pregnant or nursing. However, many parents prefer to pursue natural alternatives before considering psychiatric medication. You can find accurate and useful information on supplements at the National Institutes of Health (*www.nih.gov*) and the National Center for Complementary and Alternative Medicine (*www.nccam.nih.gov*).

Alert!

It is *extremely* important that you check with your child's doctor or a qualified naturopathic or homeopathic physician before starting a supplementation program. The doctor will help you determine proper dosing for your child's age, and check on potential medication interactions, side effects, or other precautions.

Herbs

Herbal (or botanical) supplements are dietary supplements that are used for a medicinal purpose. They generally support a specific aspect of the body's health, such as the heart, bones, or digestive system. However, just because a product is labeled as "natural" does not mean that it is safe or without side effects. In fact, many herbal supplements can produce strong effects in the body, particularly if taken improperly or at high doses. People with anxiety should be especially careful when using herbal formulas. Remember also that the levels of standardization in dosing, labeling, and added ingredients are not regulated by the FDA in the same way that pharmaceutical products are and can be dangerous to infants and children.

Vitamins

Vitamin supplements provide extra supplies of micronutrients the body needs for growth, digestion, and mood regulation. Different food sources contain different vitamins and minerals, and a wide and varied diet is the best way to make sure you and your child get enough of them. Supplements can be used in special conditions, under the care and advice of a qualified physician. Vitamins and minerals that are especially important in managing mood and anxiety include:

- **B Vitamins:** Effective in helping maintain adequate serotonin levels, which improve mood and combat the effects of stress. These vitamins lessen the body's tendency to become overstimulated by adrenaline, such as might occur in panic attacks or prolonged states of anxiety associated with PTSD. A good B-complex supplement should contain the essential B vitamins, which are thiamin, riboflavin, niacin, vitamin B_6, vitamin B_{12}, and pantothenic acid. Generally, B vitamins are found in meat, fish, grains, legumes, liver, bananas, and some dairy products.

- **Vitamin D:** Supports normal levels of calcium and phosphorus; found in cod liver oil, fish, fortified dairy products, eggs, and sun exposure.
- **Vitamin C:** Antioxidant that supports connective tissue, nervous tissue, mitochondria, and is plentiful in citrus fruits and green veggies. Over-the-counter products like powders and chewables are convenient and kid-friendly.

Mineral Supplements

Mineral supplements provide micronutrients found extensively in bone and teeth. In addition, minerals help the body create new cells and enzymes, distribute fluids, control nerve impulses, and bring oxygen and take away carbon dioxide from cells. One important mineral to help regulate anxiety is magnesium. Magnesium can relax nerves and muscles, and is a natural sleep-inducing element found in legumes, dark leafy vegetables, almonds, and whole grains.

 Fact

Check with your alternative health care provider or local health food store for powdered products, which can be mixed into tea or hot water at bedtime to aid sleep. These calcium/magnesium blends are easy to take and help relax muscles and soothe nerves, decreasing pain and creating deeper and more restful sleep. Be sure the one you choose is safe for children.

Essential Fatty Acids

Essential fatty acids (EFAs), sometimes referred to as Omega 3s, are natural nutrients that improve communication between brain cells. Their importance in cardiovascular health has been clearly established, and there is good research supporting the use of EFAs/Omega 3s to manage anxiety, depression, and bipolar disorder. EFAs are available in coldwater fish such as salmon, tuna, trout, and others. Flaxseed oil contains alpha-linoleic acid, which converts to the EFAs found in fish oils. There are many health benefits to increasing fish in the diet, and flaxseed oil is easy to incorporate into the diet as well. The size of the capsules can be daunting for children, so you may have to add the oil to a food. Some products (especially flax) need refrigeration, and many people can't take fish oils without other food, due to stomach upset and "fish breath." If either occurs on a regular basis, consider changing your child's supplement or switching to flax.

Exercise and Yoga

Exercise, including yoga, alleviates mental stress, increases blood flow to the brain, improves mood, energy, and sleep, and can create an overall sense of well-being. It can provide distraction from emotional distress, help your child tune into her body, and enhance her sense of physical strength, endurance, mastery, and confidence.

Exercise Guidelines

The 2005 USDA and Department of Health and Human Services guidelines recommend that all children two years and older should get sixty minutes of moderate to vigorous exercise on most, if not all, days of the week. Exercise should include the components of endurance, strength, and flexibility, and should involve both structured and free play. Encourage regular exercise to help your anxious child optimize mood-boosting brain chemistry, and to "blow off steam." However, if your child has trouble sleeping, she should avoid exercise within two to four hours before bedtime because it can be overstimulating.

Buddy System

Your child will be more likely to enjoy exercise and adopt it as a life habit if your family engages in physical activity together. Easy ways to accomplish this are to toss a ball in the backyard, shoot some hoops at a local park, bike, hike, walk, skate, swim, or ski. Gardening, yardwork, and housework can also be good exercise, and provide opportunities to enhance your child's sense of belonging in the family by making her work efforts important.

It Needs to Be Fun

Nobody really likes exercise if it isn't fun. Help your child enjoy exercise by being positive about physical activity and modeling how much fun it can be. Be creative! Dance, jump rope, make an obstacle course in the backyard, create your own ball game, or turn on some lively music for your child if he uses a treadmill or stationary bike at home. Create your own triathlon by walking or running, swimming, and biking, all in the same day. Find out what your child likes to do, and encourage him: If he likes to skateboard, or inline skate, make sure he has the proper safety equipment and help him hook up with some buddies. Take smaller children to the playground so that they can climb, slide, swing, run around, and just plain have fun.

Sleep Routine and Ritual

It is very common for children with anxiety to have trouble transitioning into sleep, sleeping independently, and falling and staying asleep. Most experts agree that adults and children sleep better when they establish regular sleeping and waking times (even on the weekends), and develop a routine for sleep.

Winding Down

It is important to help your child, with anxiety or not, to find ways to ramp down his level of physical, mental, and emotional stimulation so that he can drop off to sleep easily and naturally. As discussed in Chapter 15, an hour or more before bedtime, you can help your child to wind down by having him finish homework and computer gaming time, lowering the volume on music and television, and dimming the lights.

Avoiding TV, computers, or videogames maximizes the production of sleep hormones. Reading and music can be good transition activities, but make sure that your child avoids watching or listening to anything aggressive.

Bedtime Snack

Another part of the bedtime ritual for many families includes a bedtime snack. For optimal sleep, your child's snack should include a bit of protein and carbohydrate, possibly including milk or other tryptophan-rich foods, which encourage melatonin production. An example of a good sleepytime snack might be a bit of cottage cheese or yogurt and some canned, fresh, or dried apricots, or a slice of turkey on a piece of bread with a glass of milk. Avoid cocoa at bedtime; most have too much sugar and caffeine and may prevent your child naturally drifting off to sleep.

Check-Out

You may wish to use snack time to "check-out" with your child at the end of the day. That is, take a few minutes to review with your child how her day went. Try to focus on what went well for your child, and set up positive intentions for tomorrow. After your child has had a snack, you might want to incorporate positive imagery along with breathing and relaxation so that you can send your child off to sleep feeling relaxed and confident, rather than worried and overwhelmed. A few gentle yoga stretches before bed can also help muscles to relax easily into sleep.

Creature Comforts

Help your child let go of the day's anxieties by creating a calm and nurturing environment for sleep. Research indicates that people sleep better when a room is slightly cool, (about sixty to sixty-five degrees; slightly warmer for babies) and when their bed is supportive, but comfortable. Smaller children, especially, do well with cozy blankets, and may feel more secure if their stuffed animals, or "lovies," are with them in the bed. Use nightlights in your child's room if he is afraid of the dark, and provide additional nightlights in the bathroom and near your room so that your child feels secure once everyone goes to bed.

Managing Insomnia

Insomnia is usually seen as a nighttime problem, involving trouble falling or staying asleep. However, insomnia causes daytime problems as well, such as tiredness, lack of energy, difficulty concentrating, and irritability. If your child is not sleeping well, she may feel out of step with the world around her. Prolonged sleeplessness can cause health troubles, depression, and can even increase the potential for accidents and injury. Interestingly, the experience of insomnia has as much to do with the actual amount of sleep as it does with one's perception of not sleeping well.

 **Alert!**

Melatonin, a readily available herbal supplement for sleep, may have applications for older children with insomnia, for example, in adolescents receiving steroids for chemotherapy. Even though melatonin is a naturally occurring hormone, it must be used with caution, and with a recommendation from your child's doctor.

Get Up Early

One of the simplest ways to combat anxiety is to get up earlier. Moving up your "start time" will help your body to be more ready for "quitting time" when the day is done. Depending on your child's age, you can adjust the time he gets up by fifteen to thirty minutes each day, and see how he responds after a week or so. Remember to factor in the amount of sleep your child needs by age (see Chapter 2) when balancing bedtimes and rising times. An additional bonus of awakening earlier is that the extra time can be used for exercise or yoga, meditation, organization, and ensuring a good breakfast.

Increase Activity

Regular exercise boosts serotonin, making melatonin more available. It also tires and relaxes muscles, provides an outlet for stress, regulates blood sugar, and supports other bodily processes important to sleep. It is best to avoid exercise for several hours before bedtime, and some experts feel that morning activity boosts mood the best. If your child has insomnia, make sure she has some time to be active each day. You may want to increase the recommended exercise guidelines for your child's age, in combination with some of the other strategies in the chapter, to see if your child's sleep and overall anxiety level improves.

The Bed Is for Sleeping

Most sleep specialists agree that it is best to reserve the bed, and even the bedroom, if possible, for sleeping. If your child uses her bed for reading, studying, drawing, or play, the sheer power of behavioral patterning may make it more difficult for her to turn her mind off and fall asleep easily. Make sure your child's bed is comfortable (try laying on it yourself) and that she has cozy blankets, pillows, and other comfort items that create a nighttime oasis.

 Fact

In the Ayurvedic (Indian) and other systems, honey promotes sleep, and may be a natural and palatable cure for insomnia. The general recipe is one teaspoon to one cup of water, or you can add the honey to warm milk or calming tea to enhance its effect. Remember, never give honey to children under the age of two due to the risk of botulism.

Stories and Music

Many kids find the distraction of music, books, or stories on tape an invaluable tool in falling asleep. The external focus gives busy minds something other than worry to attach to, and, if the themes or images in the audio promote serenity and relaxation, the body will respond to these cues. Guided imagery for sleep can also be very helpful, but make sure you choose a program your child will use only for sleep, and have another for general relaxation. Make sure the volume is at a comfortable level and that your child will not be startled awake by a tape player flipping off. Some children find they can go back to sleep on their own if they awaken during the night simply by turning their audio selection back on.

White Noise

Adding ambient sound such as a fan, fountain, or white noise machine can help your child turn down the volume on anxious thoughts and create an external reference point which helps him to drop off to sleep. There are inexpensive sound machines available at many drug or department stores that can be set to any number of natural or created sounds. Tapes or CDs with ocean waves, crickets, or running water can also be helpful. If you are working on decreasing bedwetting, you may want to avoid water sounds, which might subconsciously affect your child's urge to urinate.

CHAPTER 19

Create Your Own Toolbox

Like going to a hardware store to stock up on tools so you can confidently build a home project, having a toolbox of information can help your child and you feel confident as you rebuild or strengthen skills. Remember, any time you work on changing habits it can feel uncomfortable, so help your child use the thought-stopping techniques discussed in Chapter 16 with encouragement and support, to ease the transition.

Using Baby Steps to Build Confidence

As discussed in the beginning of the book, your child may believe that he cannot prevent his anxious feelings because they come so fast and furious. Using baby steps can help your child manage anxiety and panic and shift attention from the panic to the task at hand.

Managing Piece by Piece

As discussed previously, small steps are key with a child who has anxiety. By creating change in little doses, managing a situation in steps builds a confident mindset. Using this tool, your child's coping statement might sound like, "I'm really nervous because I have to give a speech in front of the whole class next week; how can I make this feel less scary? Well, I could write it first, and just concentrate on making it a good paper. Then, when it is done, I could ask to practice it in front of my mom and dad, and after I do that, a few times I could say it in front of the whole family. When I am feeling better about it, if I want, I could also call my friend, and say it in front of him too." Planning and preparing in small pieces allows your child to reap better results and achieve his goals without becoming overwhelmed.

 Essential

Some of the main keys to building confidence include focusing on your achievements, setting reachable goals, preparing thoroughly, acting as if you are confident, rewarding yourself when you are successful, and facing your fears.

The 70 Percent Rule

The 70 percent rule is featured in the book *Living with Anxiety*, by Drs. Montgomery and Morris, and can be helpful when working with older children and teens. Just like the importance of taking baby steps, their rule aims for success by allowing your child to face her fears until the discomfort level has reached 70 percent out of a max of 100 percent. That means she never has to reach the "out of control, it is too much, I can't do it," stage while making changes. Ask her to imagine what going into full-blown panic would feel like; that will be 100 percent. Then have her imagine what 50 percent of that might feel like, and push just a little more past that. The example cited in the book is about a person's inability to tolerate dirt on their hands, stating, "You might deliberately rub some dirt on your hands and leave it there until you reach your 70 percent" level of discomfort. "Then wash it off and give yourself a break, as well as a pat on the back." You can ask younger children to visualize how big their fear looks on a scale of 1 to 10, with 10 being the biggest. Or, ask your child to think about how "full of fear" he is. You can use a balloon, and each puff you blow into the balloon is another step closer to "full." You also can encourage your child to use his body as a way to visualize. For example, full "up to my knees" is not so worried, "up to my stomach" is more worried, and "up to my head" is truly petrified. With the 70 percent rule, your child learns he can tolerate some dirt, stays in control, and does not have to reach the panic state associated with all-or-nothing thinking.

Building Self-Reliance

A child who is self-reliant is able to move forward with a sense of independence and competence, trusts in her own judgment, and is confident about her inner resources to cope. For a child with anxiety this tool is essential because it will increase her ability to have the internal locus of control discussed earlier, which, for a child with anxiety, is so important.

Parenting Do's

Encourage your child to take baby steps in an area that does not have big consequences just in case it does not go well. Your child can be given the responsibility to brush his teeth without your asking, or tie his own shoelaces without your immediate intervention. Instead, try encouraging and guiding affirmations: "I see you remembered to make a bow with your shoelace, good for you." Older children and teens can help with chores, decide on a paint color for their bedroom, help make dinner, manage their own time schedule for homework, and choose clothes for the next day. These are all non-threatening ways your child will gain a sense of personal mastery.

Parenting Don'ts

A child who is growing in trust for herself so she can feel more in control, and therefore less anxious, will need parents who do not hover. When you stand over children, they will feel as if you are waiting for them to fail and do not trust them to complete the task or get through the situation. Constant instructions about the right way to do things is also not helpful. Rushing to their aid when things become difficult, even if they are scared, also needs to be avoided until at least they have reached their 70 percent discomfort threshold. Other "don'ts" include setting impossibly high expectations for children, or giving them responsibility they are not ready for. Both are set-ups for failure.

A Balancing Act

Your child's ability to build self-reliance is a balancing act. Encouraging independence and freedom to think is great, but not if it goes against your values about respecting others and/or established family rules. Yet, if you do not give your child enough independence and freedom to explore, you risk creating a dependent child who is afraid to think for himself, feels insecure and anxious, and is not confident in his ability. It will be important to assess your child's changing age, developmental ability, and skills to find that balance. It is usually different for each child, especially if one has an anxiety disorder.

 *Question?*

My children are upset because they say I have different rules for each of them. Am I doing something wrong?
No, you are not. Rules usually are different for each child, especially if one has an anxiety disorder. Continually assess your child's changing age, developmental ability, and skills as you make rules. Consider a family meeting to discuss the differences, and how you can build self-reliance, with each child in the family.

Use Positive Reinforcement

The foundation of positive reinforcement is to catch your child when she is doing something that pleases you, and then give her positive feedback about it. It was developed based on the premises that a child's feelings of esteem and confidence are connected to, and influenced by, their relationship with their primary caregivers.

At first it may seem as if it is a lot of work because you need to be constantly attuned to your child's behavior in order to catch her doing it right, and downplay what she is doing wrong. Research shows that, when used correctly, positive reinforcement will inspire confidence in your child and help her adopt that important "can do" attitude.

The Shift

When you use positive reinforcement, you shift your focus from reminding and reprimanding your child for what he is doing wrong and therefore how he is disappointing you, to acknowledging and showing him that he is loved, appreciated, and valued. Watch for the desired behavior to occur and then reinforce it with praise, a pat on the back for a job well done, and/or follow up with a special privilege. By accentuating the positive, you address the action the child took, rather than making a value statement about him as a person. For example, "Wow, I see you wrote that paper for school and asked everyone to gather in the family room to hear it; boy, are you working hard!" instead of "Wow, I liked what you wrote for your school paper, great job." The de-emphasis on your like or dislike demonstrates to your child an understanding and support of their effort. This also reinforces your appreciation of what it took to push through their fear, instead of how well the job was done, which can seem judgmental, subjective, or arbitrary.

Other Positive Reinforcements

Besides verbal reinforcement, what is motivating varies for each child, so be aware of what your child values, and use it. Is it extra TV time, computer time, phone time, or time at the mall? You can use rewards when you feel your child has accomplished a task that is directly related to coping through a situation they have in the past feared. This does not mean you offer money or treats for tasks they can normally do. It does mean you find a motivator or incentive to make the challenge of facing a fear easier to swallow. And remember you are rewarding the effort, not the outcome.

 Essential

Social research on family communication has repeatedly confirmed that caregivers spend less than twenty minutes a day, on average, communicating with their children. Researchers also found that when parents do talk with their children it is usually to state a complaint, give them a command, or request they do something. This negative communication style seems to peak during the middle to late teenage years, fueling grounds for a poor relationship.

Here are some examples of communication using positive reinforcement: "You challenged yourself to make a phone call to get your math homework; I know that wasn't easy for you. How about when you are done with those math problems we play your new board game?" Or, "I know you felt anxious about joining the play at school and you did it anyway. Why do not you ask one of the girls you met there if they would like to go for ice cream tomorrow after rehearsal?"

So, a reinforcer can be a verbal praise, a hug, ice cream, or anything that is meaningful to your child. Social reinforcers, for a child with anxiety, can pack double the punch. Not only will your child get increased playtime, he will get additional social interaction, which can increase confidence and self-esteem.

Some behavioral psychologists suggest increasing the value or impact of a goal over time. This might involve starting with your child choosing a favorite homemade meal, then a trip to the park, then a movie rental, then a meal out, then a more expensive toy or outing. The idea is to build momentum by increasing the "wow" factor as your child increases his success rate. However, remember that the ultimate reward should be your child's sense of pride in accomplishment, NOT what he can earn for following the plan, so you may elect to keep reinforcers modest.

Question?

I told my son that if he faced his fears and went with his class to the zoo, I would get him the new bike he wanted. Is that positive reinforcement?

No, that would be considered a bribe. A reward happens after the fact. Let's say your son is doing the best he can to fight his fears and chooses to go to the zoo. He is not going to the zoo *for* the reward; he is going for the pleasure of achievement. Your reward is an unexpected bonus, and a bribe is used to motivate a child in advance.

Using Logical and Natural Consequences

Natural consequences are the automatic results of an action, and the parent usually plans logical consequences in advance, sometimes together with the child. Allowing logical or natural consequences to occur helps your child develop an internal understanding of self-control, which as you have seen, can be very helpful. You want your child to feel empowered and capable of working through his anxiety, which usually cannot happen if you overfunction, make decisions for him, or punish him. Choices are more hopeful and positive if you allow your child to make a decision, and be responsible for the consequence for that choice, all the while overcoming his personal issues with anxiety. The choice then becomes a structured learning opportunity that preserves the dignity of the child. This is because there is no punishment or shame attached to the outcome, just an opportunity to take baby steps and grow in trial and error.

Doing Too Much

This point has been mentioned multiple times because of how singularly important it is. Parents often fall into this trap and it can severely affect and limit how your child will develop if you are not careful; so here it is again: Although your desire is to help your child, especially when she is stressed or anxious, don't. Do not do for her what she can, if given the time, do for herself. Yes, sometimes it is easier to clean up for her if she is already running late, cover up her mistakes to save her self-esteem, or do her homework for her because she's having a meltdown. Children really do learn best from natural and logical consequences, not from you giving them a lecture and then doing it for them with frustration and resentments.

Natural Consequences

Natural consequences for your child's actions are most effective as long as certain criteria are met, and will often make more sense to your child than punishment. The definition is exactly as it sounds—the natural outcome of our child's choice in behavior. For example, when a child does not finish his homework a natural consequence will be a zero for the assignment, given by the teacher, and falling behind in the class. Another example might be that during the winter if your child insists on going outside without his coat, he will be cold and learn he needs to wear the coat. The natural consequence is not life-threatening and it avoids a power struggle between parent and child. This scenario will allow the natural course of events to become the teacher. An example for an older child might be that, if your teenager gets a speeding ticket, he will have to pay for it himself, and have points against his license.

The exceptions for using natural consequences are as follows: The consequence is dangerous, the consequence will be delayed for a long time (consequences work best when immediate), or the consequence causes emotional, legal, or physical problems for other children or adults.

Logical Consequences

Logical consequences do not "naturally" occur because of behavior, but are deliberately created by the parent, and as mentioned earlier, sometimes with the help of the child. Most parents already use logical consequences every day. For example, if your child is dawdling during dinner, she does not get dessert, or if she does not pick up her toys and instead plays with the dog until it is time for bed, the toys are put on a shelf for a specified amount of time. The rules for setting up logical consequences are as follows: First, announce the consequence beforehand, then relate the consequence to the issue and fit the consequence to your child's development level. Make sure that you do not negotiate, do not wait, be consistent, make sure everyone is on the same page, and be calm and respectful—no shame, no blame.

 Fact

The best you can do as a parent is to provide opportunities for growth that are realistic, supportive, and educational while not sacrificing responsibilities and values. When you allow your child to experience logical and natural consequences, you are doing just that.

One alternative that many parents and children alike find positive is to engage the child in the consequence. This makes your child a part of the problem-solving process and feels a little less controlling. You can say to your child, "You seem to have difficulty getting yourself to bed on time, what are you thinking the consequence should be?" This does not mean you will do what your child says, but rather will take into account his thoughts. "It feels like you are pushing for a later bedtime, which is not an option; can you think of a consequence?" Depending on your child's response, you might say, "It sounds like you feel a consequence would be to turn off the

TV fifteen minutes earlier so you get yourself moving. That sounds reasonable to us."

Natural and logical consequences allow your child to be in control, because the consequence is not arbitrary; it is also direct and requires no questioning. The structures they provide are extremely important factors for a child who has anxiety.

Managing Anxiety Away from Home

Being away from home, whether for an afternoon or a vacation, can be a challenge for an anxious child. The following is a list of techniques that will lessen anticipatory anxiety and meltdowns, thereby helping your child stay engaged with his peers and other family members. Much of the information you have received in this book can be applied to all children, anxious or not; just understand the pace will need to be slower with a child who has anxiety and should be focused on process rather than outcome.

Communicate
First, help your child break down tasks into smaller steps that feel reasonable, with a timeline, as a way for him to see it can be accomplished. Part of this process can include role-playing the possibilities, and communicating what each of your needs will be for that outing. Openly discuss how you both want it to go, along with the worries and perceived obstacles. Discussing concerns aloud is often helpful and can make your child feel more confident and safe. It is similar to cognitive rehearsal. For example, "Remember today after school you will have just enough time for a snack and then we will be leaving for soccer. When soccer is done, I will make dinner and you can use that time to do your homework. This will give you the free time you asked for so you can watch that new show. Let's just take a minute to write down the time schedule, and talk about how it will work best for us." Notice that the conversation is direct, does not suggest there is room for any negotiation, and speaks as a team, not just about the

child. In other words, "Let's" is used, instead of "Do *you* need," and "What will work best for us," not "For *you*." This is important if you want your child to feel as if he is warmly understood and not an irritation, or as putting others out, for being anxious.

 Essential

Be sure your child is ready for what she says she wants. If it is for a sleepover at a friend's house, is she sleeping through the night in her own bed without waking? If it is to join a team sport, does she feel comfortable with groups and competition? If you are taking a family trip, is she open to new experiences and comfortable leaving the house for an extended period? Without these things in place first, you could be setting everyone up for failure.

Be Prepared

Part of being prepared to ensure the success of your outing, trip, or lifestyle means looking at possibilities, and being truthful with yourself and your child. Saying, "The drive is only two hours, you do not need your blanket," will not work out well for anyone if your child feels best having his blanket at his side. Sometimes it is "just in case" for them. Not allowing it will increase your child's anxiety, maybe unnecessarily. Some suggestions are:

- **Do a dress rehearsal.** If you are going to a new doctor, drive by the office so your child can visually relate to what is coming, or if you have an especially tight schedule coming up, do a practice run over the weekend, in the car, and show your child it can be done.
- **Buddy up.** Research shows kids feel safer and happier away from home if they know at least one other child. It could be a sibling, someone from the neighborhood, school, religious

organization, or team sport. This person does not have to be a best friend; it can be an acquaintance that she can hang with or just know is there.

- **Pack a few "security items."** A few special and familiar items can make even the most worried child a little less anxious. A favorite stuffed animal, blanket, picture, touchstone, or flashlight can increase your child's confidence, especially when sleeping over at someone else's house. Ask your child what she needs to feel more secure and comfortable wherever she is going.

- **Talk to or meet with the adults your child will be spending time with no matter how old she is.** Just make the connection, clarify how you can be reached if there is a concern, and let your child know it has been done.

- **Have a positive sendoff and do not make a big deal of it.** Be cheerful and optimistic as you and your child pack, discussing the positive aspects of the outing. If you are doing a dropoff to school, sporting practice, camp, or party, do not wait until your child looks settled. Give her a big hug, kiss, and leave unless it was decided beforehand that you would stay for a designated amount of time. Do not linger.

- **No matter what happens, it has been a success.** So, what if your child does not make it all the way through the night? Remember, it is all about baby steps, slow and steady. Just the fact that your child tried is a big step.

- **Use praise freely.** Praise your child when she takes part, in spite of her worry. Openly share how impressed you are with her ability to "do."

Emotional Resilience

As discussed at the beginning of the chapter, self-reliance is the ability to solve one's own problems, creating an underlying sense of autonomy and independence. Emotional resilience is the capacity to face normal, everyday hurts and disappointments to one's self-confidence, without losing self-esteem in the process. It is the ability to "bounce back."

Characteristics of Resilient Children

It is not that emotionally resilient children are more intelligent, know more, or have superior coping skills than do nonresilient people. Rather, the difference lies in their ability to apply the coping skills that they have attained, keep a good perspective, and persist long after less resilient children become disheartened and give up. In order to help your child become a more resilient person, it is necessary to work on cultivating certain beliefs and attitudes. First, your child must believe that it is possible to cope. Resilient children trust that they have the potential to control and influence outcomes by their thoughts and actions.

 Fact

Your child needs to know that occasional frustrations can have positive results in the long run, and they are not to be feared. Experiencing some hardship actually provides your child an opportunity to develop immunities, or strengths, and is no different than allowing your child to play with someone who has a cold because it builds his immune system.

Other characteristics of resilient children are that they have realistic expectations and goals for themselves, are thoughtful rather than impulsive, are effective communicators, are able to learn from past experiences, have care and concern for others, and are optimistic.

How Parents Can Help

The author Robert Brooks, Ph.D., who wrote *Raising Resilient Children*, believes that the most important quality we can instill in our children is resilience. It has been found that the best way to assist your child to grow in those characteristics is to use appropriate limits because children actually feel more secure and have better outcomes with structure, to give verbal reminders so your anxious child can grow in emotional resilience, and to remember to teach your child how to use calming behaviors. Additionally, express your love, praise accomplishments often, provide continual opportunities for growth so your child with anxiety can learn to manage himself better, be a good model, and finally, encourage open, nonjudgmental and nonshaming discussions that seek alternative options.

I Have, I Can, I Am

A helpful exercise that connects your child with his ability to grow in resilience is to ask him to write down three to five endings for each of the following queries: I have, I am, and I can. If he cannot write, you can brainstorm possibilities with him, write out his answers or draw them, and hang the list somewhere in his bedroom. This list can be updated as often as he likes, but at least once a month, fostering a continued ability to see himself in a positive light and be reminded of his accomplishments. For example:

I Have . . .
Many people who love me
A best friend that I can tell everything to
Remembered to use my breathing when I got scared

I Am . . .
Stronger every day
Allowed to be nervous sometimes
Fun to be around
Proud of myself

I Can . . .
Ask my parents for help if I need it
Manage my feelings if I try
Think of ways to make things better for myself
Make good choices
Learn new things
Be confident if I want

Your child's ability to be resilient will not make his problems go away, but will give him the ability to see beyond them. Also, keep in mind that if you and your child look at experiences that created worry and anxiety in the past, you can learn what strategies are needed to increase personal strengths and resilience for the future.

CHAPTER 20

Create a Confident Future

The ultimate goal of learning to manage anxiety is twofold: First, your child needs to gain the core confidence that she is capable enough to meet just about anything that life throws at her. Second, she needs the reassurance that she can overcome internal and external obstacles, even if this means tolerating a certain amount of discomfort. One of the best gifts you can give as the parent of a child with anxiety is to help her stay on the road once a course of recovery has been established, and to ensure that you and your family create an obstacle-free course your child can eventually run on her own.

Letting Go

Many of you have heard the serenity prayer, used at Alcoholics Anonymous and Alanon meetings worldwide: "God, grant me the serenity to accept the things I cannot change, the courage to change the things I can, and the wisdom to know the difference." Though this mantra may have become trite for some, it has much to offer in both learning to manage anxiety itself and in fostering your child to grow into her own as she leaves anxiety behind.

Trust Yourself

You, as a parent, know your child better than anyone else in the world. If you are able to see yourself clearly as well, you are in a great position to use your intuition and a bit of courage to know when to step back and hand your child the reins. This means that sometimes you may have to stand by as your child struggles a bit, let him experience his own consequences, and manage your own anxiety all the while. You may also have to encourage other family members to do the same. Trust your instincts also if you truly feel your child is overwhelmed by the treatment and other goals you've set, or if the pace of therapy is moving too rapidly, or too slowly. Remember that you are your child's best natural resource for health and security.

Launching

Just as the job of a good therapist is to prepare a client to end therapy, your job as a parent is to make sure your children have the skills they need to fledge, and use their new wings to become more and more successful when they are away from you. For many parents, a child's increasing independence can be scary, lonely, confusing, and sad. Sometimes it helps simply to reassure yourself that it's nature's plan for your child to leave the nest and continue to do your best to allow your child to soar. As covered earlier in the book, use your family, friends, and the professional community for support; do not depend on your child to offer reassurance, because this is what she most needs from you.

Gossamer Strings Make Stronger Wings

As you learn to let go of your child, it is important to stay flexibly attached, connecting securely but not too tightly. Gossamer does just this; its filaments are light, airy, and flowing, creating obvious but gentle tethers. It is important for parents to be prepared to handle strong emotions as children become less dependent on them. This can be especially true when separation anxiety is an issue. As you've learned, it is always best to try not to let your fears interfere with your child's desire and need to push forward. Draw on your inner and outer resources, and know that you and a million other parents have learned to let their children go on to be competent, productive, happy, responsible adults.

Knowing When to End Therapy

Ending therapy can be a bittersweet experience, and one that is often dreaded by both parents and children who have come to trust in the therapist, rely on the care given within the relationship, and take pride in the forward moving process of change. Some schools of therapy stress that it is never too early to address the eventual end of treatment, and, indeed, it can be helpful to paint a picture of what "success" will look like for your child as you begin therapy.

Practice Makes Perfect

Scientists have known for years that learning involves physical changes in the brain. Eric R. Kandel, who received the Nobel Prize in Medicine in 2000 for his groundbreaking work, proved that as learning occurs, the release of neurotransmitters increases, creating new neural structures and connections, which multiply and further enhance learning. It has also been established that learning inter-personal skills and social interaction is more complex, and therefore requires more repetition to acquire. This, of course, has applications to social anxiety, assertiveness, and learning when and how to seek support from others.

 Essential

> Conventional wisdom has it that it takes twenty-one attempts at a new behavior before it becomes a habit. However, the rule of twenty-one actually has no basis in fact. There are simply too many intervening factors to make a sound prediction on anyone's learning curve. So, keep the faith and encourage your child to be patient and to keep trying while her brain is busy rewiring!

Also, keep in mind that your child is unlearning old, unhelpful behavior at the same time he's learning new skills. Following Kandel's observations, though it does not take long for the brain to store a new image or idea, new cell growth and connection does require quite a bit of repetition and reinforcement to truly take root. For these reasons, it is important for your child to continue therapy until you and the therapist are assured that your child has truly mastered new skills such as better self-talk and self-calming skills.

Taking Stock of Your Toolbox

As you consider ending therapy, you may wish to use the following checklist as a guide if you believe it is appropriate:

- ❏ Have you and your child learned what anxiety is, and what your child's particular triggers are?
- ❏ Have you addressed any medical, nutritional, or environmental concerns that contribute to your child's anxiety?
- ❏ Has your child improved in his ability to identify and express his needs and feelings effectively?
- ❏ Are you and other family members more able to share your needs and concerns without undue upset or conflict?
- ❏ Have you, as a parent, addressed any personal or family patterns that may perpetuate anxiety?
- ❏ Does your child use skills such as breathing, relaxation, and imagery with minimal or no prompting from you?
- ❏ Can your child self-soothe in other ways, such as bathing, music, or distraction?
- ❏ Are you and your child satisfied with the amount of symptom relief being experienced at home, at school, and with friends?
- ❏ Has the relief been relatively consistent for at least two to four months?

If you were able to check off the majority of these questions, it is likely time to consider ending therapy. Although the process may sound scary, your child's ability to go it on his own is actually a learning experience in and of itself.

Weaning

When your child is recovering from anxiety, she may need ongoing reassurance, and reminders to use the skills she has learned. This can easily be accomplished by gradually lengthening the time between therapy sessions as she becomes more able to manage her symptoms on her own, with your support. It is often very encouraging to hear from the therapist that your child does not need to come in as often, and for many children, this can be a great source of pride and accomplishment.

 Essential

> When ending therapy, keep in mind that your child (and you) may have developed a strong attachment to the therapist. Honor the effort and the relationship, and avoid ending therapy abruptly, unless you have reason to believe it is harmful or inappropriate for your child to continue.

To help with closure and acknowledge your child's accomplishments, consider planning something special with the therapist for the final session, or ask about exchanging touchstones.

Knowing When to End Medication

As you've seen, changing, adding, or stopping a medicine during the course of therapy can provide particular challenges (see Chapter 11). Research shows that many people are able to maintain control over their anxiety effectively after stopping medication, typically if they have received therapy to learn ways to combat their symptoms. Specific data on exactly how this applies to children with anxiety is less conclusive, due to the fact that children's development is dynamic and ongoing, along with the current lack of longitudinal research.

Basic Guidelines

In general, it is common practice for a child to stay on a medication for at least six to twelve months for maximum benefit to occur. However, timeframes vary depending on the class of medication. For example, it is typical to see benefits from antidepressants in around four to six weeks, while an anxiolytic will have more of an immediate effect. In addition, if it takes time to reach the therapeutic dose of the medicine, or if another is added, it may take longer to see optimal effects. Your child's age, the length and severity of her symptoms, and the co-occurrence of other mental health issues, will also determine when it is reasonable to discontinue a medication.

 **Question?**

Are there any times when my child should *not* go off medication?
Yes, in fact. It may be beneficial for your child to stay on medication through times of transition or particular stress, during anniversaries of loss or trauma, or during the fall and winter months if seasonal affective disorder is a concern. It is unwise to risk further unbalancing your child when times are already difficult.

Though most medical professionals would agree that a child shouldn't take medication she no longer needs, there are just as many reasons to continue until full benefit can occur. Unfortunately, it can sometimes be difficult to determine just when to discontinue a medication, especially if it has been used for an extended period of time.

Your Child's Signals

Ultimately, of course, you might want your child to be nearly symptom free for as long a time as possible before ending medication. However, this may not be practical for several reasons, including cost, health concerns, or even the need for a trial without medication so that your child can test her wings. Though medications have been proven effective in reducing symptoms, it is often difficult to determine whether the medication has itself been effective, or whether your child may have improved as the result of positive events, extra attention, or the simple passage of time. So, what does this mean in practical terms? First, review the questions in the toolbox section above. Then, depending on your answers, approach your child's doctor and consider your options together.

Transitioning Care

It may be important for your child to stay on medication after ending therapy. As long as your child is stable, and you maintain regular contact with whoever is prescribing, you should have nothing to worry about. Once children are stable on a medication, they can often transition to a less specialized level of care, for example, from psychiatrist to general practitioner, or pediatrician to nurse practitioner. Whoever is prescribing your child's medication should offer this option if they feel it would be more beneficial or practical; raise the issue yourself if you feel a change would be helpful.

Offering Smother-Free Support

Throughout the book, you've received many pointers on how not to let your own fears and needs interfere with your child's recovery. This is especially important once your child has finished treatment, so that he will be able to maintain his gains without constant outside reminders or reinforcement.

Encourage Independence

As you've learned, in order for your child to have the confidence that he can manage on his own, he needs to feel that you believe that he can. Always let your child make an attempt, no matter what his age, before you step in. This applies all the way from learning to walk, to applying for college. If your child seems to have trouble managing on his own, offer support while respecting his growing independence by considering the tip below.

Ask Before Offering

This strategy can be applied to young children, and is especially important to cultivate as your child ages. If you see your child struggling, simply ask her if she needs feedback, assistance, or direction. If she does, help her make a plan by using the "baby steps" concept presented earlier. As your child becomes stronger and more independent, she may begin to decline your assistance; take this as a sign of growth and accomplishment, not as rejection! As mentioned previously, the best strategy is always to allow your child the time and space to figure it out on her own before you step in. This is especially important for young adult children who have moved out or gone away to college. Always be sure to lend a sympathetic ear, but use your best reflective listening skills to guide and encourage, not to control or dictate.

When to Return to Therapy

Research indicates that overall recovery from anxiety is enhanced when people return to therapy periodically to reconnect with an understanding coach, and revisit coping skills, which can naturally fall by the wayside as life's challenges interfere. Also, keep in mind that as your child matures and develops, what she will be able to handle will increase and new or deeper work can be done. For example, if she was abused at age six, she will only be able to deal with certain parts of the trauma depending on her developmental age, and may need to go back to therapy at a later date, when she is more equipped to handle certain aspects of it emotionally. This is partially due to the fact that, as her brain develops, she will become more and more able to handle the complex and abstract concepts involved in emotional healing. Because it is often hard to gauge, here are some thoughts about when or if a return to therapy might be indicated for your child.

Have a Plan

When ending therapy or medication, it is advisable to make a plan for when a return to care might be indicated. If your child experiences a trauma, major transition, or an especially stressful period, she may need a mental health tune-up to make sure that she stays on course. Other signs your child may need to return to therapy or restart medication include an increase in the frequency, intensity, or duration of anxiety symptoms, such as worry, perfectionism, panic attacks, or insomnia. It may help to take some measurements of your child's symptoms as you conclude therapy so that you have a baseline to work from.

The Tune-Up

As children mature, different developmental challenges present themselves. The demands of a new school, extracurricular activity, or peer group may temporarily unbalance your child, causing an increase in anxiety symptoms. Most providers will be agreeable to scheduling an appointment or two for your child to check in periodically. This approach can be especially helpful during transition times, such as at the beginning or end of the school year, or during stressful periods such as holidays.

Switching Modalities

Sometimes, even if your child has been successful in individual therapy and seems generally able to use the skills he's acquired, he may encounter an increase in discomfort, with or without readily identifiable symptoms. If you feel this is the case, you may want to consider group therapy, or find a class such as relaxation or assertiveness to help your child regain a sense of confidence and security. You may wish to consider or revisit marital or family therapy if the level of conflict in your home has increased, if communication problems are occurring more frequently, or if you and your partner aren't seeing eye-to-eye. Remember that the functioning of your family system as a whole can make or break your child's ability to manage anxiety. In fact, your child can act as a barometer for family troubles, his anxiety rising and falling with the level of strain in the system.

 Essential

If your child's progress seems to stall out, or if you've lost momentum with your treatment or aftercare plan, consider reviewing reading material you've found helpful, focusing on improving a specific skill, or taking a class to breathe new life into your level of creativity and motivation. Have a chat with your co-parent to make sure you are still working as a team toward the same objectives.

Changing Therapists

Once you've established a trusting relationship with a therapist, it can be daunting to consider working with someone new. Unfortunately, changes in insurance, residence, or schedule may make this transition unavoidable. If your child needs to change therapists, be sure to sign the appropriate releases so that the new provider can have, at minimum, a summary of the work your child did with her previous therapist. Often, a brief telephone consultation between therapists can be a reassuring bridge of security for both you and your child. If you are transferring care within an agency, you can request a joint session with both providers if you feel this would be helpful.

Moving Away and Other Life Transitions

For some children with anxiety and their parents, the prospect of leaving home can be troublesome, painful, and confusing, even after a successful course of therapy and/or medication. The unknowns of college, work, a new residence, and new social connections can seem insurmountable at times. As you've seen, when addressing most anxiety-related concerns, your best bet is to help your child compartmentalize to minimize the overwhelm; that is, help your child identify smaller steps toward the ultimate goal, and support her as she meets each milestone.

Moving Out

Whether it is a new apartment, shared housing with friends, or the transition to college, your child may experience his first real sense of independence when he moves out of your home. For some, this can be exhilarating, for some, frightening, and for most, a combination of the two. To help your child manage separation and general anxiety, make a plan for how you'll stay connected, and acknowledge that this is a big change for both of you. Clarify guidelines for how often you will talk on the phone, and set limits if you feel either you or your child is too dependent on the contact. If your child will be living nearby, you might consider starting a Sunday dinner ritual, a monthly night at the movies, or Saturday coffee break. Children are often comforted by care packages, impromptu grocery deliveries, or occasional offers to help with housework. Remember, though, to ask before you offer, and respect your young adult's need for privacy and the right to establish a life of his own.

College

Along with a new residence and all of the associated freedom and responsibility of living away from home, moving to college adds the combination of increased academic and social demands. Your child will need to manage her time largely independently, make choices about classes, friends, and lifestyle, and she may also work and pay bills on her own. Many young adults experience anxiety and depression at the start of college, and many schools offer academic and counseling support to assist students in the transition process. Other sources of support include student organizations, athletics, theater, music, and other extracurricular activities. As always, have a plan for how you'll stay connected, and what supports you can offer. It is important that you and your child have a clear picture of what to watch for, should her anxiety return. This will be specific to your child's pattern of anxiety, but should include a way to monitor the frequency, intensity, and duration of her symptoms. It may help your child to identify specific ways she can use her skills, such as exercise and meditation. Finding ways to reinforce skills along with supportive peers can be especially powerful.

 Essential

Many colleges have functions and activities that give parents opportunities to visit their child on campus, experience a meal, and perhaps meet professors. You can stay connected with your child by attending performances and sporting events, and perhaps by volunteering in some way.

Moving Back In

It has been suggested that the children in the United States have the most extended adolescence of any culture in the world. This can be especially true for children with anxiety (most specifically separation anxiety), who may have trouble launching and return home after brief periods away at college or their own residence. Sometimes, the best medicine for a young adult who can't seem to separate is a bit of tough love. If your child moves back into your home, make a clear plan for how long it will be that he can stay, and the steps he will take to regain his independence. A return to therapy, and the expectation that your child will attend school, hold a job, and contribute to the functioning of the household are all reasonable and responsible approaches when your child has returned to the nest. Remember, as bittersweet as it can be for both of you, your ultimate goal is to help your child use the wings he's been developing all along.

Challenges of Adulthood

Moving into adulthood naturally presents marvelous opportunities, as well as challenges. Getting married, starting a career, establishing a home, and having children can be great times for your child to enhance his sense of self and increase competence, but the added stress can cause symptom relapse. Using the approaches above, along with others in the book, you will be equipped to support your child through any number of challenges. Here are a few final tips to help you stay on course: Practice and model good boundaries, communication, and self-care. Ask before offering, but offer often. Remember, gossamer strings make stronger wings. Above all, you can never love your child too much.

Anxiety Questionnaire

If you think your child may have an anxiety disorder, please answer the following questions, and show the results to your child's health care professional:

Yes ◯ No ◯	Does the child have a distinct and ongoing fear of social situations involving unfamiliar people?
Yes ◯ No ◯	Does the child worry excessively about a number of events or activities?
Yes ◯ No ◯	Does the child experience shortness of breath or a racing heart for no apparent reason?
Yes ◯ No ◯	Does the child experience age-appropriate social relationships with family members and other familiar people?
Yes ◯ No ◯	Does the child often appear anxious when interacting with her peers and avoid them?
Yes ◯ No ◯	Does the child have a persistent and unreasonable fear of an object or situation, such as flying, heights, or animals?
Yes ◯ No ◯	When the child encounters the feared object or situation, does she react by freezing, clinging, or having a tantrum?
Yes ◯ No ◯	Does the child worry excessively about her competence and quality of performance?
Yes ◯ No ◯	Does the child cry, have tantrums, or refuse to leave a family member or other familiar person when she must?
Yes ◯ No ◯	Has the child experienced a decline in classroom performance, refused to go to school, or avoided age-appropriate social activities?
Yes ◯ No ◯	Does the child spend too much time each day doing things over and over again (for example, handwashing, checking things, or counting)?
Yes ◯ No ◯	Does the child have exaggerated fears of people or events (for example, burglars, kidnappers, car accidents) that might be difficult, such as in a crowd or on an elevator?
Yes ◯ No ◯	Does the child experience a high number of nightmares, headaches, or stomachaches?
Yes ◯ No ◯	Does the child repetitively re-enact with toys scenes from a disturbing event?
Yes ◯ No ◯	Does the child redo tasks because of excessive dissatisfaction with less-than-perfect performance?

Diagnostic and Statistical Manual of Mental Disorders, Fourth Edition. Washington, DC, American Psychiatric Association, 1994.

APPENDIX B

Resources

Books

Wagner, Aureen Ph.D. *Worried No More: Help and Hope for Anxious Children.* (Rochester, NY: Lighthouse Press, Inc., 2002).

Ellsas Chansky, Tamar. *Freeing Your Child From Anxiety.* (New York, NY: Broadway Books, 2004).

Mansee Buel, Linda. *Panic and Anxiety Disorder, 121 Tips, Real-Life Advice Resources and More.* (Poway, CA: Simply Life, 2001).

Nardo, Don. *Anxiety and Phobias.* (New York, NY: Chelsea House Publishers, 1992).

Burns, David D. *When Panic Attacks: The New Drug-Free Anxiety Therapy That Can Change Your Life.* (New York, NY: Morgan Road Books, Random House, 2006).

Foxman, Paul Ph.D. *The Worried Child: Recognizing Anxiety in Children and Helping Them.* (Alameda, CA: Hunter House Publishers, 2004).

Foa, Edna B. Ph.D., and Wasmer Andrews, Linda. *If Your Adolescent Has an Anxiety Disorder.* (New York, NY: Oxford University Press, 2006).

Fox, Bronwyn. *Power over Panic: Freedom from Panic/Anxiety Related Disorders, 2nd Edition.* (NSW, Australia: Pearson Education Australia, 2001).

Lee, Jordan. *Coping with Anxiety and Panic Attacks.* (New York, NY: The Rosen Publishing Group, Inc., 1997, 2000).

Gardner, James M.D., and Bell, Arthur H. Ph.D. *Overcoming Anxiety, Panic and Depression.* (Franklin Lakes, NJ: Career Press, 2000).

Bourne, Edmund J., Ph.D. *The Anxiety and Phobia Workbook, Third Edition.* (Oakland, CA: New Harbinger Publications, 2000).

Web Sites

About Our Kids, New York University Child Study Center
Articles, research, programs, and education about children.
✍ www.aboutourkids.org

American Academy of Child and Adolescent Psychiatry
Information about diagnosis and treatment of developmental, behavioral, and emotional disorders that affect children and adolescents.
✍ www.aacap.org

American Academy of Family Physicians
✍ www.aafp.org

American Psychological Association
Helps you find a psychologist in your area.
✍ www.helping.apa.org

Anxieties.com
Self-help site with tests, publications, and information.
✍ www.anxieties.com

Anxiety Disorders Association of America (ADAA)
Comprehensive Web site about anxiety.
✍ www.adaa.org

Anxiety Disorders: The Caregiver
Web site for caregivers and support people.
✍ www.healthyplace.com/communities/anxiety/strong/index.asp

Healthy Place
Offers information, live discussion, and chat groups.
✍ www.healthyplace.com/index.html

Mental Health Net
Resource for consumers and professionals.
✍ www.mentalhelp.net

National Alliance on Mental Illness (NAMI)
General mental health resource includes opportunities for support and networking.
✍ www.nami.org

National Institutes of Mental Health (NIMH)
Up-to-date news, research, and treatment information about anxiety.
✍ www.nimh.nih.gov/HealthInformation/anxietymenu.cfm

Psych Central
A mental health Web site that has created a social network that is run by mental health professionals.
www.psychcentral.com

Specialty Resources

Communication
Advocates for Youth Web site provides a good resource for multiple issues with children.
www.advocatesforyouth.org/youth/health/relationships/feelingwords

This Web page gives a list of feeling words to help you and your child learn ways to express emotions.
www.psychpage.com/learning/library/assess/feelings.html

Massage
Massage Magazine has articles of every kind about massage and studies about the health aspects of massage for children.
www.massagemag.com

Biofeedback
Association for Applied Psychophysiology and Biofeedback, with information about providers, research, and treatment.
www.aapb.org

Conscious Living Foundation has books, CDs, and movies to guide children in relaxation techniques, stress tools, and understanding how the body works.
www.cliving.org/children.htm

Aromatherapy
Aromatherapy and Children article by Kathi Keville, Mindy Green (Excerpted from *Aromatherapy: A Complete Guide to the Healing Art* found at the Health World Web site).
www.healthy.net/scr/Article.asp?Id=1714

Chiropractic
The International Chiropractic Pediatric Association is a resource that provides an accumulation of research and a membership directory for the layperson interested in chiropractic care for his or her family.
www.icpa4kids.org

Resource to find studies and articles on chiropractic care for children.
www.chiro.org/pediatrics/ABSTRACTS/Chiropractic_For_Children .shtml

Homeopathic Medicine

The National Center for Homeopathy has created a Web site to help one access studies, resources, and practitioners.
www.homeopathic.org

National Center for Complementary and Alternative Medicine is an excellent resource for alternative options.
www.nccam.nih.gov

Insurance Terms

Accreditation An evaluative process in which a health care organization undergoes an examination of its operating procedures to determine whether the procedures meet designated criteria as defined by the accrediting body, and to ensure that the organization meets a specified level of quality.

Annual maximum benefit amount The maximum dollar amount set by an MCO that limits the total amount the plan must pay for all health care services provided to a subscriber in a year.

Appropriateness review An analysis of health care services with the goal of reviewing the extent to which necessary care was provided and unnecessary care was avoided.

Case management A process of identifying plan members with special health care needs, developing a health care strategy that meets those needs, and coordinating and monitoring the care.

Claim An itemized statement of health care services and their costs provided by a hospital, physician's office, or other provider facility. Claims are submitted to the insurer or managed care plan by either the plan member or the provider for payment of the costs incurred.

Claim form An application for payment of benefits under a health plan.

Claimant The person or entity submitting a claim.

Claims administration This is the process of receiving, reviewing, adjudicating, and processing claims.

Clinical practice guideline A utilization and quality management mechanism designed to aid providers in making decisions about the most appropriate course of treatment for a specific clinical case.

Co-insurance A method of cost-sharing in a health insurance policy that requires a group member to pay a stated percentage of all remaining eligible medical expenses after the deductible amount has been paid.

Consolidated Omnibus Budget Reconciliation Act (COBRA) A federal act that requires each group health plan to allow employees and certain dependents to continue their group coverage for a stated period of time.

Co-insurance The amount of coverage the plan will pay usually based on a percentage. Additional costs are then paid by you.

Coordination of Benefits (COB) When a person is insured under two contracts, and the sequence in which coverage will apply (primary and secondary).

Co-payment A specific dollar amount that a member must pay for a medical expense out-of-pocket.

Credentialing The process of obtaining, reviewing, and verifying a provider's credentials—the documentation related to licenses, certifications, training, and other qualifications.

Deductible The amount a member must pay before the insurer will make any benefit payments.

Diagnostic and treatment codes Special codes that consist of a brief, specific description of each diagnosis or treatment and a number used to identify each diagnosis and treatment.

DSM-IV *The Diagnostic and Statistical Manual of Mental Disorders, Fourth Edition.* This is the standard guide for mental health professionals to diagnosis, code for insurance purposes, and set up a treatment plan.

EOB (Explanation of Benefits) A statement mailed to a member or covered insured explaining how or why a claim was paid or not paid.

Fee-for-service (FFS) payment system Insurer pays for its own service.

Fee schedule The fee for a service the provider agrees to accept as payment in full.

Generic substitution The dispensing of a drug that is the generic equivalent of a drug listed on a pharmacy benefit management plan's formulary.

Health Insurance Portability and Accountability Act (HIPAA) Federal legislation that improves access to health insurance when changing jobs by restricting certain pre-existing condition limitations and guarantees availability and renewability of health insurance coverage for all employers regardless of claims experience or business size.

Health Maintenance Organization (HMO) A prepaid medical group practice plan that provides a comprehensive predetermined medical care benefit package.

Indemnity insurance Often called "fee for service," this type of insurance plan allows patients to go to any doctor or hospital that they select, anywhere in the United States or abroad.

Lifetime maximum benefit amount The maximum dollar amount that limits the total amount the plan will cover for health care services in the subscriber's lifetime.

Managed care A health care program that controls utilization of health care services, providers, and the fees charged for such services.

Medicaid Administered by the states and funded by the federal government. Within certain guidelines and income requirement will pay certain medical expenses.

Medical advisory committee Committee whose purpose is to review general medical management issues brought to it by the medical director.

Medical director Manages a health care organization and is responsible for finding providers, provider relations, quality and utilization management, and medical policy.

Medicare A federal government hospital expense and medical expense insurance plan primarily for elderly and disabled persons.

Medicare supplement A private medical expense insurance plan that supplements Medicare coverage.

Open Enrollment Period The period when an employee may change health plans; usually occurs once per year.

Patient Bill of Rights Refers to the Consumer Bill of Rights and Responsibilities, a report prepared by the President's Advisory Commission on Consumer Protection and quality in the health care industry. This was created to ensure the confidentiality of patient information, promote health care quality, and improve the availability of health care treatment and services.

Precertification The process of obtaining authorization from the health plan utilizing medical benefits and treatment.

Pre-existing condition Physical and/or mental condition that existed prior to becoming insured. Some plans may cover certain conditions after a waiting period of six months to a year.

Preferred Provider Organization (PPO) A PPO allows patients to see a doctor from the plan's network of physicians for a small co-payment fee.

Premium A prepaid payment or series of payments made to a health plan by purchasers, and often plan members, for medical benefits.

Primary Care Basic or general health care as opposed to specialist care.

Prior authorization Provider must obtain authorization before treatment for the service to be covered.

Psychiatrist A physician who specializes in mental, emotional, and behavioral disorders and can provide medication.

Psychologist A health professional (not a physician) who specializes in the mental or behavioral health and counsels.

Usual, customary, and reasonable (UCR) fee The amount used by traditional health insurance companies as the basis for physician reimbursement.

Utilization management (UM) Managing the use of medical services to ensure that a patient receives necessary, appropriate, high-quality care in a cost-effective manner.

Utilization review (UR) The evaluation of the medical necessity, efficiency, and/or appropriateness of health care services and treatment plans.

Utilization review committee Committee that reviews utilization, coverage, and providers.

Index

THE EVERYTHING®
PARENT'S GUIDES SERIES

Expert Advice for Parents
in Need of Answers

All titles are trade paperback, 6" x 9", $14.95

The Everything® Parent's Guide to Childhood Illnesses
ISBN 10: 1-59869-239-9; ISBN 13: 978-1-59869-239-6

The Everything® Parent's Guide to Children and Divorce
ISBN 10: 1-59337-418-6; ISBN 13: 978-1-59337-418-1

The Everything® Parent's Guide to Children with ADD/ADHD
ISBN 10: 1-59337-308-2; ISBN 13: 978-1-59337-308-5

The Everything® Parent's Guide to Children with
Asperger's Syndrome
ISBN 10: 1-59337-153-5; ISBN 13: 978-1-59337-153-1

The Everything® Parent's Guide to Children with Asthma
ISBN 10: 1-59869430-8; ISBN 13: 978-1-59869-430-7

The Everything® Parent's Guide to Children with Autism
ISBN 10: 1-59337-041-5; ISBN 13: 978-1-59337-041-1

The Everything® Parent's Guide to Children with Bipolar Disorder
ISBN 10: 1-59337-446-1; ISBN 13: 978-1-59337-446-4

The Everything® Parent's Guide to Children with Depression
ISBN 10: 1-59869-264-X; ISBN 13: 978-1-59869-264-8

Available wherever books are sold.
Or call 1-800-258-0929 or visit us at www.everything.com.

THE EVERYTHING® PARENT'S GUIDES SERIES (CONTINUED)

The Everything® Parent's Guide to Children with Dyslexia
ISBN 10: 1-59337-135-7; ISBN 13: 978-1-59337-135-7

The Everything® Parent's Guide to Children with Juvenile Diabetes
ISBN 10: 1-59869-246-1; ISBN 13: 978-1-59869-246-4

The Everything® Parent's Guide to Positive Discipline
ISBN 10: 1-58062-978-4; ISBN 13: 978-1-58062-978-2

The Everything® Parent's Guide to Raising a Successful Child
ISBN 10: 1-59337-043-1; ISBN 13: 978-1-59337-043-5

The Everything® Parent's Guide to Raising Boys
ISBN 10: 1-59337-587-5; ISBN 13: 978-1-59337-587-4

The Everything® Parent's Guide to Raising Girls
ISBN 10: 1-59869-247-X; ISBN 13: 978-1-59869-247-1

The Everything® Parent's Guide to Raising Siblings
ISBN 10: 1-59337-537-9; ISBN 13: 978-1-59337-537-9

The Everything® Parent's Guide to Sensory Integration Disorder
ISBN 10: 1-59337-714-2; ISBN 13: 978-1-59337-714-4

The Everything® Parent's Guide to the Strong-Willed Child
ISBN 10: 1-59337-381-3; ISBN 13: 978-1-59337-381-8

The Everything® Parent's Guide to Tantrums
ISBN 10: 1-59337-321-X; ISBN 13: 978-1-59337-321-4

Everything® and Everything.com® are registered trademarks of
F&W Publications, Inc.